The Performative Presidency

The Performative Presidency brings together literatures describing presidential leadership strategies, public understandings of citizenship, and news production and media technologies between the presidencies of Theodore Roosevelt and Bill Clinton, and details how the relations between these spheres have changed over time. Jason L. Mast demonstrates how interactions between leaders, publics, and media are organized in a theatrical way, and argues that mass mediated plot formation and character development play an increasing role in structuring the political arena. He shows politics as a process of ongoing performances staged by motivated political actors, mediated by critics, and interpreted by audiences, in the context of a deeply rooted, widely shared system of collective representations. The interdisciplinary framework of this book brings together a semiotic theory of culture with concepts from the burgeoning field of performance studies.

JASON L. MAST is a global research fellow at Warwick University's Institute for Advanced Study.

Cambridge Cultural Social Studies

Series editors: JEFFREY C. ALEXANDER, *Department of Sociology, Yale University, and* STEVEN SEIDMAN, *Department of Sociology, University at Albany, State University of New York.*

Titles in the series

MABEL BEREZIN, *Illiberal Politics in Neoliberal Times*

LINDA NICHOLSON, *Identity Before Identity Politics*

MARGARET R. SOMERS, *Genealogies of Citizenship*

FUYUKI KURASAWA, *The Work of Global Justice*

TAMIR SOREK, *Arab Soccer in a Jewish State*

JEFFREY C. ALEXANDER, BERNHARD GIESEN, AND JASON L. MAST, *Social Performance*

ARNE JOHAN VETLESEN, *Evil and Human Agency*

ROGER FRIEDLAND AND JOHN MOHR, *Matters of Culture*

DAVINA COOPER, *Challenging Diversity, Rethinking Equality and the Value of Difference*

KRISHAN KUMAR, *The Making of English National Identity*

RON EYERMAN, *Cultural Trauma*

STEPHEN M. ENGEL, *The Unfinished Revolution*

MICHÈLE LAMONT AND LAURENT THÉVENOT, *Rethinking Comparative Cultural Sociology*

RON LEMBO, *Thinking through Television*

ALI MIRSEPASSI, *Intellectual Discourse and the Politics of Modernization*

RONALD N. JACOBS, *Race, Media, and the Crisis of Civil Society*

ROBIN WAGNER-PACIFICI, *Theorizing the Standoff*

(*list continues at end of book*)

The Performative Presidency

Crisis and Resurrection during
the Clinton Years

Jason L. Mast

CAMBRIDGE
UNIVERSITY PRESS

CAMBRIDGE UNIVERSITY PRESS
Cambridge, New York, Melbourne, Madrid, Cape Town,
Singapore, São Paulo, Delhi, Mexico City

Cambridge University Press
The Edinburgh Building, Cambridge CB2 8RU, UK

Published in the United States of America by Cambridge University Press, New York

www.cambridge.org
Information on this title: www.cambridge.org/9781107026186

First published 2013

Printed and bound in the United Kingdom by the MPG Books Group

A catalogue record for this publication is available from the British Library

Library of Congress Cataloguing in Publication data

Mast, Jason L., author.
  The performative presidency : crisis and resurrection during the Clinton years / Jason L. Mast.
    pages cm – (Cambridge cultural social studies)
  ISBN 978-1-107-02618-6 (Hardback)
  1. Clinton, Bill, 1946– 2. Clinton, Bill, 1946–Public opinion. 3. United States–
Politics and government–1993–2001. 4. Press and politics–United States–History–20th
century. 5. Mass media–Political aspects–United States–History–20th century. 6. Mass
media and public opinion–United States–History–20th century. 7. Communication in
politics–United States–History–20th century. 8. Political culture–United States–History–
20th century. 9. Public opinion–United States–History–20th century. I. Title.
  E885.M38 2012
  973.929092–dc23

                                                                          2012021050

ISBN 978-1-107-02618-6 Hardback

To my mother and father, Nancy and Louie, for doing supportive and encouraging things with their words

Contents

Figures

Acknowledgments

In its transformation from a germ of an idea into a book, this project traveled from America's west coast to its east coast, where it made periodic trips to the University of Konstanz in Germany, and it came to fruition at Zeppelin University, Konstanz's neighbor on the Bodensee. Along the journey, many people helped shape its ideas and contributed emotional support for the endeavor. I turn to Wonderland's King of Hearts for instruction on how to thank the many people who helped me along the way; I will start thanking them from the beginning and go on till I come to the end, and then stop.

The seeds for this book were sown during impassioned discussions about politics and theory with Steven J. Sherwood on the Venice Beach waterfront. Sherwood, a committed neo-Durkheimian and the last Parsonian, helped me curb my intoxication with action theory and pragmatism. Many thanks to Steve for those moments, and to the other members of UCLA's iteration of the Culture Club, who welcomed me into their community dedicated to studying meaning.

Jeff Alexander moved the Culture Club to the east coast, and, along with Phil Smith and Ron Eyerman, and with assistance from Nadine Amalfi, turned a club into a center: namely, the Yale Center for Cultural Sociology. Thanks to Jeff, Ron, and Phil for establishing this ritual core; when individuals gather to discuss their projects at the CCS, a sort of electricity is generated. Participating in the CCS's workshops continually revitalized the productive impetus that sustained me throughout this project, and I am grateful for the feedback I received from the workshop's student members and visitors during my stay.

Other faculty members at Yale exercised considerable influence on my development as a scholar and on this project, most likely without knowledge of their contributions. I take this opportunity to thank Julia Adams, who I came to admire as a model of academic integrity, and for how she balanced the demands of intellectual rigor and collegiality. Also during this time Joe Roach provided a critical intervention in this project by welcoming me into his seminar on Writing Performance History, which was supported by a grant from the Mellon Foundation. Thanks to Joe for providing me with this opportunity and for sharing his insights, both of which were pivotal in deepening my knowledge of performance, theatre, and literary studies.

This project is deeply influenced by the turn to performance that Jeff Alexander and Bernd Giesen undertook during recent years. Collaborating with them while assembling our coedited volume, *Social Performance: Symbolic Action, Cultural Pragmatics, and Ritual* (Cambridge University Press, 2006), convinced me that a book-length treatment of Clinton's tenure could prove illuminating, and, more importantly, they helped shape many of the analytical tools that permeate this work. In addition to these two scholars, I am also grateful for their students' support and encouragement, which was expressed during several seminars and conferences.

Caroline Gray, Sam Nelson, Ates Altinordu, and Sarah Egan provided much needed camaraderie, and I thank them for sharing their sharp minds and wits with me. I am additionally thankful to Caroline for repeatedly offering critical feedback on several sections of the manuscript. If the drama of book writing includes a character who will respond to seemingly unlimited requests that begin with the phrase, "I'm sorry to ask again, but would you read," who seems to know intuitively when to offer a sympathetic ear and when to offer stern encouragement, then Caroline inhabited this role with a Meryl Streep-like kind of fusion.

Thanks to Nico Stehr for providing a supportive environment at Zeppelin University in which I was able to complete this project, and to our colleague Marian Adolf, whose passion for theories of the media provided welcome moments of inspiration.

Thank you John Haslam, Carrie Parkinson, and Lorenza Toffolon for providing perfect measures of structure and flexibility as this manuscript moved through the production process. And special thanks to Joanna Pyke for helping me to express more clearly what I have endeavored to communicate, and whose deft copy-editing refined the manuscript's prose considerably.

Jeff Alexander's guidance, support, and wisdom were a constant throughout this journey. To Jeff I offer my heartfelt appreciation for being a generous and patient mentor, and for showing me what a creative intellectual spirit looks like when it puts its mind to writing.

An earlier version of Chapter 2, "Presidential Leadership under the Conditions of Defusion," was translated into French and published in *Cahiers de recherche sociologique*, in a special issue on Theatricality and Society, under the title "The Rise of Performance in Mass Democratic Politics."

A modified version of Chapter 3, "Character Formation," was published under the title "Cultural Pragmatics and the Structure and Flow of Democratic Politics" in *The Oxford Handbook of Cultural Sociology* (ed. Jeffrey C. Alexander, Ronald N. Jacobs, and Philip Smith, Oxford University Press, 2012).

The empirical analysis in Chapter 7, "The Second Term," was published in a chapter titled "The Cultural Pragmatics of Event-ness," in *Social Performance: Symbolic Action, Cultural Pragmatics, and Ritual* (ed. Jeffrey C. Alexander, Bernhard Giesen, and Jason L. Mast, Cambridge University Press, 2006).

1

Introduction

In "World of Wrestling," the literary theorist Roland Barthes (1972 [1957]) describes how professional wrestling communicates its stories to audiences through dense symbolic clusters that define an event's protagonists and their relationships to one another, and render obvious a bout's plot. "The physique of the wrestlers," Barthes comments, "constitutes a basic sign, which like a seed contains the whole fight. But this seed proliferates, for it is at every turn during the fight, in each new situation, that the body of the wrestler casts to the public the magical entertainment of a temperament which finds its natural expression in a gesture. The different strata of meaning throw light on each other, and form the most intelligible of spectacles" (18). When thinking about the politics of 1998, the year of the Clinton–Lewinsky scandal, it is difficult not to imagine the president on television, wagging his finger at the national audience and denying the affair, or the heavily circulated image of Kenneth Starr confronting reporters while carrying a bag of garbage to the curb of his street (see Figure 1.1 and Figure 1.2). These images helped define the year's events, and while the political battle was of a more contingent dramatic structure than those displayed in the wrestling ring, the characters' meanings nonetheless played a critical role in determining the outcome.

A pattern emerged when I watched television in 1998. Sitting with friends, family, or in a public space, I would routinely overhear people saying, "I hate that guy," when President Clinton, Ken Starr, or Newt Gingrich appeared on screen. Monica Lewinsky's image would shade the atmosphere with blue humor, while Hillary Clinton's image seemed to produce more complex reactions, headshakes of skepticism and disbelief being the foremost expressed. Admiration, respect, hope, fondness, pride – feelings not commonly associated with politics today except,

Figure 1.1   With a gesture that mixed signs of forceful conviction and the assignment of shame, President Clinton stabbed his pointed finger in the air while denying having a sexual relationship with Monica Lewinsky, January 26, 1998.

perhaps, following a national election – were entirely absent, or only voiced with irony. The people onscreen were recognized by everyone – they seemed to be on the television all the time – and their appearances stirred passions. Viewers seemed to know a lot about these characters, as if written all over their suits and skin were stories telling us who they were. And yet one viewer could read Clinton's image and express disgust, while sitting next to him another person would grimace at Starr's image. The reading metaphor, in fact, is too cumbersome; a briefly televised image alone communicated a density of meaning, instantly. Reading takes time; these people's images communicated at a rate that would defy measurement by a hummingbird's watch. What viewers knew was not entirely clear, but their knowledge was clearly not simply based on political policy and legal precedents. The knowledge was not merely cognitive; rather, it was thicker, suggesting something more akin to an understanding. And the emotional registers these images struck, though

Figure 1.2   In an image that combines in one frame the private sphere of his personal home and the garbage he is handling at work, Independent Counsel Kenneth Starr talks to reporters while taking out the trash at his house in Virginia, April 2, 1998.

not always hate or love, were not always shallow either. Like a social fact, one could love it or hate it, follow it closely or try to ignore it, be captivated by it or simply want it to go away. But there it was, the national political drama, on the news, in late night television comedy monologues, in newspapers, and on the expanding internet, and it forced a way into everyone's attention, regardless of whether or not it inspired outrage or boredom, awe or indignation. It was an event.

These people on screen clearly meant something greater than their simple human selves. They were characters with complex, multifold meanings, and the simple, quick projection of their images onto the television would lift these meanings into the awareness like dust fleeing a beaten rug. What we saw in these clouds of debris were constellations of characters and relationships: Clinton and Starr had an obviously adversarial relationship, as did Clinton and Gingrich, but the latter one seemed to have more dimensions, and, in some ways, the two who appeared to spar on the playground seemed like they could just as easily have been buddies of some sort. The mystery of Bill and Hillary's relationship, so obviously under great stress and in flux, was reduced to a handful of possibilities: a political and career agreement, a nontraditional romantic partnership, or a deeply flawed marriage struggling with the ideals of love and loyalty. All of these people and their relationships developed meaning in relation to one another; take one away, and the remaining characters' meanings would change to some degree. Their characters had developed over the years in the public spotlight, and their relations to one another had galvanized into a story with a particular structure. What the public experienced, however, was not the unfolding of one singular plot, but competition between multiple plots, developing stories that aspired and pretended to tell us who each of these people really was, what their motives were, and what was actually, really going on in the nation's center. Their images on the television screen reflected neither chaos nor a perfectly stable order, but coherent characters with discernable relationships, whose futures remained uncertain.

Every time these actors appeared on screen their images were accompanied by a news reporter, anchorperson, media critic, or entertainer who would reduce and simplify the story, and move it forward, however incrementally. I was lucky enough to see David Brinkley, the longtime newsman and recently retired host of the ABC Sunday morning news program *This Week*, exiting a plane one summer during Clinton's second term. Brinkley had left the news business by this time, but it was still through his prior years on *This Week* that I had developed a sense of who these current political actors, the ones still living the drama, were. Brinkley had been an important part of my Sunday morning ritual. I trusted him, and enjoyed his commentary and onscreen presence, even though by the time I began to identify with his show he had largely adopted the posture of a bemused elder statesman or father figure, who would listen patiently to Cokie Roberts, George Will, and Sam Donaldson joust about the meaning of the week's latest developments. A year or two priorly, commenting on Clinton's re-election while on air, Brinkley had proclaimed Clinton a "bore" and declared that the forthcoming four years would be filled with "pretty words" and a lot of "goddamn nonsense!" I laughed out loud at Brinkley's candor; it did not matter if I agreed with him or not, I simply enjoyed seeing him express himself thus, and I felt closer to him for having witnessed it.

Standing in the luggage retrieval area of Jackson Hole, Wyoming's airport, I wanted to express to Mr. Brinkley my fondness for him. My taken-for-granted assumptions quickly unraveled: "Hey, I know this guy!" turned into, "Well, I know this guy's on-air persona," which was followed by perhaps the most obvious realization, "This man does not know me at all." It produced an unsatisfying feeling that signaled no clear norms of how to proceed. It is this odd paradoxical sense of knowing and not knowing, of having an understanding about someone based on a thoroughly mediated relationship, and of the emotional attachments I felt that, in part, this book seeks to explore. The experience of politics in America is a lot like this encounter: we develop understandings, feelings of certainty, about political actors and media critics from political actors and media critics, but at a step removed. These understandings feel intuitive, have emotional components, and just like my memory of this chance meeting with Brinkley, they present themselves and then disappear, only to be recalled in future analogous moments. Where do these understandings and feelings come from, how do they take form, and create feelings of certainty, and passions of hatred and affection? A structure is certainly erected through this dynamic relationship between state actors, media critics, and publics, but nothing is known in any concrete terms. Collective life makes something from nothing, and then we get up and make a near replica again the next day. The nothing has a structure: namely, culture. We are born into it, and we think and feel through it. It is the structure and flow of American political culture that this book seeks to illuminate.

This project began as an attempt to explain the events of 1998 through the metaphorical lens of Watergate, as representing a national ritual in which a counter-democratic element had been identified in the nation's center, thus sparking a redemptive, purifying process through which the normative ideal would be restored. Watergate morphed from representing a bungled break-in into a widely shared understanding that Nixon had abused the power of the office and obstructed justice. The House hearings and Senate proceedings forced Nixon to resign. As a symbol, Watergate came to connote presidential power run amuck. Monicagate erupted with an intensity that resembled the heights of the Watergate hearings proceedings, and it had an initial symbol – an affair with a White House intern – that had the potential to morph into far more dangerous and polluting understandings. Yet for the majority of the American public, Monicagate failed to mature symbolically, or to suggest that far more seriously threatening meanings lurked beneath the originating charge. Between initiating event and impeachment, Monicagate became enmeshed and mired in enervating details, and due to the long-standing, unfulfilled charges of corruption against Clinton, its symbolic boundaries appeared opaque and fuzzy.

A ritual is a ceremonial process with an identifiable beginning, middle, and end. It invites its participants to join in the celebration and reaffirmation of shared meanings. While the eruption of Monicagate in January 1998 signified a beginning, Clinton's impeachment by the House of Representatives in December later that year represented a false and sputtering ending to the event. The Senate's acquittal in the spring of 1999 was already a foregone conclusion, an anemic coda to a failed performance. While the ritual model illuminates the event in many respects, it fails to successfully capture the deep divisions and combativeness on display throughout the year. Like experts offering authoritative yet contradicting testimonies at a trial, some media critics and political actors said that Clinton's actions were the same as Nixon's, while others argued that they had absolutely nothing in common. Understandings had developed and hardened into consensuses, but they were staunchly opposed to one another, and the understanding that no purifying ritual was needed came to dominate. While the impeachment process moved forward, it failed to bring national publics into sympathetic participation. The impeachment was a ritual, but it was in many ways a mechanical process rather than an organic event generating emotional attachments and reinvigorating senses of collective identification. Given these conditions, it is little wonder that Clinton was able to remain in office to finish his second term. In sum, Monicagate and Clinton's impeachment were ritual-like; they represent a ritual process, but they demarcate a ritual within a larger social dramatic context. They were the culmination of events – of character development and plot formation – six years in the making. They were spectacles capping years of spectacle, and, in retrospect, a fitting if unfortunate crystallization of the decade's ongoing drama through which the nation's political fabric was continually rewoven.

Marx famously paraphrased Hegel to suggest that these types of grand historical events seem to happen twice, the first time as tragedy, the second as farce. As tantalizing as the formulation is, invoking it to interpret Monicagate in relation to Watergate would obscure critical, fascinating processes. The point of the following pages is to take this formulation not as a statement of historical law, but to understand these results as contingent, interpretive outcomes, and to investigate how these understandings are achieved through the constant interactions between political actors, media institutions and critics, and a nation's publics. Late-modern politics occurs in highly differentiated and complex social and cultural conditions. Powers that used to reside naturally in positions and personages no longer inhere so effortlessly in the social statuses, like the presidency, that simply assumed them in the past.

Public understandings of the boundaries separating the real and the artificial, the public and the private, and the notions of authenticity have shifted, as the people's emotional reactions to the televised images of national figures I described above, and my experience of meeting Mr. Brinkley, suggest. Under these fluctuating cultural conditions, in which power has become more "defused" and diffuse, national politics unfolds as cultural performances, with actors, mediating critics, and audiences working through symbolic means to narrate, define, and interpret the nation's current status and future trajectory.

Clinton's presidency and the mystery of his impeachment amid high public approval ratings compel the generation of a new explanatory framework, a macro-sociological approach based on a dramaturgical sensibility. Recently a new kind of sociology has emerged from the cultural turn in the social sciences. Called cultural pragmatics (Alexander 2004), the framework identifies how social and political processes in highly differentiated societies are the product of the complex interplay of six elements of cultural performance: actors, audiences, collective representations, means of symbolic production, mise-en-scène, and power. While continuously narrated by media critics through various news outlets, politics today often takes place through televised performances, in which these elements of performance are brought together and used to stage communicative moments. Embedded in deeply structured collective representations that define what is democratic and what is counter-democratic, what is right and wrong, and sacred and profane, political actors craft scripts, and use means of symbolic production, like props and signifying objects, to communicate with their audiences and to shape public understandings. Such a televised moment is the mise-en-scène, the actual performance before a camera, which is broadcast in real time to Americans, who, as audiences, are themselves skeptical and critical, and pulled in multiple directions by the demands of contemporary everyday life. Media critics interpret and critique these performances, and subsidiary political actors spin them to sharpen talking points, and to either reiterate or oppose the presidential narrative. Political power operates through the interplay of these dramatic elements. It is performative in its exercise, and it is always shaped by the other elements of cultural performance. Power – institutional, material, and social – can be exercised in ways that allow or disallow such performances, that enhance or detract from them. But the usage of power always contains a performative dimension, and its usage is interpreted by audiences in important and highly consequential ways. Political power operates through performative power. As such, power is always held in check and shaped by the other elements of social performance.

I approached Mr. Brinkley, offered him my hand, and said, "I've really enjoyed your work." He accepted my hand, smiled a warm, crooked smile, and said, "Thank you." We carved a script out of the cultural milieu, performed it, and it worked.

What follows is a sustained social scientific investigation of a presidential tenure. Many presidential historians, political scientists, sociologists, and even scholars from the humanities have analyzed the sources of social power, and the exercise of presidential power in particular. However, none have offered a systematic, detailed sociological history of how a president, media institutions, and publics interact to shape the everyday processes by which we sustain, contest, and remake democratic life. Policy choices, political careers, and the public's fortunes are structured by the cultural dimensions and performative processes detailed in the pages that follow. Without embedding the practice of presidential power within the complexities and flows of performance, we fail to see that the office is more than a mere state institution, and its incumbent embodies more than a biography of the person is able to capture.

The cultural pragmatics of the Clinton years

In January of 1998, President Clinton appeared on live television to deny having an affair with former White House intern Monica Lewinsky. In August, after testifying about his relationship with Lewinsky via video-link to a Grand Jury, Clinton appeared on television again to admit to an inappropriate relationship with the former intern. In September, nearly 500 pages of Independent Counsel Kenneth Starr's investigative report were released to the public on the internet, radically increasing web traffic to sites offering the report for public downloading.[1] A little over a week later, Clinton appeared on television again, as Congress released his taped testimony before the Grand Jury for public airing. In December, Clinton was impeached by the House of Representatives, whose hearings were broadcast live on television. In February 1999, after being acquitted of the charges of impeachment by the Senate, Clinton said to his close advisors: "Thank God for public opinion" (Woodward 1999: 513).

American publics learned an incredible amount of detail about Clinton's public and private lives throughout 1998 and the congressional impeachment processes. Over the prior six years, political actors had developed character structures, and plots had formed, eroded, and formed again. These symbolic structures would be activated again during 1998: Clinton had been framed as "Slick Willie" on the one hand, and as an intelligent, compassionate, Horatio Alger-like character on the other; Newt Gingrich and Kenneth Starr had become vessels for restoring dignity to the White House as well as corrupt investigators bent on enacting a political coup. Plots about the "politics of personal destruction" and "vast right-wing conspiracies" battled against plots detailing personal and political corruption of such severity that socialist schemes, complicity in murder, and real-estate and banking boondoggling had been constructed. Political battles were waged daily, and in 1996, when FOX News and MSNBC joined CNN and CSPAN as available cable news channels, and as the internet became present in a rapidly increasing number of American homes, a complex symbolic distribution network formed an available and eager mediating environment prepared to narrate and critique, and in many ways sustain, an explosive political storm.

What follows is not just an explanation of the Clinton presidency, and indeed one of the few sustained social science investigations ever attempted of an eight-year presidential term itself. It is also a decidedly new and different kind of approach. It is an explanation of power shifts that is rooted in culture. Over recent decades, social science has undergone a cultural turn, but this seems hardly to have disturbed studies of power, and has intervened only sparsely in studies of the president. What would it mean to make meaning central to power struggles in general, and to the Clinton presidency in particular?

To answer this question, I introduce a cultural sociological understanding. This will be a new kind of cultural sociology, however, one that offers a clear break with both classical (Van Gennep 1960 [1908]; Durkheim 1995 [1915]) and modern approaches (Shils and Young 1953; Warner 1959; Bellah 1967; Douglas 1966; Turner 1974, 1977 [1969], 1982; Alexander 1988; Smith 1991; Roth 1995; Edles 1998; Marvin and Ingle 1999). At the core of cultural sociology is the insistence that social action is neither interest based nor contingently calculated in an interest-based way, but that action is meaningful and that, to be meaningful, is carried out in relation to structures of understanding that are social, collective, and extra-individual in nature (Alexander and Smith 1993, 2001). In classical and modern forms of cultural sociology, however, the understanding of cultural structures and meaningful action focused on ritual behavior, highly stylized moments that created parallels with actions in primitive societies. Except for Clinton's impeachment, the Iran-Contra Affair (1986) that occurred during Reagan's second term is the closest America has come to revisiting the ritual dynamics so vividly displayed in the Watergate proceedings. Yet even when the Administration was revealed to have engaged in profoundly counter-democratic activities, the proceedings failed to rise to a level of crisis that could foster widespread ritualization. Social conditions were defused to the extent that even when the polluting symbolic framework of a soldier "just following orders" was so readily available a sizeable portion of the proceeding's audience reacted to Oliver North's performance by interpreting him as representing a hero as opposed to a villain.

Concluding his analysis of Watergate, sociologist Jeffrey Alexander (1988) observes that "achieving the form of modern ritual is contingent ... for modern rituals are not nearly so automatically coded as earlier ones" (190). Indeed, the problems with applying the ritual framework to the Clinton case are clear: (1) it imposes too rigid a structure on the event's processual flow, (2) it tends to assume a unidirectional relationship between ritual producers and their intended audiences, (3) it presupposes that rituals either succeed or fail to achieve their theorized social functions, (4) it does not allow for exploring ambiguous, complex, or multifaceted outcomes, and (5) it suggests that only big events have meaning. Recently there has developed a radically new form of cultural sociology that promises to maintain the emphasis on meaning while avoiding the drawbacks of ritual theory. This is cultural pragmatics, which has initiated the performative turn in sociology (Alexander 2004; Alexander, Giesen, and Mast 2006).

Cultural pragmatics pays attention to background structures of meaning, but takes a pragmatic understanding of whether actors can effectively embody them (e.g. Turner 1982, 1986; Carlson 1984, 2001; Schechner 1985, 1990, 1993, 2003 [1988]; Aston and Savona 1991; Taylor 1995; Roach 1996, 2000). Scripts have to be forged out of these background representations, and this requires creativity, and in modern politics this occurs in teams. Even when scripts are developed, however, they must walk and talk – actors need a place to stand, a stage, and access to means of symbolic production. Actors must create a scene, compel media attention, and communicate their messages in real time. Put another way, teams must create an event's mise-en-scène. Finally, teams need a sense of audience, which in performative terms is filled with agency of its own.

In this way cultural pragmatics draws attention to six elements of cultural performance: actors, audiences, systems of collective representation, means of symbolic production, mise-en-scène, and social power.

Actors: Symbols and plots are given life and communicated to publics by men and women inhabiting their political roles, striding the stage. In and through the symbolic contestation, actors make choices that vary from prescient to poor, and embody or speak their symbolic intentions with varying degrees of deftness. Actors control their own meanings through their speech and comportment, but they are never fully in control over their entire semiotic domain. Actors take on meanings in relation to other actors in the drama, and in relation to the settings, plots, and vagaries of everyday life that can be picked up by a video camera. In the age of the "public relations presidency" (Brace and Hinckley 1992, 1993), politicians have become increasingly aware of their telegenic potentials and limitations. Goffman elegantly explored "the problem of misrepresentation" (1951: 298) throughout his work (1959, 1963, 1967), bringing to light how people have the ability to project meanings that can be misleading or disingenuous. Actors and audiences are attuned to this social fact, that an actor's motivations in relation to the words and deeds she communicates are contingent (Alexander 2004: 531). "Authenticity" is prized, but it is an interpretive category, not an ontological state. Audiences can attribute the virtue to an actor or not, and the qualities that evoke notions of authenticity change over time and across cultures (Peters 2000).

Audiences: Audiences decode what actors have encoded (Hall 2005 [1980]). Scripts and performers must communicate culturally familiar content, messages that audiences can interpret and understand. Audiences interpret performances in variable ways (Alexander 2004: 531), depending on their social, cultural, and biographical familiarity or symbolic distance to the material being performed. Symbolic content communicates on both a cognitive and emotional level. Audiences can agree or disagree with factual content, but have conflicting emotional reactions to other symbolic cues by, for instance, appreciating the message but not liking the messenger. Audience members must be able to psychologically identify with performers and recognize character traits at some level. In this volume I specifically use the term audiences, in the plural, to draw attention to the multiple groups that form, and along group lines, interpret messages similarly, and seek out productions with similar messages and aesthetic qualities. Broadly speaking, American political dramas create three to four audiences, one for each major party and ideological position, a giant, swayable middle that remains more autonomous from specific party productions, and, at times, a fractional group associated with an emerging third party.[2]

Systems of collective representation: In the ongoing flurry of actors acting and audiences interpreting, critics, analysts, and laypersons alike can feel compelled to dismiss the political arena's symbolic battles as shallow and illusory, and be moved to search for more meaningful depths in institutional logics, the instrumental exercise of power, or the veiled pursuit of material interests. But, to paraphrase Marshall Sahlins

(1976: 166), compartmentalizing the symbolic would mean ignoring the cultural code that specifies the concrete properties governing claims to and uses of political authority. The rhythmic cycles of scheduled political contests and the periodic eruptions of events do not obscure but rather draw to the fore the structuring effects of a symbolic order and logic in and according to which these processes unfold. The cultural universe is lent order and organized around collective representations, or potent symbols that Emile Durkheim (1995 [1915]) argued express collective realities (9), constitute facts and "objects of experience" (436), and shape people's conduct "with the same necessity as physical forces" (229). Collective representations matter in that they define circumstances and influence the determination of consequences.

Like constellations in the night's sky, or the anchoring radii of a spider's web, collective representations order the symbolic worlds into which we are born and socialized. Collective representations order the political universe too in the form of deep structures like the binary codes of civil society, which specify the characteristics of social actors, relationships, and institutions that connote either liberty or its antinomy, repression. Yet this symbolic world is also composed of more ephemeral sign formations, such as a party's "talking points" which are crafted so that they will be reiterated across a Sunday morning's broadcasting of news shows and in newspapers' editorial pages. Some collective representations are deeply constitutive, enduring, and operate at a level beyond reflexive consideration, while others, the ones that receive most attention in public discourse, are more tangible, obvious, and ephemeral. In social performance, the discursive goal is to wrap oneself in a metaphorical flag that connotes the narratives of democracy and liberty. But because of the cultural system's relative autonomy and immutability, this goal is far more easily engaged in than won.

Means of symbolic production: The means of symbolic production refers to the material environments from which actors project their meanings. The material objects that surround the actor, from the stage and setting, to props and costumes, all contribute to the meanings a performance will project. Performances also require that actors ensure that the means of symbolic distribution are in place in order to project their messages to distant audiences. The relative autonomy separating the state from the media means that political actors must be seen as compelling enough to warrant attention, and be seen as interesting enough for media to decide to devote its communicative spaces to distributing the performance, let alone reviewing or critiquing the event, and thereby devoting to it extra communicative space.[3]

Mise-en-scène: Making a text walk and talk upon a stage requires spatial and temporal choreography, bringing actors, props, and cameras together, and putting them into motion in a predetermined way. Mise-en-scène refers to the bringing together of all of the dramatic components and putting them into action for the moment and practice of performance. The mise-en-scène is what ends up on screen at any particular time. All political performances are directed and produced to some degree, with commercials and conventions representing the height of choreographed control, and live debates and town hall meetings representing the other end of the controlled/contingent performance continuum.

Social power: Forms of power are distributed unequally, of course, and social performances are enabled and constrained accordingly. Access to the variety of forms of social power (Mann 1986, 1993) influences the size, scope, and reach of performances, but in no means determines their effectiveness. Challengers beat incumbents, the latter of which hold more symbolic and political power. Gandhi and Martin Luther King Jr. demonstrated the power of performance from below, and performance is used by a variety of disenfranchised groups to protest against the powerful and to make claims for social justice (Taylor 1995). In the political sphere, the office of presidency affords a vast array of forms of power, yet his ("his" as of this writing) exercise of power is continuously interpreted and critiqued through the performative lens. The current study is about the extravagances and the limits of political power, in each of the three American branches of government.

Contemporary politics is the product of a constant interaction between teams of performers and audiences. Political actors experience, react to, and work to gain control over "micro-events" within a broader effort to project stable images of power and legitimacy. Politics flows in episodes, and actors work within and between episodes to control micro-events so that they are well positioned when large-scale events, which compel broad public attention, form and appear to take on a life of their own. Audiences are bombarded by these micro-events, or political "occurrences" (Molotch and Lester 1974), which, while meaningful, exist only temporarily and relatively discretely in people's awareness. Political occurrences do not transcend their originating contexts or take root in the larger public's consciousness; they do not become part of the narrative of history. Yet political actors are always engaged in mediating them in an effort to control their potential future meanings in case they do, in fact, become plot points in an "event" writ large. For instance, after the Democrats ceded control over Congress to the Republicans in 1994, President Clinton began narrating the Republicans as mean, uncaring, anti-government revolutionaries. His efforts received little attention until six months later, when domestic terrorists detonated a car bomb at the federal building in Oklahoma City, killing and injuring dozens of citizens. Due to Clinton's prior symbolic work, the event reversed his downward slide in public opinion, and vastly improved his position entering the late-fall showdown over the federal budget with Speaker Newt Gingrich and congressional Republicans. The stalemate over the state's future economic plans was thoroughly dramatic in nature, and profoundly emblematic of how politics operates under the conditions of defusion. Contrary to John R. Zaller's (1998: 185) *a priori*, "bottom-line politics" assumptions about public opinions, the budget's contents were shaped by political actors' readings of public desires, and the public's understandings of the budget's contents were shaped as much by subjective feelings about each political actor's character as by any knowledge of the plan's economic details or its potential consequences for the nation's trajectory. The battle over the budget was interpretive and performative, and Clinton's prior symbolic work enabled him to allow for the federal government to shut down while shifting responsibility for the dramatic event to his opposition, Newt Gingrich, who was promptly caricatured in the *New York Daily News* as a crying, diapered baby.

Clinton's dramatically improved performative politics in 1995 also helped him secure his re-election in 1996 (see Chapter 6). For political actors, controlling "events," or narratively interconnected occurrences that achieve "generalization" (Alexander 1988; Smelser 1963), means securing one's own favorable interpretation over potent, historically influential political symbols. The cultural pragmatic framework outlined here reconstructs the meaning-texture of these flows, showing how occurrences are transformed into culturally meaningful events, as characters emerge and plots are formed, and the meaning-texture of political life is continuously rewoven.

To analyze politics as a flow of occurrences and events, cultural pragmatics attends to the internal structure of political sequences both diachronically, in terms of the overall flows of dramatic phases, and synchronically, by looking at variations within phases. Diachronically, for instance, public understandings of House Speaker Newt Gingrich and Independent Counsel Ken Starr were critical to shaping opinions about the investigative and political actions aimed at Clinton in 1998. Gingrich's and Starr's characters, and their emplotments in the social drama, had been forming for years prior to the scandal's eruption in January 1998. Likewise, Republicans and partisan opinion makers had been crafting plots against Clinton since he first took office, promising to reveal a smoking gun that would have Clinton's fingerprints on it, and that this evidence would reveal Clinton's "true" corrupt and undemocratic self. The Republicans would have profited by being mindful of the rule of "Chekhov's gun," named after the late-nineteenth-century dramatist Anton Chekhov, who pointed out a critical maxim about crafting compelling drama. If a gun is introduced in the first act, Chekhov instructed, then it had better go off in the second or third act, otherwise the gun should not be introduced in the story at all. This insight identifies a critical weakness in the structuring of the Republicans' dramatic efforts during the Clinton years. They began promising to reveal evidence that would unravel Clinton's presidency so early in the drama – the promise of the smoking gun that would be proof of damning corruption – that by the time Monicagate erupted in 1998, the plot's dramatic tension had profoundly eroded.

Turning to synchronic analysis: isolating each dramatic phase facilitates identifying unpredictable opportunities that arise in an event and analyzing how they may be seized upon and narrated to influence the larger event's flow and outcome. For instance, Ken Starr's and the Republican House's highly dramatic, televised release of Clinton's taped testimony before the Grand Jury in 1998 backfired on their production efforts and intentions, both repulsing audiences and further delegitimating the Republican impeachment narrative in the eyes of many. The Clinton team seized on this unexpected backlash and used the video's release to further symbolically pollute the Republican effort (see Chapter 7).

Within the flow of events, multiple forms of audience-to-production relations develop. Cultural pragmatics conceives of audiences as – to a greater but qualified degree – more interpretive, critical, and agentic than the ritual framework's theorized audiences. Audiences can actively participate in productions, or they can contemplatively absorb and reflect on them. They can cheer or hiss at productions, or they can simply ignore them or turn off their televised images. Political teams strive to draw in their audiences and to win over new audience members, and they effect changes during the event's flow to accomplish these ends.

Through accounting for alternative theatrical modes of presentation, cultural pragmatics allows for analyzing how various genres cultivate different audience-to-production relationships. A farcical production may succeed to the extent that the audience laughs at the production, or shrugs it off, thus compelling the audience members to return to their various individual routines. Alternatively, tragedies and melodramas can lead to highly ritualized processes, drawing their audiences in to the degree that the line between production and audience is erased – the audience comes to identify with the production, and thus liminality may develop, potentially affecting social- and culture-structural transformations.

In the following pages, I will demonstrate how these ideas offer a new approach to a democratic politics, and specifically to a major episode in American political life. I begin with the working hypothesis that any effort to gain power or sustain political power in American society must situate this effort in terms of a public, civil binary discourse that divides the world into the democratic sacred and the anti-democratic profane (Alexander and Smith 1993; Alexander 2006).[4] The codes of civil society are empirically derived cultural codes that structure the ways social actors attempt to frame themselves and their foes to influence spectators' interpretations of them. The codes have an evaluative dimension that when applied by motivated contestants in the political or public realms plays a key role in the determination of public contestations. The codes have proven remarkably stable over time, and are evidenced in political contestations ranging from debates over Ulysses S. Grant's fitness for holding the presidency in the 1870s, to political battles during the Teapot Dome Scandal in the 1920s, to Watergate in the 1970s, and the Iran-Contra Affair in the 1980s (Alexander and Smith 1993).

The codes are present in the Clinton presidency as well. But – and this is an all-important qualification – from the perspective of cultural pragmatics, this background code is only a place to begin, not end. The efforts and struggles of actual politics are entirely contingent: each side must place the other in terms of the profane, and itself in terms of the sacred. To do this is difficult, in itself. It is made even more difficult with the fragmentation of audiences and the multiplicity of actors, the differential and continuously shifting access to means of symbolic production, and the incessant mediation by journalists and critics, conditions which define turn-of-the-century American politics.

It is these concerns that will be our primary focus in the pages that follow. I begin by setting American politics of the 1990s within an historical context. I bring together literatures that describe presidential leadership strategies, public understandings of citizenship, and news production and media technologies, between the presidencies of Theodore Roosevelt and Bill Clinton, and I detail how the relations between these spheres have changed over time. I argue that interactions between these spheres are currently organized in a theatrical way, and that mass mediated plot formation and character development play an increasingly determinative role in structuring the contemporary political arena. I conceptualize politics as a process of ongoing performances, staged by motivated political actors, mediated by critics, and interpreted by audiences, all in the context of a deeply rooted, widely shared system of collective representations or webs of signification.

The central empirical mystery this study explains is how Bill Clinton finished his presidency with high approval ratings after being impeached by the House of Representatives in 1998. Explaining Clinton's popularity during and after Monicagate requires that we analyze the particular cultural and political context out of which the social drama erupted. I begin my investigation of the Clinton years with the struggle for the Democratic nomination in the 1992 presidential primaries, when Bill Clinton makes his initial steps onto the American political stage. Early in Clinton's first term, congressional Republicans, with the support of an exuberant, solid quarter of the nation's citizens, began to construct Clinton's assumption of power as representing a counter-democratic threat, and as a national "fall from grace" drama (see Chapter 4). After meeting with some narrative success that enabled significant political victories, the persuasive power of the Republicans' dramatic narratives began to erode (Chapter 5). Toward the end of its first term, the Clinton administration became increasingly effective at controlling social dramas. The Administration's newfound social dramatic acumen enabled it to weather the Right's relentless symbolic and political onslaughts. The Administration's narratives shored up support from its Democratic base, and increasingly secured the sympathy of the silent, swayable, middle majority of American citizens (Chapter 6). In the final empirical chapter, I analyze the cultural pragmatics that produced Monicagate's frenetic beginning and shaped the contours of the event's unfolding (Chapter 7). In so doing, I show how the cultural pragmatic framework explains the apparent paradox of how Clinton, though impeached by the House Republicans, remained in office to finish out his second term with high approval ratings, and the sympathy and support of a majority of American publics.

2

Presidential leadership under the conditions of defusion

The focus of this study is the public life of democratic politics: the performative dimensions, causes, and consequences of the struggle for political power in a fragmented and differentiated society committed to democracy and regulated by open and unabashed competitions for influence and public legitimation. Formerly nestled in the state, party leaders, economic and religious institutions, and social elites, political power and authority have splintered and become more diffuse over the course of the twentieth and early twenty-first centuries (Schudson 1998; Alexander 2004; Gorski 2006; Kernell 2007; cf. Mann 1993), as mediating institutions have insinuated themselves between former sources of power and the nation's publics (Altheide and Snow 1979; Schudson 1995a; Zelizer 1992). The assumption and exercise of power have become more complicated, as media elites and opinion makers have increased their interpretive power, and as the American imagined community has transformed from a mass society into a system of interlocking and overlapping yet differentiated publics (Neustadt 1990 [1960]: 73; Alexander 2006). As a consequence of these transformations in the social bases of authority, politics at the turn of the twenty-first century increasingly operates through performative power, which has both an interpretive and a constitutive dimension.

These are the conditions of defusion (Alexander 2004), in which the authority to name, narrate, proscribe, and prescribe is no longer the sole province of office holders, party leaders, social elites, and experts. While the United States is still constituted by a shared, overarching American cultural structure (Alexander and Smith 1993), it is also more symbolically differentiated and complex than at any other time. These conditions have turned the practice of politics into performances. Contemporary politics demonstrates a performative logic, but

I do not mean this in a pejorative sense, or to suggest that those in power act solely in duplicitous and inauthentic ways simply to achieve their desired ends, which the "politics as theater" metaphor can oftentimes suggest (Apter 2006). Rather, politics are like performances in the sense that agents of power must work in a more consciously symbolic way to communicate their ideas to publics, which, as audiences with critical distance, are more capable than ever of accepting or refuting, embracing or ignoring, messages from on high, and whose reactions shape, in turn, the future actions of the powerful.

For political dramas to even occur, the actors and audiences must share a broad system of cultural understandings so that they can communicate and understand one another. Culture is composed of deep structures and collective representations that structure our shared understandings, on the one hand, as well more tangible symbols such as words and material objects that we use intentionally to communicate our ideas and intentions with others, on the other. Assisted by teams of advisors, political actors carve scripts out of this cultural milieu, and stage their performances with symbolically powerful objects and settings in ways that show they identify with their audiences, and in hopes of stirring them cognitively and emotionally in a favorable way. With scripts on teleprompters, and surrounded by evocative means of symbolic production, political actors perform before the television cameras their scenes, which are instantly interpreted and spun by media critics and diffused throughout the nation's and, increasingly, the world's publics (Thompson 2000: 71). This is the structure and flow of politics under the conditions of defusion. Clinton's rise to power, his early struggles, political rebirth, and battles with Republican opposition over the course of the 1990s demonstrate that contemporary politics operates through performative power, a social force composed of efforts to constitute and shaped by processes and structures of interpretation.

A cultural and social context produces particular arrangements and relations of power and obedience, and as social and cultural conditions change, the practice of politics changes as well. Max Weber created the field of political sociology when he identified how the social foundations of authority change over time in conjunction with varying degrees of social differentiation. The authority to exercise one's will over a populace, Weber argued (1968: 212–300), has been rooted in tradition, charisma, and constitutive of the modern epoch, in rational-legal systems of formal rules and laws institutionalized in bureaucracies. Weber developed these categories to delineate broad historical epochs and trends, and his descriptions of the sources of power in the rational-legal context tell us very little about the actual structure and flow of contemporary political dynamics. Politics today does occur within a rational bureaucratic context. However, Marx (1963 [1851–2]) had earlier observed that even when members of a collectivity seem poised to create a more rationally just social and political order, they "anxiously conjure up the spirits of the past to their service, borrowing from them names, battle slogans, and costumes," and thus fashion the new arrangements "in time-honored disguise and borrowed language" (15). Marx was describing the French Revolution (1789–1814) and the popular election of Louis Bonaparte in 1848; however, his insight into the cultural underpinnings of political action remains true today. In less lyrical prose: while contemporary politics occurs within a rational bureaucratic context as Weber suggested, political imaginings, ideals, concerns, calculi, and contests are nonetheless constructed and interpreted with reference to the cultural names, slogans, and borrowed languages of the past.

When Emile Durkheim (1995 [1915]) laid the foundations for a cultural sociology in *The Elementary Forms of Religious Life*, he indicated that Marx's observation is more appropriately interpreted as an astute insight into social ontology than merely a normative lamentation or superstructural distraction. The most "rational" of human concerns, Durkheim's work suggested, including the economic, political, scientific, and emotional, are embedded in a cultural milieu, structured by collective representations, and enmeshed in webs of signification. Weber (1946 [1922–3], 1958 [1904–5]) was aware of culture's power to shape social action and institutions, of course. Yet Durkheim added a much more explicitly cultural dimension to the understanding of authority and social order when he theorized that rituals are the means through which social systems of understanding are reproduced, the symbolic boundaries of solidarity are redefined, and internal hierarchies are reaffirmed. Durkheim's emphasis on rituals, as structured, ceremonial proceedings, drew attention to the *processes* by which collective representations and symbol systems are translated into material realities in people's everyday actions and in the reproduction of social institutions. All societies, regardless of complexity, he concluded, must engage in ritual dynamics to reaffirm collective representations and redraw the ties to, and boundaries of, collective solidarity (Durkheim 1995 [1915]: 429). Modernist and contemporary sociologists attentive to culture have demonstrated the analytical purchase of the ritual framework, examining how ritual processes are central to the construction of national identities (Shils and Young 1953; Warner 1959; Spillman 1997), and how they are manifested during extreme moments of social and political cleavage, such as revolutions (Sewell 1985, 1996; Kertzer 1988; Edles 1998), crises of democracy (Alexander 1988), and modern warfare (Smith 1991).

Yet the very mediated public-ness and narrative combativeness demonstrated in the United States's contemporary political culture are indicative of how the status of legitimacy and projection of authority have become increasingly contingent, and how collective rituals struggle to affect widespread interpretive consensuses and feelings of group solidarity at the turn of the twenty-first century (Mast 2006). Achieving and maintaining legitimacy becomes an increasingly difficult task, given that multiple competing plots, instant mediation, and a fierce competition for people's attention are the order of the day in late-modern America. The ritual process has become more complicated and contingent in this context, and while collective social action continues to generate ritualized dynamics and structures, these events and proceedings are more likely to achieve a "ritual-like" structure than the stable, consensus-generating manifestations of the past (Turner 1982; Wagner-Pacifici 1986; Alexander 2004).

By examining how the structure of collective symbolic action has changed over the *longue durée*, Jeffrey Alexander (2004: 528, 533) created a theory of cultural performance that offers both a means of bridging Weber's typology of authority and Durkheim's theory of culture and ritual, and a model for analyzing the relations between the state, publics, and media in the ritual-like United States. Collective symbolic action, Alexander states, can be analyzed in terms of six elements of cultural performance: actors, audiences, the means of symbolic production, systems of collective representation, power, and the mise-en-scène. The exercise of power, Alexander's theory suggests, has transformed from (a) fused performances,[1] in which the elements of performance work together to create a kind of synchronicity in process and authenticity in role embodiment characteristic of rituals in tightly bound, socially and culturally homogenous social groups, to (b) contingent performances under defused conditions, in which political actors struggle to persuade audiences by seeking to strike the right constitutive chords in their scripts, by crafting them with an ear sensitive to the familiar background cultural tunes long found in a collectivity's songbook. In the real, empirical world, the challenge of cultivating and inhabiting political legitimacy under the conditions of defusion becomes one of "re-fusing" the elements of cultural performance. Analytically, understanding the nature of political power under the conditions of defusion means considering how easily, or problematically, these elements of performance affect or relate to one another during political exercises like, for instance, political campaigns and elections, routine and combative legislative processes, and during heated battles over political actors' claims to legitimacy, all of which the Clinton presidency evidenced in dramatic fashion.

With Alexander's theory of the shift from ritual to performance in hand, we can turn to examining how scholars have narrated the cultural expectations of citizens and leaders over time, and highlight some of the changes in the empirical world that helped give rise to the defused conditions that shaped the politics of the 1990s. Power and legitimacy suggest a binary relationship of leadership and obedience. Legitimacy refers to how the parties on each side of this binary construct and interpret their expectations of both role positions, and these role positions are themselves given cultural form by the collectively specific narratives of citizenship and nationhood in which they are embedded. Through the lens of cultural pragmatics, studies of citizenship (Tocqueville 1969 [1835–40]; Lippmann 1965 [1922]; Dewey 1954 [1927]; Mills 1962 [1953]; Dahl 1961, 1989; Bellah et al. 1985; Lichterman 1996; Eliasoph 1998; Schudson 1998; Putnam 2001; Skocpol 2003; Alexander 2006) can be read as examinations of audiences' expectations, while studies of leadership styles (Kernell 2007; Tulis 1987; Neustadt 1990 [1960]; Brace and Hinckley 1992, 1993; Ryfe 2005; Greenstein 1993–4, 1994, 1998, 2000; Renshon 1994, 2000) can be read as descriptions of political actors' understandings of their roles in the drama of democracy. However, because leadership and obedience constitute one another, studies of one subject tell us something about the expectations of the other as well.

Studies of leadership styles, models of citizenship and assent, and news journalism have demonstrated that substantial transformations have occurred regarding how publics and political actors understand their role positions over the course of the country's history. The studies characterize this transformation as a movement from a broad consensus on the purpose of politics, tight bonds of group solidarities, and centralized, insulated political power practiced at a remove, to more fragmented understandings of what politics is for, solidarities rooted in more abstract cultural codes, and a more visible, immediate, and reciprocal relationship between the sovereign and the citizenry. In his examination of how understandings of citizenship have changed over the course of America's history, for instance, sociologist Michael Schudson (1998) characterizes this relationship's transformation as one initially shaped by "an organic view that the polity has a single common good" (5), which shifted to a framework dominated by parties "more devoted to distributing offices than to advocating policies" (6), and finally to contemporary circumstances, in which "individual claimants compete to set the standards of political life" (8), and "all bid to define what counts as politics and what the experience of politics might mean" (9).[2]

Political scientists and scholars of the presidency have focused on changes in the ways that political actors understand, derive, and exercise their power, and have also narrated a movement toward conditions of defusion and the rise of performative politics. Jeffrey Tulis (1987) argues that "a true transformation" (7) occurred in the early twentieth century regarding how political actors relate to their publics, when presidents began to see popular and mass rhetoric as "a principal tool of presidential government" (4). Prior to this, presidents constrained the sources of their authority to the model espoused by the Founders, who "discouraged any idea that the President should serve as a leader of the people who would stir mass opinion by rhetoric," and envisioned the president as representing a "constitutional officer who would rely for his authority on the formal powers granted by the Constitution and on the informal authority that would flow from the office's strategic position" (Ceaser et al. 1981: 161–2). Numerous examples of "mere suggestions by the president that particular legislation be enacted" were met with "congressional antipathy," Greenstein (1988: 298) suggests, and "even the veto could not legitimately be used as an expression of policy preference by the chief executive." Theodore Roosevelt changed this orientation, and actively started "going over the heads" of Washington elites and appealing to publics for support of his initiatives, a practice that Woodrow Wilson later adopted, initiating what Tulis calls the era of the "rhetorical presidency."

In his hallmark book *Presidential Power and the Modern Presidents*, Richard Neustadt (1990 [1960]) characterized mid-twentieth-century politics as operating within an autonomous, institutional Washington, and the president's political authority as rooted in his ability to get congressional and other Washington elites to agree to bargain with him and acquiesce to his will. First published in 1960, the book argued that "the power to persuade is the power to bargain. Status and authority yield bargaining advantages" (ibid.: 32). In later editions Neustadt attributed more significance to public opinion, acknowledging that it shaped political power, but he maintained that it was mediated through how Washington elites gauged the president's popular prestige (ibid.: 73). Because "Washingtonians" think about the president's popularity, Neustadt suggested, "public standing is a source for [the president], another factor bearing on [elites'] willingness to give him what he wants" (ibid.). Albeit in a footnote, Neustadt also acknowledged the power of public opinion polls, stating that they "are very widely read in

Washington. Despite disclaimers, they are widely taken to approximate reality" (ibid.: 81 fn. 9; cited in Gronke and Newman 2003: 501). Presidential power remained tethered to bargaining power for Neustadt (1990 [1960]: 264), even when television's impact on the political process was in full bloom:

A President's capacity to draw and stir a television audience seems every bit as interesting to current Washingtonians as his ability to wield his formal powers. Their interest is his opportunity. While national party organizations fall away, while congressional party discipline relaxes, while interest groups proliferate and issue networks rise, a President who wishes to compete for leadership in framing policy and shaping coalitions has to make the most he can out of his popular connection. Anticipating home reactions, Washingtonians ... are vulnerable to any breeze from home that presidential words and sights can stir. If he is deemed effective on the tube they will anticipate.[3]

The sources of political power shifted again during the 1970s and 1980s, political scientist Samuel Kernell's work indicates (2007: 33), from operating within the context of "institutional pluralism" so well described by Neustadt, in which "political elites, and for the most part only elites, matter" (12), and the public "normally pays little attention to what politicians do or say" (25), to one of "individualized pluralism," in which the political center is no longer organized by strong loyalties rooted in hierarchical protocoalitions, but by independent congresspersons who are free to "resort to their own devices to secure their political fortunes" and "to pursue private career goals" (30). In the context of individualized pluralism, Kernell (ibid.: 121) asserts, presidents more routinely "go public" in order to bypass Washington elites and appeal directly to the public to further their agendas.[4] It should come as no surprise that Kernell (2007, first published in 1986) and Tulis (1987) crafted their insights about the "rise of the rhetorical presidency" and the increasingly employed strategy of "going public" during "The Great Communicator" Ronald Reagan's presidency, during what Brace and Hinckley (1993) described as the era of the "public relations presidency," in which "president watchers worry that the office has become dominated by public relations goals" (382). Masterfully cultivated by Reagan and further institutionalized by Clinton, the "public presidency" now operates within a context of performative politics, in which an incumbent's public-ness is not simply a means or strategy of pursuing policy agenda goals. In the late twentieth century, "Americans simply expect presidents to communicate often and at great length about every public issue of the moment," political scientist David Ryfe (2005: 1) asserts, "no matter how far removed from the formal concerns of the office," such as coming out "in favor of school uniforms and against the use of steroids in baseball."

The metaphors used in these studies of state actors and citizens create a singular narrative arc: the country started with a polity that shared a broad consensus of a common good and power was rooted in station, which gave way to conditions in which political identities became tightly tethered to parties. While presidents began increasingly to court public opinion, in the early and mid-twentieth century an institutionally autonomous Washington represented a mass public, whose members were becoming models of the rational, informed citizen. Under contemporary conditions, Washington elites and citizens are defined foremost by one characteristic: they act and think of themselves as individuals. This, in a nutshell, is a narrative of America's movement toward the present conditions of defusion.

The current study decenters the state in the analysis of political power (see Friedland and Alford 1991; cf. Skocpol 1985) and embeds the practices of presidential actions and politics more generally within the conditions of defusion, which suggest that the shape of a democratic nation's trajectory is produced through the interactions of three social spheres: the state, media, and publics. These interactions are manifested in constitutive and interpretive efforts to shape public meanings and understandings, and they occur within broad cultural frameworks into which all of the actors have been born. As illuminating as studies of presidential leadership styles and strategies have been, and while presidents certainly do act strategically to pursue desired ends, the president's function is as much semiotic and performative as executive (Norton 1993: 87), and studies of political power must approach political practices and strategies as embedded and structured by a semiotic logic as well as by institutional and executive ones. Politicians, media critics, and citizens make decisions and identify their own preferences; however, they do so within cultural conditions that they neither create nor choose. Rhetoric and the art of persuasion are shaped and shadowed by the narrative and discursive formations in which they are practiced. Structured around the theory of cultural pragmatics, the performative presidency folds rhetoric and bargaining within a theory of culture as discourse; it draws to our attention the collective representations, the symbolic reservoir, from which political rhetoric is drawn, by which it is evaluated, and through which it is made meaningful.

The rise of the conditions of defusion and performative politics

The conditions of defusion and the rise of performative politics are rooted in changes in the political landscape that occurred in the 1890s and the first two decades of the twentieth century. Cautious of demagoguery, and with the intent of preserving representative republicanism, nineteenth-century presidents played only slight roles in the legislative process, and during the rare occasions when they spoke directly to the public, they remained general and vague in their statements. Congress dominated the legislative agenda, while political parties exerted great influence over the distribution of political offices and the promotion of political candidates, and represented the principal organizing symbols and institutions governing citizens' political identities. News journalism was shaped by party loyalties as well, with editors shaping their commentaries to support party goals, and reporters functioning as recorders or stenographers of institutional proceedings and congressmen's thoughts and deeds.

Progressivism began to erode party domination over political offices, and cultivated the understanding that citizens should participate directly in the political process, their political identities unmediated by party loyalty. Guided by the discourse of scientific management, political appointees were to become skilled, professional administrators of public office. The symbol of the citizens' representative in government shifted from congressman to president, and presidential candidates initiated the practice of speaking directly to voters – that is, of campaigning for office (Tulis 1987: 182–3).

In his analysis of press coverage of State of the Union messages, Schudson (1995a) notes that during this period news reporters shifted their self-identities and adopted a narrative form that continues to structure political news story telling to this day. News reporters gained autonomy from their editors and began to exert interpretive power: reporters "increasingly took it as their prerogative to assert something about the larger political meaning of the messages" (ibid.: 60), and political commentary, "once a partisan activity of the newspaper editor," increasingly became "a professional activity of the journalist" (66). These newly empowered interpreters of the political arena professionalized, creating their own press clubs and journals, forming internal hierarchies and elevating some of their members into an elite stratum, and reiterating the template of the journalist with wide name recognition if not celebrity-like status (ibid.: 67; see Stephens 2007: 279). Just as political administrators were transforming into public management experts, news journalists too were becoming expert critics of their subject.

In addition to the status of the reporter changing from recorder to interpreter, the subject of news journalism changed as well. The president became the central actor in the political drama, and was increasingly framed in news narratives as a "representative of the nation, a national trustee" (Schudson 1995a: 60). In addition to the office being narrated into the center of the political and national story, Schudson notes that in this era's news stories, "the President is treated as a person, and is mentioned by name in both the lead paragraph and the headline" (ibid.), and that his State of the Union message was increasingly treated as "an indicator of the President's personal program and political career" (61).

Translated into cultural pragmatic terms, the political drama was becoming more complex: the office of presidency was transforming from a marginal role into a central one, becoming the main symbol of citizen identification and, most interestingly, within the office itself, the role of incumbent was becoming defused. Schudson's keen empirical detail, noting that the president is treated as a *person* with his own program and career trajectory, indicates that the news reporters, flexing their interpretive skills, were beginning to distinguish increasingly between the person and the office (see Kantorowicz 1957). The institutionalization of this distinction in narrative form represents the process of defusion *in media res*; it signifies the creation of an interpretive and critical space in which the office holder is, in part, two distinct characters. This distinction increases the potential to analyze the two characters in relation to one another, to juxtapose the incumbent to the role, and critique the person with regard to the office, its predecessors, and its normative ideal representations. Claiming that late-twentieth-century politics operates under the conditions of defusion means that actors inhabiting the presidential role more routinely and consciously work to manage the critical distance between person and office. Their project becomes one of re-fusing person with presidential role. Indeed, presidential campaigns are exercises in cultivating in audiences exactly this understanding, that the person *is* presidential, the person will become, will seamlessly fuse with, the role of president.

As mentioned above, nineteenth-century presidents had been reluctant to engage in discursive practices that could excite mass sentiments. Tulis (1987) and his colleagues (Ceaser et al. 1981) demonstrate that it was in the first decade of the twentieth century that presidents changed this understanding of executive political power and began using popular rhetoric as a strategy for overcoming political opposition. While Theodore Roosevelt "presaged this change by his remarkable ability to capture the nation's attention through his understanding of the character of the new mass press and through his artful manipulation of the national press corps," it was Woodrow Wilson who "brought popular speech to the forefront of American politics" (Ceaser et al. 1981: 162). Wilson interpreted the presidential role as representing a national vessel of performativity:

A nation is led by a man who ... speaks, not the rumors of the street, but a new principle for a new age; a man in whose ears the voices of the nation do not sound like the accidental and discordant notes that come from the voice of a mob, but concurrent and concordant like the united voices of a chorus, whose many meanings, spoken by melodious tongues, unite in his understanding in a single meaning and reveal to him a single vision, so that he can speak what no man else knows, the common meaning of the common voice. (Wilson 1908, quoted in Ceaser et al. 1981: 163)

Wilson's statement is a performative to establish the president's performative authority, and it represents the archetype of the performative presidency. The president, in Wilson's view, "has no means of compelling Congress except through public opinion" (ibid.). To exercise the power of his office, the president must be attuned to the collective representations that structure the understandings, desires, and moods of his followers. As a social actor, the president must be a competent performer: "It is natural that orators should be the leaders of a self-governing people" (ibid.). And it is through performances to the public, his audience, that the president leads the nation in pursuit of a particular vision. To paraphrase the poet Wallace Stevens, Wilson imagines the presidency as representing the single artificer of the nation in which he leads: "There is but one national voice in the country and that is the voice of the President," he proclaimed (quoted in Ceaser et al. 1981: 163). The president must have an ear for both the background cultural milieu and the specific cultural moment; he must fold his policy objectives within the contours of this discursive formation to create his script, and he must perform it to the public, however mediated, in order to exercise power over his institutional counterpart. The president, in Wilson's view, has interpretive and constitutive authority, and he must be capable of performing this authority persuasively to his audiences.

Wilson's vision of the presidency belies the utter contingency of such performative efforts. While he foresees the possibility that performances can fail by suggesting that presidents will need to be good orators, he is also offering a vision of the fused presidency; for him, performative power inhered in the office and the person holding it. To the contrary, presidents can and do misinterpret public culture and moods, and regardless of the anthropological accuracy of their interpretations and the acuity of their scripts, their actual embodied performances can and do fail as well. In the latter half of the century the performative presidency has developed institutional mechanisms organized to reduce and control the greater degrees of performative contingency that define the conditions of defusion. Over subsequent decades presidents would bring political strategists, speech writers, communications directors and departments, and pollsters into their administrations, all of whom engage in the business of trying to perfect exactly Wilson's goal – namely, of re-fusing the person with the ideal presidential role.

While Wilson presaged the performative presidency, it would be another decade before the strategy took its next substantive foothold and became further institutionalized. Fred Greenstein (1988) argues that Franklin Delano Roosevelt's assumption of office represents the breakthrough that established the modern presidency, a mode of presidential authority defined by the "practice of advocating, backing, and engaging in the politics of winning support for legislation" (298). FDR's active orientation toward shaping legislation combined with his confident comportment, high oratory, forceful challenges to Congress, ebullience, and decisiveness to encourage the semiotic process whereby citizens "think increasingly of the president as a symbol for the government" (ibid.: 299). FDR faced national and international crises when he took office, and he met the challenges by promoting a "relentless succession of legislative enactments," policy initiatives that were passed by a special session of Congress during the president's first one hundred days. "One way to deal with the increasing complexity of government was to personify it," Greenstein states, and FDR met these conditions by wedding "his own great powers of personal communication to the general sense of national urgency, channeling what had hitherto been a static patriotic sentiment – American veneration of the great presidents of the past – into a dynamic component of the incumbent's role" (ibid.). Schudson (1995a) identifies the press's practice of personifying the incumbent. FDR's leadership orientation cultivated the association of the president's persona with the office, and as the presidency increasingly came to symbolize the government, the president's persona became part of this symbolic formation as well. Greenstein proposes some potential consequences of this semiotic process:

In initiating this characteristic of the modern presidency, he undoubtedly enhanced his ability and that of his successors to muster public support in times of perceived national crisis. But he also undoubtedly established unrealistic and even contradictory standards by which citizens tend to judge both the personal virtue of presidents and their ability to solve the typically controversial social and political problems that arise during their administrations. (Greenstein 1988: 299–300)

To return to the language of cultural pragmatics, FDR's personification of the presidency reiterates the person/office symbolic association, as well as the person/office/state conflation. As these signs fuse with one another, they also establish the symbolic fault-lines by which they can become defused; these fault-lines establish spaces of critique and evaluation. Presidents are rendered citational; the incumbent is constantly "ghosted" (Carlson 2001) by imaginings of how past political leaders – real, fictional, and mythical – inhabited the office (see Alexander and Mast 2006: 15).[5]

Far from the conditions of defusion, the politics of the Roosevelt era conjures images of the opposite, a moment in which politics, publics, and communicative technologies came together in ways that strengthened the American collective identity and bonds of national solidarity. Kernell (2007: 29) invokes a quintessential metaphor of fusion, the clock, when he characterizes the politics of the era: "The reciprocity of exchange and the complementarity of tasks between presidents and protocoalitions – especially when the latter equitably represents the interests of the nation – render institutionalized pluralism the look of a finely regulated clock. The synchronization of such a system of cogs and escapements would gratify those Newtonian mechanics whom we call our Founding Fathers." FDR's use of the radio to address his public conjures fused conditions as well.

While FDR epitomized a bargaining president in the Neustadt model, he also understood the power of cultivating a favorable relationship with the broader public. In an era without a national newspaper, and in which the local newspaper was the primary vehicle for conveying the news (Mickelson 1998), FDR took to the radio airwaves thirty times to communicate directly with the American public to shape popular understandings and build public support regarding such matters as banking reform, expanding the Supreme Court, and to communicate about the prospect and progress of war. Benedict Anderson (1983) argued that the novel and the newspaper were pivotal in establishing conditions for the rise of the national identity. Made available for public and commercial use in the early 1920s, radio enabled FDR to use the communicative technology to cultivate a national identity and strengthen solidarity during an era in which a mass public faced the enormous collective challenges of the Great Depression and World War II. Far from conjuring imagery of the cold hand of rational bureaucratic authority, FDR used the radio to cultivate a more intimate relationship between the president and his citizenry. In his fireside chats, he crafted his relationship with his audience by identifying with them personally and in terms of national identity, frequently referring to listeners as "my friends" and "my fellow Americans," thus rendering the "president's fireside … more accessible than the mayor's" (Stephens 2007: 272). In addition to speaking directly to the American public, FDR also cultivated informal and collegial relations with newspapermen with whom he conducted biweekly press conferences, and he created the White House Press Office to facilitate information exchange between the state and the news media (Maltese 1994: 4). He also carefully crafted and managed his public image – for instance, by seeking to project strength and vigor by hiding the effects of polio. On the other hand, FDR also set in motion some practices that would become powerful political tools in contemporary conditions of defusion. In terms of his formal presidential powers, FDR exercised "executive privilege" to resist sharing documents with Congress, and he started to use the office's veto power for partisan interests, a practice that had been reserved for addressing issues of constitutionality (Tulis 1987: 7).

At the time of FDR's death in 1945, newspapers, radio, and cinema newsreels were the principal technologies for disseminating narratives and images to the greater public. The production of television sets and network development had been halted by the war, and in 1948 roughly 400,000 Americans owned one of the new receivers. Television entered the political domain by broadcasting the Truman and Dewey political conventions in the summer of 1948; however, because the broadcasting infrastructure was still in its formative stages, the proceedings were only viewable by receiver owners within the regions bounded by Boston, Washington DC, and Pittsburgh. These conditions would change rapidly and dramatically as television ownership exploded during the 1950s: roughly 3 million American homes (9 percent) contained a set in 1950, whereas by 1960 approximately 46 million American homes (86 percent) housed a set. Television signals spread from regional access to blanketing the country during the decade (108 stations in 1950, to nearly 1,000 stations in 1960),[6] news content increased its portion of daily programming, networks' news staffs grew exponentially, and competition between networks to dominate the prestigious news programming sector heated up. Whereas high-status radio newsmen like the "Murrow Boys" had shunned the medium in its infancy, televised news broadcasts quickly began to displace the most popular news programs broadcast over the radio (Mickelson 1998).

While FDR courted public support for his initiatives over the radio and his successor, Truman, used the railcar and "whistle stop tours" to communicate directly with voters to retain power,[7] the rise of television in the mid-1950s shifted the relationships between the state, media, and publics, and altered the dimensions through which performative power could be projected and the terms by which it could be critiqued. As a communicative technology, television and its impact on the political process have been interpreted through cultural discourses that situate it as representing either a potential source of clarifying realism or as a source of distortion, as a tool that enables liberation or enslavement (see Alexander 2003). More frequently, television is narrated as representing the latter. In the early 1980s, for instance, political scientist Austin Ranney (1983) argued that television corrupts and denigrates the integrity of the political process, and encourages the erosion of public trust and confidence in government actors and institutions. More recently, postmodern theory has cast television as representing as another instantiation of a pervading hyperreality, a condition in which images and sound bites displace and vanquish substance and meaning. "During the past decades," Best and Kellner (1997: 108) argue, "all the major political battles in the United States have taken place in the media, in a hyperreal world of media image and spectacle," in conditions that convert "falsehood into 'truth,'" and in which "audiences [are] hooked on simulation." Schudson (1995a: 53), on the other hand, offers a welcome moderating insight, noting that while television became the "central locus of activity in American culture and politics," its political news productions represent less a distortion or triumph of image over substance than a crystallization of "political narrative that was well established in the print media decades before" the technology found its way into so many rooms in American homes (cf. Robinson and Sheehan 1983).

Indeed, television would establish a place in the nation's ritual center. The vast majority of Americans would turn to the device for political news, and they continue to do so today (Bennett 2007: 92–3). Most obviously, television added the visual to the media experience, and placed the images of political actors' bodies in the living rooms of news consumers. Print news journalism introduced the distinction between the presidency and the person holding office at the turn of the twentieth century (Schudson 1995a: 60–1), and presidents like Theodore Roosevelt, Woodrow Wilson, and FDR cultivated this distinction during their tenures (Ceaser et al. 1981; Greenstein 1988). Television draws to the fore this distinction as well, by bringing the bodies of presidents and presidential candidates into the visual spectrum for more routine interpretation. While television does not represent a radical intervention into the shaping of political narratives, as Schudson (1995a) suggests, it does change the performative interface between narrative authorities and citizens by adding another layer of interpretive material to the processes I am emphasizing. The body becomes a symbol from which a vast array of interpretations may be derived, cued by comportment, facial expressions, and gestures, let alone the signifiers of race, gender, and, given the effects of polio on FDR's body, interpretations of able-ness (Gray 2009).

Even when television news was in its developmental stages, a couple of noteworthy events foreshadowed transformations to come: threatened by scandal and pressured from within his party to resign, a candidate would turn to the television airwaves to perform his own narrative to the American public, and a news journalist would challenge a politician's constitutive power, and thus reiterate a mythical template casting the journalist as a heroic, everyman defender of democratic ideals. In 1952, when presidential candidates Dwight D. Eisenhower and opponent Adlai Stevenson first employed television campaign commercials matching simple animation to catchy tunes, Senator and vice presidential candidate Richard Nixon turned to the television airwaves in an attempt to deflate a rising personal finance scandal. For means of symbolic production, Nixon appeared on screen sitting behind a desk, with his wife, Pat, sitting in an armchair nearby, in a middle-class American living-room set designed by admen and constructed on a Hollywood studio. His script involved discussing in detail the taboo topic of his personal finances, and included references to his humble past, his 6-year-old daughter, his wife's "respectable Republican cloth coat," and, most famously, the new family dog, Checkers. From being pressured to resign as Eisenhower's vice presidential candidate, Nixon's Checkers broadcast secured his place on the ticket and brought in campaign contributions and messages of support from his audience. In effect, Nixon had "gone public" to circum-vent and challenge the sources of political authority in the context of "institutional pluralism" dominated by Washington elites at the time. A year later, Edward R. Murrow had transitioned over from radio to television, and skewered Senator Joseph McCarthy on his television program *See It Now*. While McCarthy was already being discredited by print journalists like Drew Pearson (Campbell 2010), Murrow's perfor-mance has become a powerful contemporary symbol of the press's capacity for staging counter-performances.

Television's ability to reshape the political arena was brought to the fore in the first broadcast presidential debate in 1960. The media savvy John F. Kennedy projected youthful vigor juxtaposed against Nixon's shadowy mug shot appearance. The debate's mise-en-scène prompted then president of CBS Frank Stanton to comment, "Kennedy was bronzed beautifully, wearing a navy suit and a blue shirt ... Nixon looked like death ... His color was terrible; his beard was not good and he didn't want any makeup. I felt sorry for him" (quoted in Minow and LaMay

2008: 28). Over the subsequent decades Kennedy's telegenic appearance vis-à-vis Nixon's would solidify into a symbolic structure representing the power of the televised image to shape public political consciousness. The consequences of this debate are profound, less in terms of its impact on that year's election, but more so as an iconic moment in television history: it has encouraged political actors and media elites to focus on the candidates' images, their personas and bodies before the cameras, and to attribute to television an immense power to constitute (Schudson 1995b: 121).[8] While the 1960 debate lingers as a potent symbol, it was through Kennedy's assassination in 1963 that television news journalism asserted and institutionalized its interpretive and constitutive power. "Figures in the television industry, particularly television journalists, regarded Kennedy as a midwife to their own birth," states communications scholar Barbie Zelizer (1992: 29), and the "Kennedy assassination ... was a turning point in the evolution of American journalistic practice ... because it legitimated televised journalism as a mediator of national public experience" (4).

Television not only reduced the time between an event and its public representation, it created a visual immediacy that allowed television news journalists to emphasize their presence "at the scene," a presence that the viewers' eyes could immediately and intuitively confirm. Combining techniques such as repeatedly broadcasting powerful images and setting them against the backdrop of authoritative narratives, and through the techniques of editing, juxtaposition, and simplification, television news anchors and reporters transformed themselves into the directors and actors in citizens' experiences of collective events. Events could now be viewed in real time and repeatedly, and each event came with a familiar, authoritative anchorperson or reporter narrating the event's details and meaning. The televised image was framed as a window on reality, and its news performers cast themselves as neutral mediators bridging the state and the public, and as the vanguard and repository of interpretive truth.

While television would become the dominant performative interface linking political actors, media interpreters, and publics, neither in the 1960s nor now does its news production represent the entirety of the journalistic enterprise. The television created a space for performing the news, but it should not obscure the variety of efforts and sources that contribute to crafting the contents of its narratives, be they performed in print in newspapers and magazines or on the television screen. Field reporters, in fact, were critical in precipitating one of the most profound shifts in the march toward defusion. Reporting from abroad, in the field in Vietnam, and domestically, covering the Johnson

Administration's reports on the conflict, news reporters responded to the gross disparities between the two sites by narrating the powerful symbol of the "credibility gap," a contradictory discursive environment that precipitated a journalistic movement toward investigative reporting (Schudson 1995c: 185). It was in 1964 that *New York Times* associate editor James Reston penned the oft-cited (Karnow 1997 [1983]: 429; VanDeMark 1991: 118) and powerfully evocative representation of the discrepancies between the savagery of the Vietnam battle arena and the Johnson Administration's version of the events: "The time has come to call a spade a bloody shovel," he wrote. "This country is in an undeclared and unexplained war in Vietnam," he continued, and, challenging the Administration's preferred genre symbols of clinical bureaucratic administration, he narrated a space in which more visceral imagery could enter the story, stating, "[o]ur masters have a lot of long and fancy names for it, like escalation and retaliation, but it is war just the same." Johnson was furious with reporters' counter-narrations, and Republican candidates exploited the narrative device in their 1966 midterm campaigns. In an article titled "The Inevitable Credibility Gap," *New York Times* columnist Tom Wicker reported that Republican candidates invoking the credibility gap metaphor were "likely to turn up some votes ... because most political observers believe that a good part of the public does believe there is a suspicious gap between the Administration's statements and the facts of the war" (August 12, 1966).

Public support for the war effort and Johnson's presidency eroded throughout the mid-1960s. Constantly following public opinion polls and engaging in narrative combat with the press, Johnson also "stationed three television sets in his office, so he could monitor coverage on all three networks" (Barnouw 1990, cited in Stephens 2007: 278). Indicative of defusion and the Johnson Administration's attentiveness to controlling the nation's master narrative, Barnouw reports that "[m]any an evening, after Walter Cronkite would finish anchoring the CBS Evening News, Cronkite would find his secretary waiting to hand him the telephone. 'White House on the line'" (ibid.).

"By the late sixties, television had come of age as the preferred medium for news," Zelizer (1992: 29) reports, and its growth "lent stature to the people who inscribed" the news narratives in the American collective conscience along the way (5). Within the decade, television news had established its place near the ritual center of American society as a legitimate interpretive and constitutive force. Roughly five years after this new realm of cultural power emerged from the Kennedy assassination, news anchorman Walter Cronkite returned from a visit

to Vietnam just after the Tet Offensive to editorialize his experience
on the CBS *Evening News.*

Who won and who lost in the great Tet Offensive against the cities? I'm not sure.
The Vietcong did not win by a knockout, but neither did we. The referees of
history may make it a draw ... We have been too often disappointed by the
optimism of the American leaders, both in Vietnam and Washington, to have faith
any longer in the silver linings they find in the darkest clouds ... For it seems now
more certain than ever that the bloody experience of Vietnam is to end in a
stalemate ... To say that we are closer to victory today is to believe, in the face
of the evidence, the optimists who have been wrong in the past. To suggest we are
on the edge of defeat is to yield to unreasonable pessimism. To say that we
are mired in stalemate seems the only realistic, yet unsatisfactory, conclusion.
(February 27, 1968)

Cronkite's performance represents an instance of the shift toward conditions of defusion: it is an example of a ritual, but the ritual center had
shifted however incrementally from the president and the state to the
nightly news anchorman. Interpretive and constitutive authority was
shifted, in part, to the CBS evening news anchor, the "most trusted man
in America," who was understood to be unencumbered by political
demands by virtue of his code to represent things as they are, most
powerfully reiterated by his signature closing line, "and that's the way it
is." In his Tet Offensive broadcast, Cronkite reconstituted his appeal to
neutrality and realism by raising the most pressing question – "who is
winning?" – and then suggesting that he did not have the knowledge to
answer it. Reality is more complicated than our leaders have led us to
believe, Cronkite asserted, and appealed to "evidence" – namely, his experience in the field – to buttress his interpretive authority. Through his
performance, Cronkite mapped the civil society terrain, identifying himself
with the citizenry by stating that "we" have too often been misled by the
nation's leaders. Yet he also distinguished himself from the citizenry,
and thereby indicated that his interpretation held more authority than
the everyday American's, because of the very fact that his editorial was
the product of having traveled to and witnessed the war in Vietnam first-
hand. The "story" in the editorial was as much about Cronkite asserting his
interpretation of the war's trajectory contra the state's; Cronkite was
reporting that the public had been misled, and that it should turn to
television news for interpretive and constitutive truth as opposed to state
officials. Cronkite was suggesting the only "realistic conclusion" was that
he could be trusted to tell you the truth and others could not.

   White House press officer Bill Moyers reported that President Johnson
said to his aides in response to the broadcast, "If I've lost Cronkite,

I've lost Middle America."[9] President Johnson took to the airwaves a month later to announce that he would not seek to represent the Democratic party in the forthcoming November's presidential election. Of course, Cronkite's Tet Offensive performance was but one factor among a myriad of others in shaping Johnson's decision, factors such as Eugene McCarthy's strong showing in the New Hampshire Democratic primary on March 12, and Robert Kennedy's decision to challenge for the position a few days later. And Cronkite was simply expressing an understanding that had been narrated in the press for years; his performance, however, crystallized the interpretation and lent it greater authority. In fact, the Moyers anecdote has been challenged as representing more myth than reality (Campbell 2010). The transformation of a story into myth is emblematic of the rise of a new source of cultural power, the very point that this chapter is endeavoring to demonstrate: the rise of the collective representation, the truth-telling media critic, who gained and assumed interpretive legitimacy at the cost of some state constitutive authority. Broad public belief in the collective representation transforms the symbol's content into a social fact. For the present study, the point is not what one single thing caused another; it is that the communicative space that is the civil sphere had been radically transformed during the decade by changes in presidential leadership styles and strategies, a divided and increasingly differentiated public, and a strong challenge to the narrative center by print journalism's and television news production's emboldened interpretive authority. By asserting that reality is more complex than state leaders had led us to believe, Cronkite was complicating the cultural center, challenging the dominant understanding of what was occurring in the collective endeavor, and presenting himself as an alternative "constituter" of national experience.

Johnson departed the executive branch having primed news journalism's investigative skills and sensitized its practitioners to signs of evasiveness and falsity. Into this environment stepped Richard Nixon, who earlier in the decade had blamed the media for his failed bid for the California governorship and had famously burst into the room in which his press secretary was to deliver his concession announcement and declared to the gathered reporters, "You won't have Nixon to kick around anymore." David Gergen, a member of Nixon's speech-writing team, described the president as a person with a "side to his nature" that was "insecure, secretive, angry, vindictive," and as someone who "thought there were times when he needed to be mean in order to retain power in the face of countless hostile forces" (Gergen 2000: 89). During the ascendancy of the public presidency, into the role stepped a person with a personality particularly ill-suited to the presidential character's demands. Under the conditions of defusion, presidents, as lead actors in the political drama, must work more routinely to re-fuse their persons with the symbolic expectations of the presidential role and character. Combined with his suspicion and hostility toward the press, Nixon's personality would render the project of re-fusion an all but insurmountable task. In contrast to Reagan, but like George H. W. Bush, Nixon even seemed to resent the notion that this project was part of the demands of office.

In addition to creating the White House Office of Communications in 1969 to facilitate speaking to the public without being filtered by the press, Nixon started in his first year to weave presidential politics into the culture of television, and continued to greatly increase the practice of using the medium to speak directly to the nation's audiences throughout his tenure (Kernell 2007: 136). Just as the rise of cable news channels in the mid-1990s created an institutional communicative environment poised to fuel and narrate the Clinton scandals and impeachment processes, in 1973 the four television broadcasters, NBC, CBS, ABC, and PBS, were well positioned to serve as an interpretive bridge linking the state investigative processes into the Watergate affair with the nation's publics. Despite resistance among investigative officials, some congressmen, and the Nixon Administration, both the Senate Select Committee's investigative hearings and the House Judiciary Committee's recommendation to proceed with three articles of impeachment drew extensive television coverage and large audiences (Alexander 1988: 190). While newspaper journalists broke the story, most famously through the collaboration of the insider informant "Deep Throat" with *Washington Post* reporters Woodward and Bernstein, it was a combination of the performances by state officials, prosecutors and defense lawyers, and witnesses on television that facilitated the symbolic transformation of Watergate the "bungled break-in" and politics as usual to Watergate the "crisis of democracy," the redolent symbol of presidential corruption that defines the era in the public imagination (Alexander 1988; Schudson 1992).

The events of 1973–4 became the constitutive symbol that is "Watergate" through complex processes of cultural shifts among public audiences, press and legal investigative efforts, and the "event-ness" (Mast 2006) created by the televised Senate and Judiciary Committee proceedings. In terms of audiences, the social and ideological polarization of the 1960s abated after Nixon's landslide re-election victory in 1972, enabling the Left to assume a more critical universalist symbolic framework, which, juxtaposed to the Right, cast the latter in more particularistic and traditional symbolic hues. Actors in the hearings demonstrated an emerging dramaturgical sensibility, fashioning themselves in time-honored disguises to signal solidarities, and to spark identification with authoritative characters of the past among their living-room audiences. Means of symbolic production like props and costumes can be chosen consciously in an attempt to effect particular reactions among one's audiences, but they need not be. Regardless of an actor's intent, one's expressive equipment is only meaningful in relation to how it has been manifested and emplotted in past events, and in relation to other symbolic patterns evoked in the present dramatic enactment. Senate committee chairman Sam Ervin, for instance, carried with him a Bible and a copy of the Constitution throughout the proceedings, facilitating interpretations of a man more oriented to higher scripts of justice than engaging in mere politicking. Administration witness H. R. Haldeman, on the other hand, who had been likened to a Gestapo agent in the press, grew his hair longer for his testimony in order to disguise himself in the expressive equipment of actors in the anti-war protests and the social justice movements of the recent past (Alexander 1988: 191). When Nixon fired special prosecutor Archibald Cox, the press borrowed time-honored language of the past to dub it the "Saturday Night Massacre" to associate the political action with the ruthless and profoundly undemocratic methods of the mob killings in 1920s Chicago – namely, the "St. Valentine's Day Massacre" (ibid.: 197).

Television placed the state proceedings in American living rooms. In contrast to the multitude of entertainment and news options, on the one hand, and the competitive, more ideological tenor of cable news editorializing in the late 1990s, on the other, four networks cooperated with one another to provide extensive, commercial-free coverage of the Watergate hearings. Every day Americans broke from their typical routines in enormous numbers to symbolically and emotionally engage with the proceedings on television. "Viewing became morally obligatory for wide segments of the population," Alexander (1988: 190) reports, and what the viewers saw "was a highly simplified drama" that "created a deeply serious symbolic occasion." The televised Senate proceedings fostered a "ritual communitas" (ibid.: 189; Turner 1977 [1969]) that drew understandings of citizenship and democracy to the fore of people's awareness, and eroded the divisions created by the polarizing issues of the recent past. Through television, ritual form was achieved.

That was the experience then. Future generations, on the other hand, would experience politics under the conditions of defusion catalyzed by the splintering effects of Johnson's credibility gap and the Watergate experience. Both affairs demonstrated that the semiotic center of the national community – a combination of both the office of presidency and the office's inhabitant – was corruptible. As a result, trust in political actors and institutions was joined by increasing measures of skepticism and cynicism (Bowler and Karp 2004). In the language of cultural pragmatics, the office and the person holding it had become defused from the cultural codes and narratives that in the past had cloaked both seamlessly in the aura of legitimacy and authority. Future presidential actors would have to work much more diligently to maintain the aura of the presidency, to embody the culturally scripted roles that cast the president as a sacred figure in the drama of democracy. Post-Watergate, presidents could much more easily fail to appear presidential; the office no longer defined the actor's social essence. Rather, Watergate helped to demonstrate that what was thought to be the president's essence was in fact the power of cultural constitution, and that future presidents would have to work much harder and continually to perform seamlessly the role of the president lest they begin to slip from the office's mantle and start to appear merely human.

Not only was there a profound erosion of the constitutive power of the state, but another powerful constitutive institution had entered the ritual center of the national community as well. Television news had institutionalized, and combined with a reservoir of powerful critics in print media, these institutions had triumphed in their professional efforts to offer a counter-narrative to those of both the Johnson and Nixon administrations. Additionally, these events groomed future political actors who would remain in the public eye, some of whom, like David Gergen and Pat Buchanan, would shift between roles as media critics and public servants. Finally, the critical sensibility – the defusing gaze – grew to inhabit audiences' subjectivities as well, as the increasingly frequent usage of the term "spin" in the 1980s and 1990s indicates.

Prior to Clinton, presidents Nixon, Carter, and Bush governed during dramatic declines in trust of political actors and institutions (Hetherington 1998: 800). Ford and Carter assumed office with the all but impossible task of reconstituting the office in the wake of the "imperial presidencies" (Schlesinger 1973) of Johnson and Nixon, and of mending the cleavage between the state and publics torn by Vietnam and Watergate. Ford's brief presidency was and is defined by his pardon of Nixon. The pardon was both a symbolic gesture to enable national reconciliation, and a politically devastating action that sparked a precipitous decline in his public approval ratings, a fall from which he was unable to recover. Ford's tenure was also defined by what *Time Magazine* called "The Ridicule Problem" (January 5, 1976): Watergate had upset the symbolic geometry that history had established, in which the office of presidency functioned unmistakably as the gravitational center of the nation's symbolic orbit. It is little wonder that Ford struggled to convincingly inhabit the office's role demands given the profound shock of Watergate to the system's cosmology. The conditions, however unfair to the man, turned Ford into the subject and wellspring of a deluge of comedic criticism, and public memory of the president is as much shaped by the comedian Chevy Chase portraying him as a bumbling oaf on NBC's late night comedy show *Saturday Night Live* as by his former athleticism or how he handled the challenges of office.

In Watergate's wake, Carter framed himself as representing the restoration of character to the White House. Yet he was faced with a symbolically contradictory situation: he had to assume a non-imperial persona while inhabiting a role that favors the projection of masculinity, assured authority, and commanding character. Carter was such a poor performer in the role of president that Richard Neustadt (1990 [1960]: Ch. 11) analyzes his presidency as one in which the actor became so defused from the office that he suffered from a "Jimmy Who?" syndrome.[10] As means of symbolic production, Carter's famous inaugural walk with his wife down Pennsylvania Avenue and cardigan sweater greatly reduced the symbolic distance between the president and the citizenry, and powerfully played against the symbolic tenor of the prior imperial presidencies. Yet the office of presidency will not afford this style of leadership; presidents cannot be just people too.

Wrapped in the vestiges of his former television and movie characters' personas of cowboy, soldier, and all around good chum, and with the acumen of a professional actor, Ronald Reagan re-fused with the office's role demands. In stark contrast to his predecessors, and Nixon in particular, Reagan had a personality and background extraordinarily well-suited for fusing his persona with the character demands of the presidential role. Guided by an extremely well-organized and disciplined communications team (Bennett 2007: 138–9), Reagan also benefited from a press that was retreating from the critical and investigative orientations it had honed so sharply in the wake of the Johnson and Nixon administrations (Hertsgaard 1988). In addition to encountering a more civil and respectful press, Reagan would also alter the media landscape by ending the fairness doctrine, which, since its inception in 1949, had required broadcasters to provide "a reasonable opportunity for the presentation of opposing views on controversial public issues" (Jamieson and Cappella 2008: 45), thus establishing conditions for the rise of Rush Limbaugh and his acolytes on AM talk radio and the ideologically organized cable news channels of FOX News and MSNBC.

Kernell (2007: 174) observes that Reagan preferred to govern by going public over bargaining with Washington and congressional leaders. While Kernell is primarily interested in identifying the rewards and pitfalls of presidents going public, his description of Reagan moves the eye to the performative dimension of contemporary leadership demands:

Try to imagine an individual better suited by experience, temperament, and ideology to lead by going public than Ronald Reagan. It is difficult to do so. Certainly not George H. W. Bush, who served eight years as his understudy but in office proved long on motion and short on vision. Bill Clinton was better than Bush at going public but perhaps not as good as Reagan. Reagan brought to the presidency ideal qualities for this new strategy of leadership, and his performance was not disappointing. (ibid.: 148)

The next chapter retraces Bill Clinton's first year in the national spotlight, and in detailing his campaign for the presidency, it also discusses George H. W. Bush's tenure in the presidential role. In the current chapter I have endeavored to retrace instances in the rise of the conditions of defusion. As the presidency moved into playing a central role in the political drama over the course of the twentieth century, the distinction between the person holding office and the presidential role itself was introduced in the press and cultivated by particular office holders. Television created a space in which presidents and candidates stood before exponentially larger audiences, a development that drew their bodies and comportments into the interpretive arena. The press sharpened its critical gaze of the exercise of political power and crafted powerful counter-narratives, and following the splintering events of the Vietnam War and Watergate, the issue of character, or the political actor's integrity and authenticity, became an increasingly central interpretive category.

Into this context stepped Bill Clinton. His presidential tenure would be characterized by historically unusual elections, a resurgence of extreme partisanship, the expansion of cable television news channels and the rise of the 24-hour news cycle, a ubiquity of scandals, and, most significantly, an impeachment. The conditions and events that defined the Clinton presidency represent not a break, but a significant extension and heightening of the historically emergent processes, changes that have increased the centrality and power of presidential performance. Clinton's presidency, historically significant in its own right, foreshadows the political dynamics of his successors (Alexander 2010), who face the challenges of re-fusing their scripts with the nation's background collective representations, embodying the presidential role in ways deemed authentic, in their efforts to project constitutive and interpretive power, and to be felicitous performative presidents.

3

Character formation: the rise of two Bill Clintons, 1992

When Bill Clinton stepped onto the national stage to announce his candidacy for the presidency of the United States the spotlight cast two distinct and restless shadows. Over the course of 1992 the American public witnessed the formation of two Bill Clintons. The Clinton that won in November appeared hopeful, empathetic, inclusive, and brilliant. The other seemed to treat the truth the way a grifter handles a deck of cards; he would play with it masterfully and deal you any hand he wanted. In this chapter I describe the formation of these two characters and explain how the positive, democratic side gained dominance and won the presidency.

The two Bill Clintons developed through a series of mini-scandals and campaign performances. "Slick Willie" dominated the stage during the first third of the year's election drama. Between January and April the Clinton presidential campaign was threatened with destruction by *Star* magazine's stories of long-running adulterous affairs and episodes of sexual harassment, the *Wall Street Journal*'s allegations of draft dodging, and Clinton's own ambiguous and clumsy confession of casual drug experimentation. A second Clinton, a previously faint but expressive character that seemed to spring naturally from a Horatio Alger story, forcefully emerged mid-year during the Democratic National Convention and the bus tour that followed. This Clinton solidified during the presidential debates and effectively stole the spotlight from the candidate's less flattering persona.

Election results indicate that Bill Clinton won in November less because he was a beloved candidate to a majority of voting Americans or even because he was considered all that desirable as a national leader. Neither of his presidential victories was accompanied by a strong voter mandate, and neither time did he win a majority of the popular vote.[1]

More so, incumbent George H. W. Bush lost the race by the summer of 1992, while Clinton and Independent candidate Ross Perot skillfully and masterfully ensured that President Bush could not redeem himself in voters' eyes. Bill Clinton's success stemmed from his and Perot's dramatizations of the slumping economy and from their principal competitor's unpopularity and apparent aloofness. Clinton's 1992 victory is in large part the story of Bush Sr.'s dramatic – in both senses of the term – failure. The explanation that follows is more than a simple list of scandals. It is a reconstruction of the processes by which characters and events were given form, and an analysis of how particular cultural structures galvanized to form a plot. Finally, it is an examination of how the lead characters brought the plot to life on the national stage and compelled voting publics to participate in the election drama.

Clinton entered 1992 on the verge of seizing control of the Democratic race and was poised to win the party's primaries outright. His chairmanship of the Democratic Leadership Council gave him a platform for reaching his party's leaders and organizers, and his southern roots and experience as governor of Arkansas made him an attractive candidate to the party. The Democrats faced Republican President George H. W. Bush, a popular wartime incumbent who had experienced record high approval ratings little over a year priorly. Despite his waning national popularity, Bush remained the contest's favorite and was expected to win re-election in November.

Over the course of the primaries Clinton would weather a serious challenge for the nomination from centrist Democrat Paul Tsongas, the former senator of Massachusetts. He would also weather a series of damaging assaults on his character from Democratic challenger and former governor of California Jerry Brown. Bush Sr.'s nomination to lead the Republicans in a second term, on the other hand, was all but guaranteed. His popularity among the Republican base, and his party's ideological coherence, however, were severely unsettled by candidate Patrick Buchanan's attacks on the incumbent from the Right. Rounding out the election's cast of characters was the third party candidate and Texas billionaire, Ross Perot, who staged an awkward yet surprisingly powerful campaign fueled by grassroots populism and the narrative appeal of the promise of reform.

Political campaigns as plot development

Campaigns work through theatrical and narrative means to impose a particular dramatic structure on an electoral competition. They seek to define the event's protagonists, emplot them into a world characterized by the centrality of particular issues facing the voting community, and to dramatize the consequences of audiences' potential voting actions. Put another way, campaigns are in the business of character development and plot construction. In an election cycle, campaigns work to dramatize the socio-political order as threatened by particular conditions or as in some crucial way deficient of the normative ideal. These conditions and social problems get reduced and subsumed under the sign of a "campaign issue." In its simplest form a plot includes an action and a reason for why it took place. As elections are dramatic events in the making, campaigns use issues as plot devices to motivate potential voters to act in the election drama's crucial, final act: the election-day vote. In addition to the issue problem, election plots include both a hero figure capable of righting the discursively constructed socio-political wrong, and a particular plan by which the wrong will be righted. As heroes, election candidates must continually perform their issues to potential voters in a manner that compels them to join the election drama by getting out to vote.

As with any election against an incumbent, the Democratic challengers could not just construct their candidates as competent alternatives. They also had to make a case for change. In their competitions against one another for their party's nomination, Democratic hopefuls Bill Clinton and Paul Tsongas established their cases for change by constructing the same issue: Bush Sr.'s responsibility for a lingering economic recession.

Early in 1992, the two leading Democratic contenders began to construct the election's plot using a particularly effective dramatic practice, turning Bush's sound bites back on him. The much-derided sound bite is actually an extraordinarily potent performance technique for introducing potential voters to an electoral narrative. The felicitous delivery of a well-scripted sound bite reduces an election's complexity to a pithy mouthful. It clarifies and facilitates understanding by dramatically emphasizing a campaign's plot point. Its performance also embeds the plot in a broader narrative that touches on more expansive cultural themes. Sound bites tell voters why they must get out and perform the drama's final act by voting.

Paul Tsongas, for instance, Clinton's closest competitor, blamed the nation's economic woes on Bush's "voodoo economics – continued,"[2] borrowing and extending the sarcastic phrase Bush leveled against Ronald Reagan during their 1980 bids for the Republican nomination. Tsongas differentiated himself from his Democratic competitor, and symbolically associated Clinton with incumbent Bush Sr., by calling Clinton's economic proposals "voodoo economics with a kinder, gentler face."[3] Clinton, on the other hand, exploited one of Bush's most intimate of political relationships to develop the same dramatic plot structure as Tsongas, stating: "President Reagan set a simple standard as to whether you get your contract renewed ... Are you better off today than you were four years ago?"[4]

This practice of turning a sound bite back on its initial issuer lends the present performance added narrative and historical depth. Just as classic dramatic roles are haunted by past actors that have inhabited them (Carlson 2001: 10; Roach 2000: 10), playing on past sound bites sparks recognition and draws the past's context and performance into the present. The citational technique encourages listeners to consider at some conscious level the ways the two situations resemble one another; in this case, to consider how the election context today is similar to that of the day Bush and Reagan first used them against one another and then against their competitors as running mates.[5]

Tsongas's and Clinton's comments symbolically linked the current election cycle with the Reagan/Bush campaign that had unseated Democratic incumbent Jimmy Carter in 1980. Tsongas's gibe parodied Bush's assertion that Reagan's campaign promises were based on "voodoo economics" because of their implausibility, promising more government services while taking less in taxes. Tsongas's mocking revival of Bush's sound bite was doubly potent – a rhetorical checkmate, of sorts – because Bush had been accused of not only passively accepting Reagan's economic strategies as his vice president but of continuing them under his own tenure as president. Bush could have disputed this charge by emphasizing that he had raised taxes, but this of course would have raised the specter of how he had contradicted his powerful 1988 presidential campaign sound bite, "Read my lips: No new taxes."

Clinton's "Are you better off now" line, on the other hand, was effective because Reagan, Bush's political father-figure, had unseated an incumbent partially due to the rhetorical strength of this criterion of judgment. In its invocation, Clinton played on Reagan's landslide victory over Carter, suggesting to contemporary audiences that if Reagan's folk wisdom was persuasive during the Carter recession it should be persuasive now during Bush's. The invocation symbolically separated Bush from Reagan, and communicated that it was possible to remain loyal to one's prior support for Reagan without necessarily supporting Bush again. After all, Clinton's performance suggested, by Reagan's own rules Bush's contract should not be renewed. With each invocation Tsongas and Clinton performed the symbolic desacralization of the incumbent.

The net effect of the 1992 primary contenders' theatrics would be the constitution of one of the election's central issues. The primaries would tell us who the party's ultimate contender would be, and the issues that emerged from the competitors' individual efforts would establish a cause for action to take place in November. That is, their performances of this issue began to define why and how supporters should participate in the drama by voting. With the economic recession cast as one of the election's central themes,[6] over the course of 1992 the Clinton campaign worked to fashion its lead as an intelligent, personable, and youthful self-made man capable of revitalizing the nation and its slumping economy. First, however, he had to win the Democratic nomination.

In social dramas, the particular means of symbolic production that a party employs to stage its performances shapes the meanings the production ultimately imparts to its audiences. Means such as clothing, handheld props, places to perform, decorative stage scenery, and other sorts of expressive equipment serve as iconic representations that help dramatize and make visible the invisible meanings the team is trying to represent (Alexander 2004; Alexander and Mast 2006; Carlson 2001: 10). Social dramatic production teams mobilize particular symbolic means to invoke certain latent, invisible collective representations; they work with symbolic objects to assemble a particular meaning structure about themselves, and, through difference, to define their opponents as well.

The meaning of a particular election campaign derives from these physical manifestations of culture structures and from the discursive practices its characters articulate. However, a campaign production's meaning is also derived through its symbolic relationships – analogical and antipathetic – to its competitors' productions. In this sense, each campaign may be seen as a particular, discrete sign carrier working to embody and evoke a particular set of meanings. The particular meaning the campaign ultimately communicates is derived from the background cultural referents and signs it intentionally associates with itself through performance, on the one hand, and from differences between its pragmatically achieved sign structure and the sign structures of its competitors, on the other. Thus a social dramatic production never fully controls its own meaning as its ultimate meaning structure is only partially the result of its own symbolic work. One production's meaning is also the product of simple juxtaposition to other productions, and in symbolic competition, of course, productions act strategically to demonize their competitors and to paint them in counter-democratic shades.

Fusing narrative and candidate, part 1: the rise of "Slick Willie"

Rumors of marital indiscretions began to cloud Clinton's campaign once he formally announced his candidacy in October 1991. Despite this, Clinton appeared the clear favorite for capturing the Democratic nomination well into January 1992. His frontrunner status changed dramatically when the tabloid magazine *Star* published a series of articles documenting allegations of Clinton's sexual improprieties while governor of Arkansas.[7]

The race toward the Democratic primaries had garnered typical if scant national attention to this date. The tabloid's articles changed this, and forced the quality of Clinton's character and integrity directly onto center stage, drawing immediate and wide public attention to the Democratic race. Perhaps most significantly, the tabloid's articles turned rumors about a candidate's private life into a durable, crystallized issue that would dominate the political stage through Clinton's tenure. After playing an important role in Gary Hart's dramatic departure from the 1988 presidential competition, the question of "character" – how one's private life shapes one's public service – returned and once again became a concrete, stable dimension of political discourse, a seemingly natural and important concern for citizens. Some critics decried character's increasing centrality in political discourse, and many more joined the chorus in 1998.[8] Despite these alternative voices, character began to appear almost as natural a political issue as the economy. More immediately, the articles almost turned rumors into the makings of a campaign-ending scandal.[9]

The contents of the *Star* stories spread immediately to other news and entertainment organizations, and through these organizations to the nation's intrigued publics. Any control the Clinton team had exercised over the symbolic framework of its main signifier – Clinton himself – promptly evaporated. While "character" was stabilizing as a seemingly legitimate issue, the content of Clinton's character was quickly transformed from a semi-stable signifier to a more fluid site of symbolic contestation. No party vied more actively for control over the meaning of this critical political object than Clinton's team itself. Taken by surprise, the Clinton team responded with immediate if ad hoc denials and deflections, calling the material "ridiculous" and the work of "the president's Republican operatives."[10] These constructions were reported but not robustly engaged by media critics, which is tantamount to being ignored. The deflections did, however, afford the Clinton team time to orchestrate a more complex, persuasive framing of Clinton's personal history.

Though the team felt deeply threatened by the stories, the campaign placed a tremendous amount of faith and confidence in their lead's ability to regain control over his character if they could arrange for him to perform on enough American television screens. "The calculation is that the issue has to be dealt with cleanly and as decisively as possible," one Clinton advisor commented. "It's necessary to focus the American people on who Bill and Hillary Clinton are, what they believe and what they think this election is about."[11] The Clinton team's dramatic strategy involved placing their strongest asset, Clinton's performative skills, on a stage voters would read as legitimate, professional, and dignified, and inserting this scene into the living rooms of as many American homes as possible.

The Gennifer Flowers scandal broke just prior to 1992's NFL Super Bowl, a television event that routinely garners extraordinarily high numbers of viewers. In a bold yet risky strategy to regain control of Clinton's symbolic framework, the Clinton team arranged for Bill and Hillary to appear directly after the game on the same network on which the game would be televised, CBS. Originally CBS planned to follow the Super Bowl with an episode of the entertainment-news magazine show *48 Hours*. While an interview directly following the Super Bowl would guarantee enormous exposure to the Clinton camp, framing their lead within the *48 Hours* format would have been only an incremental semiotic step above and away from *Star* magazine's "sleazy"[12] pages dedicated to detailing celebrities' sex scandals and weight-gain travails. An interview on *60 Minutes*, on the other hand, a news show known for hard-hitting, interrogation-like interview tactics, would lift Clinton out of the scandal sheet and place him back in legitimate news formats. "The only way to get Bill Clinton on CBS was to make it on *60 Minutes*. I don't believe Bill and Hillary Clinton would have gone on *48 Hours* because it's not their format," commented CBS PrimeTime executive producer Rick Kaplan, explaining why CBS agreed to broadcast the interview as a 17-minute version of *60 Minutes* cutting into the infotainment format of the scheduled *48 Hours*.[13]

The step was a high-stakes gamble for the Clinton campaign: the *60 Minutes* episode promised uncomfortable discussions of sexual indiscretions and testaments regarding motives and ambitions for political power with both marriage partners present. Performative success would yield high rewards and allow Clinton to regain tenuous symbolic control of his character. A poor performance would likely drive him from the race. *60 Minutes* interviews affect interrogation-like imagery and dynamics. Steve Kroft and the Clintons sat opposite each other; Kroft asked penetrating questions that the Clintons answered – and refused to answer – and Kroft critiqued and probed evasive responses.

Steve Kroft opened the segment by introducing Clinton as the Democratic frontrunner whose campaign was facing "long rumored allegations of marital infidelity" which had "finally surfaced in a supermarket tabloid." The allegations, Kroft continued, came from "a former television reporter and cabaret singer, Gennifer Flowers, in a tabloid interview for which she was paid."

Kroft's preface introduced two semiotic domains to the interview. One was the seamy world of Gennifer Flowers, a pretty face that chirps in the smoky atmosphere of a low-status cabaret and bar culture and sometimes surfaces to appear behind a local news camera or lands some cover space on a tabloid publication. This world is contrasted to the legitimate, analytical, and skeptically detached world of the interview forum itself, the objective news culture in which *60 Minutes* resides.

Kroft opened the interview by probing the connection between the two worlds: how are you, the Clintons, appearing on *60 Minutes* and sitting in a pleasant, suburban living-room atmosphere, connected to this other world? Clinton answered by positing that money spread through dirty politics in a context of economic desperation bridges the worlds:

B. Clinton: It was only when money came out, wh – when the tabloid went down there offering people money to say that they had been involved with me that she changed her story. There is a recession on. Times are tough, and – and I think you can expect more and more of these stories as long as they're down there handing out money.

Kroft: I'm assuming from your answer that you're categorically denying that you ever had an affair with Gennifer Flowers.

B. Clinton: I've said that before and so has she.

Kroft: You've said that your marriage has had problems, that you've had difficulties. What do you mean by that? What does that mean? Is that some kind of – help us break the code. I mean, does that mean ...

B. Clinton: I don't me ...

Kroft: ... you were separated?

B. Clinton: I think the American people, at least people that have been married for a long time, know what it means and know the whole range of things that it can mean.

Kroft: You've been saying all week that you've got to put this issue behind you. Are you prepared tonight to say that you've never had an extramarital affair?

B. Clinton: I'm not prepared tonight to say that any married couple should ever discuss that with anyone but themselves. I'm not prepared to say that about anybody. I think that the issue ...

Kroft: Governor, that's what – excuse me. That's what you've been saying, essentially, for the last ...

B. Clinton: But that's what I believe.

Kroft: ... couple of months.

B. Clinton: Look, Steve, you go back and listen to what I've said. You know, I have acknowledged wrongdoing, I have acknowledged causing pain in my marriage. I have said things to you tonight and to the American people from the beginning that no American politician ever has. I think most Americans who are watching this tonight, they'll know what we're saying, they'll get it, and they'll feel that we have been more candid. And I think what the press has to decide is: Are we going to engage in a game of "gotcha"? . . .
                . . .

Kroft: I think most Americans would agree that it's very admirable that you had – have stayed together, that you've worked your problems out, that you seem to have reached some sort of an understanding and an arrangement.

B. Clinton: Wait a minute, wait a minute.

Kroft: But . . .

B. Clinton: Wait a minute. You're looking at two people who love each other. This is not an arrangement or an understanding. This is a marriage. That's a very different thing.[14]

Key dynamics in this interview would be repeated multiple times during the following eight years, dynamics such as Clinton's subtle evasions and redirections, his shifts in verb tenses and ambiguous use of pronouns, Hillary's defense of, and support for, her husband, and the interviewer's frustrated attempts at clarification. Subjects raised here would live on too, such as the nature of the Clinton marriage, Bill Clinton's references to causing and feeling pain, and the relevance of the candidate's private life to his public service. All parties expressed discomfort with the issues that brought them together.[15] The journalist Kroft suggested that he was not happy pursuing lines of questioning into Clinton's personal life but insisted that the questions were fair, that they were part of public and political discourse, and that it was incumbent upon the candidate to defuse the issue honestly and convincingly. Kroft expressed his personal distaste for the subject but stated that he was duty bound to push forward and that he was inquiring in terms that were well within journalistic norms.

The Clintons voiced their distaste for the subject but argued that they were agreeing to the questioning to the fullest extent that reason, common decency, and civil society could expect. Yet Kroft would not desist in his inquiries at Clinton's desired boundaries; there were moments in the interview when he felt his questions were being evaded, but Bill Clinton would not acquiesce to the terms of access or parameters of openness pursued by the journalist. This interview, as a frustrated and frustrating interaction, launched into the public domain a long-running drama focused on marital and sexual irregularities, the tension between the right of the press to inquire and the people to know versus the right to privacy, the terms of reasonable lies and evasions, and, critically, it crystallized an adversarial relationship between the future president and segments of the press.

Though the airing secured high ratings,[16] the Clintons' performances were persuasive if insufficient against the rising tide of scandal and suspicion. Soon after the interview, in early February, the *Wall Street Journal* began reporting on the young Clinton's reactions to the Vietnam War draft, characterizing his interactions with his draft board as deceptive and his subsequent explanations of his actions as intentionally evasive and fallacious. This story too spread rapidly through news and entertainment organizations and the pace of the election drama hastened as the New Hampshire primaries approached.

As a disembodied sign, Clinton's character remained a site of contestation up to and through the Democratic primaries. During this time use of the nickname "Slick Willie" began to mushroom.[17] Heading into the New Hampshire primary, critics doubted the Clinton production's ability to redefine its lead and predicted that the rumors of infidelities and draft dodging would devastate the campaign: "the prevailing wisdom, or much of it, seems to be that they must drive him from the race, that they are burdens no candidate can bear,"[18] and Clinton's allure to Democratic leaders began to wane: "national party leaders fear the cumulative effects of these stories could erode Clinton's credibility with voters and cripple him for the fall campaign against Bush."[19]

The campaign stayed afloat by willing itself forward, leading with its strongest asset, Clinton's performative skills. "In the week before the New Hampshire primary," the campaign "embarked on a breakneck schedule of live half-hour television shows and public appearances."[20]

Clinton's closest competitors at this point were Paul Tsongas and Jerry Brown. Tsongas, described as a "comic Greek tortoise snapping at the heels of Democratic hares" heading into New Hampshire, won the primary with 34 percent of the vote; Clinton finished second with 26 percent. The bookish former senator's lead was short lived, though. The race became a competition of styles.[21] Clinton, the second place finisher, almost immediately began to perform and narrate his way into the role of lead contender for his party's nomination, as described by a reporter:

A week ago, many political pundits declared Clinton's candidacy dead. But tonight he was alive, beaming, pushing his fist into the air and saying he could not wait to take his resurrected campaign across the country.

"New Hampshire tonight has made Bill Clinton the Comeback Kid," [Clinton declared].

Sticking out his chin almost in the fashion of a young and fearless Muhammad Ali in the ring, Clinton added: "This has been a tough campaign, but at least I've proven one thing – I can take a punch."[22]

Critics reacted to Clinton's triumphal performance with irony: "For democrats who didn't win, victory has many definitions."[23] Despite Tsongas's initial victory he was forced from the race one month later. The reason for his departure lies in his performative style. Many were allured to Tsongas's ideologically hybrid message; however, primary voters read into the candidate's performances signs of insufficient strength to fill the presidential role as they expected it should be played. Tsongas, voters commented,

makes a lot of sense, and has some very interesting ideas, but he might not be strong enough to be president. If he gets a little more exciting on the podium, that would be good. He has to get a little bit sexier up there ... the appearance of a lack of forcefulness is what is holding me back from choosing [him] over Clinton.[24]

The race also became a competition of organizations, geography, and timing. Clinton's team ran the most clearly national campaign, was the best funded, and was by far the best positioned entering the southern primaries that dominated the race heading into Super Tuesday, March 10. Clinton's victories in the South, particularly in Florida and Texas, eroded the race's contingency. Reinvigorated by their successes, "the Clinton organizers were able to throw a raucous, balloon-strewn victory party for the local television cameras [in Chicago]. The party was intended to throw voters a distinct message: Bill Clinton would inevitably be the Democratic nominee."[25] Tsongas agreed, and dropped out of the race after losses in Illinois and Michigan. The Clinton team redirected its dramatic purpose: "now the job is to define George Bush."[26]

By this time critics and Republican loyalists were beginning to define Bush's re-election campaign as drifting rudderless in an "ill wind" and languishing in "a wave of discontent." Clinton had performed his second-place finish in New Hampshire by thrusting his fist in the air in a show of victory. Bush, by contrast, reacted to his 18-percentage point victory over Patrick Buchanan by issuing a statement calling the primary results a "setback."[27] Critics were more forceful: "Bush takes a pasting," declared the *Washington Post* (February 19, 1992). Bush's weak victory was framed as a "jarring political message"[28] signifying a "protest vote"[29] against the incumbent's apparent detachment from, and inattentiveness to, people's everyday concerns.

Despite reportedly being "stunned" by their limited victory in New Hampshire, a month later the Bush team still lacked an advertising team[30] and showed no signs of changing its tack: "the Republican primary seems to be conforming to the expectations of dullness. Neither President Bush nor Vice President Quayle has any campaign appearances planned."[31]

By mid-March Clinton's hold on the Democratic nomination looked secure. Tsongas's withdrawal had left Clinton the clear leader in the race's overall delegate count and the rest of the primaries began to look like formalities. Yet the social dramatic process remains contingent, and the following campaign events left lasting scars on Clinton's political skin. Five days after Tsongas dropped out, Jerry Brown, former Democratic governor of California, won the March 24 Connecticut primary largely by hammering Clinton on character issues. Consequently, New York's April 7 primary was lent renewed gravity. The Clinton team could ill afford to lose further control of their candidate's symbolic framework to Brown's "renegade"[32] efforts, particularly given the New York media organizations' ability to influence other regions' campaign coverage.

Following Tsongas's withdrawal the Clinton team blinked and "lost control over the campaign's dynamic in the crucial days leading up to the New York primary."[33] Brown had succeeded in Connecticut questioning Clinton's character and tendency toward evasiveness, two issues the New York press corps and television news outlets eagerly embraced. In an attempt to evade the press's constitutive power, the Clinton team called for six debates with Brown during the week leading up to the primary date. The team hoped to "speak more directly to New York voters [to minimize] the press's role in the April 7th primary" because, as Clinton put it, all the voters heard was "bad stuff [being] dumped on" him. The team also hoped the debates would "break the flow of unflattering sound bites that [had] made up most of his television news coverage in New York."[34]

The strategy was risky because performative gaffes were the only content certain to garner wide media coverage. In his March 29 debate with Brown, Clinton committed just such a performative blunder. In a series of questions, Clinton was asked if he had ever used drugs and if he had ever broken any state or international laws. To the latter Clinton responded:

I've never broken any state laws, and when I was England, I experimented with marijuana a time or two. And I didn't like it, and I didn't inhale and I never tried it again.[35]

His response quickly became national news and entertainment.[36] On television and in print Clinton's answer was juxtaposed to past responses to similar questions, to which he had made a practice of stating flatly, "I have never broken the laws of my country." His evasiveness, and the deftness with which he practiced the casuistry, were constructed as "the kind of verbal gymnastics"[37] that confirmed there were "two Bill Clintons."[38] On the one hand, pundits and critics examined and discussed Clinton's syntactic techniques and theorized about what this tendency to prevaricate suggested about his character. In columnist Richard Cohen's words:

This is the behavior that has earned Clinton the nickname "Slick Willie." It's a behavior so at odds with the rest of the man that we are entitled to wonder about its cause ... Is this the really smart kid who thinks he can out-talk and out-think anyone? Is this, maybe, the small-town wiz, the anointed hope of his community, who thinks the rules were made for others? Whatever the cause, Clinton's behavior is childish and troubling. It dilutes his promise, mocks the seriousness of his purpose – comes up behind him at somber events and puts up two fingers above his head as the picture is snapped.[39]

Clinton's performance was also transformed into a national punch line. During the Oscars ceremony the following night host Billy Crystal stopped the ceremonies suddenly, fixed his face intently on the camera, and joked disbelievingly, *"Didn't inhale?"* drawing boisterous laughter from the audience.

Nonetheless, Clinton won the New York primary handily and Brown, finishing third in a two-man race,[40] dropped out of the competition for the Democratic nomination. Thus, the political consequences of Clinton's over-performance would not be felt immediately. The dramatic consequences, however, became immediately apparent: the performance catalyzed the symbolic bifurcation of Clinton's symbolic framework – namely, into "two Bill Clintons." It confirmed his brilliance, but it also demonstrated that Clinton would use his skills to circumvent a question's normative thrust to deceive the questioner. He would tell a truth, but not about the exact subject normatively embedded in an inquirer's question. Consequently the performance irreversibly fused "Slick Willie" to the symbolic patchwork that was beginning to constitute his character. Use of the epithet in print and television journalism, as well as in popular culture, rose dramatically, its usage peaking in March and April 1992 and experiencing a strong resurgence in the late summer.

Fusing narrative and candidate, part 2: the rise of a presidential Clinton

Jerry Brown's departure from the race ended the Democratic infighting and allowed the Clinton team to begin rebuilding their lead's character. His formal nomination at the Democratic National Convention in New York helped this process significantly. Party nominating conventions are the height of orchestrated political theater. They are staged in venues organized to create the greatest symbolic effect, and are moments in which contingency is virtually suffocated out of the social dramatic process, if temporarily. Clinton had failed miserably four years priorly when delivering the keynote address at Dukakis's nominating convention, yet he departed his own nominating convention with a twenty-four-point lead over the incumbent in the polls, a lead unseen in the previous fifty years.

Moreover, Clinton sustained his lead during a six-day, post-convention bus tour "back to the heartland of America."[41] The Clinton team's bus tour was designed to encode a nostalgic, decidedly populist structure to the Democratic ticket. Through defining its own candidate as a traditional populist and preaching "plenty of old-time Democratic religion,"[42] the Clinton team also defined Bush Sr.'s tenure in power by playing on and exaggerating differences between the two candidates. Instead of engaging Bush Sr. within the field of institutional presidential symbolism by wrapping their candidate in signs of power and bureaucratic mastery, the Clinton team increased their lead's symbolic distance from insider Washington images. For instance, instead of exiting the Democratic convention in an executive-style jumbo jet and flying off above and beyond ordinary Americans' heads, the Clinton ticket immediately boarded a bus and headed through America's rust belt toward the breadbasket states. Through reducing the physical distance between its candidate and American people, by going out to meet voters on their local turf, the campaign strove to symbolically return government to "the people." At a deeper symbolic level, Clinton's willingness to enter into the audience suggested a willingness to sacrifice himself for the community (Marvin and Ingle 1999: 253–7). The bus tour allowed Clinton to merge with the public body, which stood in stark contrast to Bush's apparent distaste for such contact. Discourse was scripted to lend narrative symmetry to the bus imagery, to explain it plainly to the audiences that were gathered at arranged "leg-stretching" stops along the route. Costumed in sweaters and khakis, Clinton and Gore would toss the football back and forth in young Kennedy fashion at bus stops, and Bill Clinton would chew on a piece of straw while leisurely talking to locals. Clinton would explain to those gathered:

You are here for yourselves, your children and your future because you want your country back. And Al and I are going to give it to you.[43]

The Clinton team strove to portray its lead as Kennedy-esque, recalling the sense of youthful revival of politics that followed Kennedy's defeat over Nixon in 1960 and the end of the Eisenhower era of politics. Busts of

Kennedy loomed behind Clinton and Gore at their bus stops, the team stopped in John F. Kennedy Park in McKeesport, PA, and Clinton invoked Kennedy in ways that suggested that this election was about another generational change in political power. "In 1960, John Kennedy came here and said it's time to change," the candidate would proclaim.

The bus tour received considerable national coverage and was lauded by critics, and further extended the bounce in the polls that the Democratic team received from their nomination convention. In addition to the bus tour, the Clinton team made use of an unprecedented number of diverse popular television shows and networks to construct their candidate as "closer" to average Americans than their opponent. To name but a few of his more publicity-generating appearances, Clinton played the saxophone on *The Arsenio Hall Show*, he defended himself and debated the relevance of the "character issue" on the *Phil Donahue* talk show, and made an appearance to field questions from young voters on *MTV*, a network Bush Sr. shunned dismissively, stating "I'm not going on any teenie-bopper network."

In terms of character formation, Clinton's national identity was young and formative but developing quickly. Bush's national identity, on the other hand, had been developing in public imaginations for over a decade. In 1992, Bush's character was a composite of his actions vis-à-vis international relations and the global projection of American military power, his perceived lack of attention to civic and race relations, and, most crucially, his degree of concern for, and mastery over, contemporary domestic economic conditions.

Bush could have framed himself in terms of his foreign relations experience and in terms of his expertise in projecting American military power around the globe. His record was not without blemishes, but he was elected in 1988 despite the specter of the Iran-Contra scandal, and though he failed to act in the spring of 1989 when the Chinese government quashed the Tiananmen Square protests, he could have associated himself much more strongly with forthcoming US successes. For instance, Poland and Hungary broke from the Iron Curtain in 1989. And while in the popular *American* imagination it was Ronald Reagan who orchestrated the end of the Cold War, it was under Bush's presidential tenure that Americans watched the remarkable crumbling of the Berlin Wall (November 9, 1989) and witnessed the dissolution of the Soviet Union into fifteen independent countries (December 15, 1991). Between these two spectacular victories for the West, Bush oversaw the successful yet unglamorous deposing of Manuel Noriega from Panama, which was framed as an essential step in the "war on drugs." And most significantly, in January and February of 1991, Bush rebuked Saddam Hussein's projection of power onto the Arabian Peninsula in a stunning military operation that forced Iraqi troops from Kuwait in overwhelming fashion. More than any other event, the Persian Gulf War contributed to the rise and power of cable news channels, made celebrities and experts of their reporters and correspondents, and laid the groundwork for a number of potential political careers for the war's successful soldiers such as Norman Schwarzkopf and Colin Powell. Yet Bush failed to reap the benefits of the "Desert Storm" campaign and failed to capitalize politically by emphasizing his experience and expertise during this crucial time, during the formation of "a new world order."

The fall of the Soviet Union was largely understood as Reagan's victory, and Bush failed to fully separate from his political father-figure and assert himself into a similar plane of masculine and political stature. He failed to own these victories with Reagan; rather, he ceded the victories to Reagan and remained under his shadow. An understanding settled in that it was Reagan who had made the world safe for the United States and indeed that the world was now safe in an unprecedented way. The Persian Gulf War played to Americans via cameras strapped to smart bombs. The war was casualty-free and bloodless, at least as portrayed on American television screens (Kellner 1992). Due to the overwhelming military might that the United States was able to direct at Iraqi forces, combined with the evaporation of the Cold War and the death of the Soviet Bear, Americans seemed to feel comfortable with choosing a future president that had virtually no foreign affairs experience over one that had almost nothing but.

The Bush team let the Clinton team define the election: it was about "the economy, stupid." One alternative campaign approach the Bush team could have pursued would have been to emphasize that the world was still unsafe, and that it was less safe now because of the new and unusual forms of instability brought about by recent Western victories. What America needed now more than four years earlier, Bush could have emphasized more frequently and with greater pathos, was precisely a leader with worldly experience and intimate knowledge and expertise of foreign affairs. Nonetheless, instead of succeeding in framing himself as a successful wartime president, Bush's national identity was dominated by the nation's slumping economy.

Bush had fastened his political identity to economic issues during his 1988 campaign. Trailing Bob Dole in his bid for the Republican nomination, Bush famously declared that he would not raise taxes if given the nomination and elected president. He reiterated his pledge forcefully when given the nomination at the Republican National Convention: "The Congress will push me to raise taxes, and I'll say no, and they'll push, and I'll say no, and they'll push again, and I'll say to them, 'Read my lips: No new taxes.'" It was a powerful message that resonated with Republicans and enough Reagan Democrats to help Bush defeat Dukakis. It was also so powerful, however, that when Bush contradicted himself by raising taxes in the summer of 1990,[44] he severely restricted his ability to present himself to his supporters as a principled man of his word who was "above politics." The contradiction also restricted his ability to project himself as a person knowledgeable of economic forces. If he understood economic trends and processes, after all, then certainly he would have known that his "no new taxes" pledge was absurd and untenable. The contradiction seemed to force his character into representing something between a liar and a fool.

The national economy, as measured by the gross national product, slipped into negative growth between the third and fourth quarters of 1990 under the weight of the enormous national deficit that developed during the Reagan years. The negative growth continued through the first quarter of 1991, earning the trend the official title of "recession." Though the recession technically ended when the economy began to grow slowly in 1991's second quarter, its symbolic weight continued to stifle and sour the national atmosphere throughout the 1992 campaign. During his re-election bid Bush acted as though he was so stung by the embarrassment and shame of having contradicted his "no new taxes" pledge that he was absolutely unwilling to engage in strong, declarative political theater again when the economy was the subject.

Bush appeared to be at the recession's mercy despite taking the potentially bold performative steps of raising taxes and lowering interest rates to turn the economy around. Bush could have performed coherence, certainty, and mastery by, for instance, insinuating that responsibility for the recession lay in the excesses of "Reaganomics." Alternatively, he could have placed blame on Congress's shoulders and insisted that his management had shortened a potentially lengthier recession. Instead, in March 1992 Bush called his decision to raise taxes in 1990 a "mistake," and agreed with former President Reagan's statement that the tax increase was the "worst mistake of his [Bush's] presidency."[45] After contradicting one of his most powerful performances in the 1988 campaign, Bush in 1992 appeared reluctant to engage in forceful, potentially constitutive performances that would distance him from Reagan and his economics, or to portray himself as in some way a positive force in the face of the economic doldrums.

Bush instead projected incoherence, appeared out of touch, and persistently sounded apologetic when he dwelled publicly on his mistakes. He appeared, in a word, Carter-esque. For instance, in early July Bush appeared on CBS's *This Morning* to attempt to bolster his campaign and to meekly declare that the country was now in economic recovery:

I'd say we've been through the longest dragged – dragging recession in recent history, and it has been very, very difficult to stimulate growth in that kind of an environment. I still feel what I have suggested in terms of jobs and opportunity and stimulating growth is what should have been tried, and I'm going to keep on fighting to get it tried. So, one, we're coming out of a recession. We grew at 2.7 percent last month – or last – first quarter, which isn't good, but it's far better than no growth or – or recession. We're in a – we're in a recovery now.[46]

The following day news of the nation's 7.8 percent unemployment rate was released. Bush responded anemically during a news conference that the report of the rate was "not good news." One of his campaign strategists responded with more verve. "This is trouble," he stated, adding that the unemployment rate news might necessarily push the Bush team toward "a mean campaign."[47]

As the incumbent, Bush represented the Republican center. Yet, while his campaign meandered and limped along, Bush seemed reluctant to lead and hesitant to make a forceful ideological stand. This lack of strength and certainty at the center produced unease and dissension within the conservative core. Vexed by the candidate's disaffection and disinterest, conservative ideologue and Republican administrator William Bennett stated on a Sunday morning talk show in late July that Bush needed to ask himself, "Do I really want to do this?"[48] Conservative commentators Rowland Evans and Robert Novak labeled Bush's "the worst-conceived incumbent presidential campaign in memory," one that carried the "smell of defeat." "A sense of direction," they continued, "can only come from the Oval Office and there is no leadership shown there."[49] Also in late July, conservative commentator George Will wrote a column suggesting Bush reinvigorate the ticket by replacing Vice President Dan Quayle with Colin Powell. One week later Will stated that perhaps Bush himself "should withdraw from the race," and that "a startling number of significant Republicans privately say they wish he would." Will continued, critiquing what Bush's communicative style indicated about his character:

Bush's meandering rhetoric stopped being amusing long ago, when it became recognizably symptomatic of two things. One is the incoherence that afflicts a public person operating without a public philosophy. The other is Bush's belief that he need not bother to discipline his speech when talking to Americans because the business of seeking their consent is beneath him.[50]

While Bush's bid for re-election was cracking apart in the middle, it was being pulled apart at the edges by charismatic critics like H. Ross Perot and Patrick J. Buchanan. Centrists and "Reagan Democrats," who had either identified with Reagan or had some affinity for fiscal conservatism, remained only weakly committed to Bush or shifted their allegiance from his re-election bid altogether in favor of H. Ross Perot's Reform Party campaign. On the other hand, far Right social conservatives were finding a champion in Pat Buchanan's popular bid for the Republican ticket.

The Bush campaign vessel continued to drift rudderless through July and into August, its mast cracking and hull splintering under the pressure of the Clinton, Perot, and Buchanan campaigns. Trailing Clinton by an enormous nineteen-point deficit just days before the Republican National Convention would begin in mid-August, Bush tried to signal a step to the helm, a renewed and forceful command, by dramatically changing his cabinet and campaign leadership, most notably by moving his longtime friend and advisor James Baker from secretary of state to chief of staff.

Perot and Buchanan represented threats from opposing ends of the Republican ideological spectrum. Perot represented a threat from the center Right, a Republican alternative to the Clinton Democratic challenge. Preaching fiscal and social pragmatism and responsibility, Perot's personal wealth and success in the private sector conveyed a sense of fiscal knowledge and "real-life" expertise. His message was similar to Clinton's, yet his persona and biography differed markedly. Perot's folksy charisma, however, was tinged with an air of the erratic: he never officially announced his candidacy, he unofficially started and stopped his campaign three times during the year, and when he bowed out of the race for the first time he announced that he was doing so because of the efforts of a Republican conspiracy that had taken aim at his daughter during her wedding. Buchanan's challenge, on the other hand, was more dangerous to Bush's re-election bid because he was stealing energy from the incumbent's base of support.

The Bush team's strategy to chart these waters was to make the Clintons appear as frighteningly leftist as possible, and to scare core Republicans into showing up to vote for Bush, who they worked to portray as the only Republican that could realistically win in November. This late in the election contest, down 19 percentage points to the Democratic contender, the Bush campaign could not spend its energy fighting to win new voters or trying to win over undecided centrists. With Perot in the mix, there were simply too many choices at the center. Instead, they tried to turn out as much of the Republican Right and its core constituency as possible. Let Clinton and Perot split the center, the team decided, but scare Buchanan's followers into showing up to vote for Bush to ensure that the Executive would remain under conservative control. This led the Bush team to position itself alongside the divisive and racially charged wave of Buchanan-inspired conservative populism.

The Bush team shifted to "mean" tactics, stepping up its attacks on Clinton by portraying the candidate as too liberal for the American mainstream and by expanding the scope of its attack to include Hillary Clinton, whom it framed as an unreasonably radical influence and source of power in the Clinton partnership. This effort dovetailed with the start of the Republican National Convention in Houston, Texas. Demonizing the Clintons, on the one hand, the Bush team sought, on the other, to bring the disaffected conservative Republicans back into their fold by inviting Buchanan to speak to the convention on its opening, most highly viewed night.

Drawing on the Los Angeles riots for visceral imagery of white authorities facing down a black threat of social upheaval and unrest, Buchanan said:

[This election] is about who we are. It is about what we believe and what we stand for as Americans. There is a religious war going on in this country. It is a cultural war as critical to the kind of nation we shall be as the Cold War itself, for this war is for the soul of America. And in that struggle for the soul of America, Clinton and Clinton are on the other side, and George Bush is on our side . . .

To conclude, Buchanan spoke directly to the LA Riots:

. . . the mob was heading in to ransack and loot the apartments of the terrified old men and women inside. The troopers came up the street, M-16s at the ready, and the mob threatened and cursed, but the mob retreated, because it had met the one thing that could stop it: Force, rooted in justice, and backed by moral courage. You know, greater – greater love than this – greater love than this hath no man than that he lay down his life for his friend. Here were 19-year-old boys ready to lay down their lives to stop a mob from molesting old people they did not even know. And as those boys took back the streets of Los Angeles, block by block, my friends, we must take back our cities and take back our culture and take back our country. God bless you, and God bless America.[51]

While the Clinton campaign was framing its candidate as a centrist, a man of the people, a candidate of inclusion, Buchanan had associated Bush and the Republican party with one of the most socially and culturally divisive, racially charged speeches in recent convention history. Bush still felt the hangover from his racially charged Willie Horton ad that had helped him defeat Dukakis in 1988. To add to this, in 1991 and 1992, the former Ku Klux Klan leader and far Right figure, David Duke, tried and partially succeeded to associate himself with the Republican party (despite the party's and President Bush's disavowals of the figure). These factors, combined with the social atmosphere generated by the acquittal of Rodney King's baton-wielding arresting officers, the resulting riots in Los Angeles, and Dan Quayle's famous battle with the television character Murphy Brown over single parenthood, gave post-convention Republicans the air of being uncompassionate, intolerant, and exclusionary. Bush received a twelve-point post-convention bounce in the polls, which left him trailing Clinton by an almost manageable deficit.

Perot re-entered the race in time and with enough support to be invited to the mid-October presidential debates. With his re-election bid continuing to struggle, Bush needed inspired performances in these forums. Clinton, by contrast, inspired national audiences. The two leads' performances in the presidential debates cemented Clinton's symbolic dominance in the election social drama. One incident in particular captured a critical symbolic difference between Clinton and Bush Sr. As performative forums, debates have a moderate amount of contingency structured into them, and each production team lobbies extensively prior to the event to control the sources that do not play to their candidate's strengths. The second debate was structured around the candidates answering questions posed directly from audience members. This structure made the event more interactive from the voter's perspective by removing the celebrity news figures that typically ask the debate questions and thus mediate between candidates and citizens and render the forum more of a traditional television show than a town hall meeting.

During the debate, audience member Marisa Hall asked the candidates:

How has the national debt personally affected each of your lives? And if it hasn't, how can you honestly find a cure for the economic problems of the common people if you have no experience in what's ailing them?

Checking his watch while Hall asked her question, and interpreting her question literally, President Bush fumbled about awkwardly trying to relate the national debt to his personal life. The debate moderator, Carole Simpson of ABC News, tried to rearticulate the question with the national recession as its subject, but Bush was unable to adjust to the reformulation. His reply meandered awkwardly from wanting his grandchildren to be able to afford an education to reading about teenage pregnancies in a bulletin at a black church outside Washington DC. Growing increasingly agitated, Bush asked Hall defensively, "Are you suggesting that if somebody has means, that the national debt doesn't affect them?"

The Clinton team's social dramatic strategy, portraying their candidate as one of the people and the incumbent as out of touch with ordinary

Americans' lives, was forcefully brought to life in Bush's performance. The script the Clinton team had labored to wrap their opponent in walked and talked upon the stage at that moment. The debate forum brought Bush face to face with an ordinary American, and both the style and substance of his response dramatized a profound subjective distance – real or fictional – from ordinary Americans' lives. Bush grew increasingly agitated with the question, and appeared resentful of what he perceived to be its subtext – that he, as a man of means, was incapable of understanding ordinary Americans' lives. In his editorial review of Bush's performance, *Washington Post* columnist Jim Hoagland claimed Bush appeared "dispirited, disjointed, and disengaged."[52]

Clinton's response to Hall performed his campaign theme; he walked and talked "feeling the typical American's pain" that, he had argued, was the result of the national recession and Bush's failed economic policies.

Clinton began his response by approaching Hall and asking her to repeat how she was affected by the recession. His movement played with the notion of the forum's stage. It eroded the symbolic boundary separating candidates from audience members. His movement toward Hall effectively eradicated the stage and the symbolic boundaries separating them, and by asking her to repeat her personal narrative, Clinton brought her character into the debate's plot. The narrative of his response fused with his movements into a kind of symbolic symmetry in which he was a wandering sage who had personally witnessed those hurt by the recession. After symbolically removing the stage, Clinton's performance dominated the moment and the event:

I see people in my state – middle-class people, their taxes have gone up in Washington and their services have gone down, while the wealthy have gotten tax cuts. I – I have seen what's happened in this last four years when – in my state, when people lose their jobs, there's a good chance I'll know them by their names. When the factory closes, I know the people who ran it. When the businesses go bankrupt, I know them. And I've have been out here for 13 months meeting in meetings just like this ever since October with people like you all over America, people that have lost their jobs, lost their livelihood, lost their health insurance.[53]

In his response Clinton narrated the social drama's culprit, Bush's economic policy, and identified the reason for action to take place in November:

It is because we've had 12 years of trickle-down economics. We've gone from first to 12th in the world in wages. We've had four years where we've produced no private sector jobs. Most people are working harder for less money than they were making 12 years ago. It is because we are in the grip of a failed economic theory.

And this decision you're about to make better be about what kind of economic theory you want, not just people saying, I want to go fix it, but what are we going to do?[54]

In so doing Clinton's performance articulated a script to the characters that would perform the social drama's final scene: the decision the audience members were about to make, he proclaimed, the vote they would cast, could change their economic and social conditions.

Clinton beat Bush in November to become the forty-second president of the United States. He entered office, however, with a split symbolic framework. His campaign left Americans with both hope and unease. PBS's *NewsHour* conducted focus groups with undecided voters after each of the presidential debates. Commenting on Clinton's performance in the second debate, graduate student Allen Ramsay, an independent, claimed that though Clinton "did a very good job explaining" his new programs, he also "seemed overly sensitive to the audience, and it gave him a fake feeling from me, and that didn't do much to help me believe him." Accountant Robin Ganzert, a Democrat, responded to Ramsay's critique by stating, "I disagree ... I feel like he [Clinton] was much more sincere, especially in response to that one woman's question" about the recession. "Bush seemed very fake," she continued; "Clinton actually came across very sincere. He's been out talking with the people. He has been affected and seen."[55]

Where some saw authenticity and sincerity, others interpreted Clinton's mental and performative abilities with caution and concern, detecting insincerity and slickness. In a column closing the year 1992, Robert Samuelson reflected on Clinton's victory and his forthcoming presidency:

There have been two Bill Clintons in the past year. The first is Bill the Bold. He's a guy who seems eager to break with past dogmas and face the daunting problems of government. The second is Bill the Pleaser. He's someone who will say almost anything (with a few exceptions) to satisfy the audience of the moment, and as a result, he's said a lot of contradictory things. We still don't know which Clinton will govern – or if both will try.

. . .

Whatever Clinton does, it will be calculated. His economic summit told us more about his political character than about his economic policies. His vast knowledge of policy means that any inconsistencies in his positions almost surely reflect deliberate choices, not inadvertent confusion. He may try to skip deftly around all of his promises. But too much fancy footwork could spawn cynicism and resurrect another Clinton: Slick Willie.[56]

4

The profanation of a president, 1992–1994: presidential character, the "climate of suspicion," and the culture of scandal

Clinton's first year offers a case study of what happens when campaign plot constructions meet the institutional constraints and organizational demands of governance; when the president must confront budgets and deficits, shape and prioritize policy initiatives, manage the competing interests of his or her supporting cast members, and attempt to control the dominant narrative of the nation's trajectory.

Afflicted by policy blunders, staff shake-ups, conflicts with the press, and developing scandals, Clinton's popularity and presidential stature failed to mature during the first two years of his first term. His approval ratings remained low throughout this time and his Administration suffered a devastating blow during 1994's midterm elections when the increasingly popular Republicans, led by rising star Newt Gingrich, took control of both houses of Congress for the first time in forty years. During 1995, however, after the Republicans' impressive congressional victories, the tides of popularity began to reverse. A symbolic inversion occurred: Clinton's tenacity and wherewithal in the face of the Republicans' unrelenting assaults, his vocal opposition to their audaciously bold policy agenda, and his move toward the political center, all cast against the devastating backdrop of the Oklahoma City bombing, earned him badly needed, deeply felt dimensions of respect among loyal supporters, swing voters, and the "Clinton Republicans" that had helped bring him into office three years priorly. The Republicans' popularity, on the other hand, suffered along a classic narrative trajectory: their successes had bred elephantine degrees of confidence, pride, and self-regard, and weakened the political inhibitions that remind powerful people to be diplomatic and civil to their opposition. When Clinton beat the Republicans in the December of 1995 budget standoff, a high stakes, winner-takes-all poker game, he convinced many Americans that the Republicans were recklessly gambling with their future, and he gained enough popularity to easily defeat Bob Dole in the November election of 1996 to secure a second term. Clinton had successfully demonized the Republicans during the budget showdown, and though the Republicans retained the fervent backing of their core supports, they had lost their ability to win over America's silent and swayable middle.

More than a mandate for the incoming president, the 1992 election represented a robust public call for change. Voter turnout was high, with 55.1 percent of the voting-age population casting a ballot.[1] For the fifth time in American history an incumbent president was unseated. In the House of Representatives, the election produced a high rate of member turnover and the majority Democrats lost ten seats. In the presidential race, third-party candidate Ross Perot ran on a platform of reform and change. Portraying himself as an outsider to Washington's insider political circles, as someone who would stand against "politics as usual," Perot won a respectable and influential 18.9 percent of the popular vote. Clinton beat Bush by 5 percentage points; however, he gained only 43 percent of the popular vote, well under a majority and the smallest portion since Nixon's 1968 victory over Humphrey. It was a year in which a lot of people voted, an incumbent was ousted, and the victor won with a historically small portion of support.[2] Exit polls indicate that all three presidential candidates, Clinton, Bush, and the folksy Perot alike, drew remarkably high unfavorability ratings. The *New York Times*'s editorial page labeled Clinton's victory a "fragile mandate … of tenuous proportion."[3]

The election was like an enormous collective gamble. People wanted to vote for change; however, they were not entirely certain that they would get what had been advertised as the alternative. Bush's tenure had enervated the populace. His leadership style had left Americans frustrated, exhausted, and with a nagging sense of stasis. The challengers' campaigns had convinced voters that change and rejuvenation were possible if not imminent. Election day represented a vote for national invigoration and rebirth. Clinton looked younger than Bush, was more personable and charismatic, and he performed an energized kind of populism when he came into contact with regular Americans. Like Kennedy following the Truman and Eisenhower administrations, Clinton's assumption of the presidential mantle represented a symbolic and institutional shift toward youth and vigor. His legitimacy and presidential stature seemed to spring from a different source than that of his predecessors. Rather than stemming from success in warfare or Cold War politicking, Clinton's was a freshly crafted form of leadership that derived from his ability to overcome his impoverished and broken familial roots, his remarkable successes in higher education, and from his public service in governing his home state of Arkansas as a young man.

The election results and post-election polls indicate, however, that many Americans did not know what to make of their new president, that they were hoping for the best but fearing the worst. Clinton had embodied many roles during his campaign, and voters' sense of engaging in a collective gamble involved finding out which Clinton they had elected: the populist he had claimed to be, the deft defendant he had so often been forced to play, or the liberal elitist his challenger had accused him of being.

Clinton entered office with a mixed symbolic framework. While most Americans hoped he would become the nation's young agent of change, many still harbored the suspicion that he was not who he portrayed himself to be during his campaign, that he remained at least in part "Slick Willie." A post-inaugural poll found that while 84 percent of respondents said that Clinton inspired confidence and 81 percent said that he "cared about people like" them, 60 percent believed that Clinton's "Slick" label still applied and 54 percent thought that he lacked conviction.[4]

For a majority of Americans, ambivalence quickly turned to pessimism. The new president started his tenure with unremarkable approval ratings that eroded to record low levels within a week of his inauguration. In historical perspective, Clinton's initial *dis*approval rating of 20 percent set the highest mark for any president since the Eisenhower Administration, when the rating scale was initiated. The average disapproval for the prior nine presidents was 6 percent.[5] While Clinton would always be able to count on a little over a solid third of the public to support him, this disapproval figure indicates that a sizeable minority would not even grant him a honeymoon phase or suspend their judgment for long enough to watch the new president at work. This minority knew that they did not like Clinton based purely on what they had learned during the campaign. The mobilizing opposition this figure portends would cause enormous grief for the president. He would need the swayable middle in order to survive conservative attacks in the future, and at his own peril, he set about alienating them right from the outset.

Clinton's favorability rating hovered in the upper 30s and low 40s through his first year and much of his second, which culminated in the Democrats' devastating loss of majority control over both the House and the Senate. While the main stories of 1993 and 1994 are about Clinton's shaky start and flagging public approval, it is essential to the overall narrative of his presidential tenure and to understanding how he survived impeachment to bear in mind that a solid 30-plus percent of Americans remained devoted fans of his presidency despite the policy blunders, missed opportunities, and the small and large scandals. Core Clinton supporters loved their candidate most of the time, though this did not prevent them from hating him periodically. Almost always, however, they hated his enemies. The same is true of steadfast Republicans and their party's leaders, of course.

The symbolic intermingling of character, scandal, and policy

Within six months of taking office, Clinton's *approval* rating bottomed out at a record low 37 percent amid constructions of his Administration as awash in policy blunders and indecisiveness.[6] In June, *Time Magazine*'s cover story, "The Incredible Shrinking President," framed the Administration as "beset since its inception with miscalculations and self-inflicted wounds,"[7] and *US News and World Report*'s headline article, "A Question of Competence," framed Clinton as "preoccupied with an astonishing series of mistakes and bungles."[8]

Three semi-distinct discursive domains dominated Clinton's first six months in office. A brief reconstruction of each indicates how Clinton lost the middle – namely, by straying from the plot that he had constructed throughout his campaign. As these three story lines developed and unfolded, Clinton's relationships with the public, the press, and the "old" and "new" Democrats on the Hill deteriorated.

First, the new president initiated his term with classically liberal initiatives that clashed with the populist and centrist tunes he had whistled throughout his campaign. The unexpectedly liberal policy tone intertwined with a sense that his Administration was in disarray and that chaos reigned in the White House, which led even sympathetic commentators to the conclusion that the new Administration's start looked like "amateur hour" (Klein 2002: 44). Though the Left-leaning ethos seemed inspired to some, the liberal cast was off-putting to middle Americans who had supported Clinton's rise to power based on his New Democratic message that emphasized middle-class economic issues over those with the ring of "special interests" or identity politics. Second, the discourse surrounding Clinton's first federal budget was dominated by references to struggles both within the Administration and between it and both parties on Capitol Hill, which the Democrats controlled. Also, the phrases "deficit reduction" and "balanced budget" were "sweeping the land" (Woodward 1994: 44), due in no small part to Clinton's and Perot's campaign declarations that the Reagan and Bush administrations had leveraged the futures of Americans' children by spending much more than the government could afford. Clinton knew he would inherit a deficit if elected. Once in office, however, it became clear to the president and to media critics that present economic conditions and political realities made it impossible for Clinton to enact his other popular economic campaign pledges, to pass an economic stimulus plan or to reduce the tax burden on the middle class. Clinton's first budget would pass by a single vote in the House with members voting along party lines, and the compromises Clinton accepted during the struggle left Democrats on the Hill questioning his sincerity and trustworthiness. Third, scandal started to emanate from the new White House.

Clinton's character as a contested sign: populist or liberal elitist?

Post-election news stories indicated to a majority of Americans that Clinton was in fact more a liberal elitist than a populist champion of the fiscally exhausted middle and lower classes. One major cause of this was the mixed messages Clinton sent as he transitioned into office. The president-elect had structured his election campaign so much around the promise of invigorating the economy that even the background stage instructions penned by campaign strategist James Carville, "It's the economy, stupid," had become a celebrated line in the onstage election drama during the year.[9] Clinton claimed he was a "New Democrat" who would emphasize fueling the economy, keeping the middle class comfortable, and raising the fortunes of the struggling classes. The campaign line "It's the economy, stupid" defined Clinton's campaign as much as that year's scandals. In his first interview as president-elect, Clinton again emphasized that the economy represented his main priority and that, in effect, all other presidential responsibilities were tied to and subservient to this one overriding issue:

I think the American people will be very clear on that as they watch the conduct of this transition ... but *I am going to focus like a laser beam on this economy.* And foreign policy will come into play, in part, as it affects the economy. Healthcare comes into play in large measure as it affects the economy, as well as the lives of millions of Americans. But we've got to keep that focus because so many of our social problems have been aggravated by economic difficulties. There's more child abuse and neglect than there would be if we had a healthier economy. There's more family breakup. There's more crime. And I'm not blaming child abuse, family breakup and crime on the economy, but the economy makes those things worse and we have got to focus on the things that we can have an impact early on and then reach out and radiate to these other things we want to bring in. (emphasis added)[10]

Clinton's "laser beam" on the economy was transformed into a sound bite by the networks, cable news, and radio news broadcasts alike, and the imagery was repeatedly invoked through the following round of Sunday morning political shows. The laser beam and economic plan, however, were quickly transformed into distant abstractions and the sound bite evaporated into the ether. The news's discursive space shifted to reports detailing the new Administration's intentions to immediately address "old" Democratic issues.[11]

On the second day of his Administration, Clinton rolled back Reagan- and Bush-era restrictions to abortions, a step taken so quickly that by taking it Clinton seemed to be signaling to pro-life conservatives that he was taking up their "challenge" to rally against him. The twentieth annual "March for Life" anti-abortion rally was held in Washington two days later. "At least 75,000 abortion opponents paraded from the Ellipse to Capitol Hill ... matching its largest crowd ever ... for what marcher Martha Donovan ... described as 'a show of force to the new president.'" The march was "an initiation for many who took Clinton's election as an affront," the *Washington Post* reported.[12]

At the same time, the Administration was drawing attention to what Ted Koppel termed "one of the most vitriolic controversies of this very new Clinton era,"[13] the Administration's determination to remove restrictions barring homosexuals from participating in the nation's armed services, or what came to be known as the "gays in the military" issue. The issue ranked very low in national polls in terms of importance and popularity, and homosexuals claimed to be more interested in workplace equality than the military issue. Military reactions ranged from an ominous, angry silence to outright hostility, and (unfounded) rumors floated through the media that the Chairman of the Joint Chiefs of Staff and rising star, General Colin Powell, had asked to leave his post early due to the controversy. Late night comedians seized on the issue and lampooned the Administration ceaselessly. By mid-year the Administration announced that the "Don't ask, don't tell" policy drafted as an interim solution would become permanent policy. The compromise was ridiculed for lacking substance,[14] and the nickname "Waffler" was increasingly applied to Clinton to describe his willingness to accept any side of an issue as long as it appeared popular.

The final issue that shaped the news discourse about the new Administration was Clinton's adamancy that his political appointments and cabinet members "look like America," a semi-coded phrase signaling that his political appointees would be comprised of women and men from all races and ethnicities. In fact, Clinton's desire to signify a multicultural and progressive approach to filling his Cabinet led him to make these appointments even before he had hired his White House staff, who are people that usually assist in and advise the president in things like selecting Cabinet appointments. The odd sequencing of hiring caused some problems for Clinton's public image.

Initially the appointment ethos was well received, particularly among core Democrats and liberal elites. The guiding ethos and the Administration itself became objects of ridicule, however, after Clinton's nominee to attorney general, Zoe Baird, revealed that she had knowingly broken the law by employing illegal immigrants and had failed to pay their social security taxes. Even greater outrage was stirred when it came to light that Baird had informed the Clinton transition team about the illegal transgressions and the Clinton team had nominated her anyway. The *New York Times*'s editorial page said her appointment would have projected "devastating symbolism," and it excoriated the Clinton team for its presumptuousness in assuming that its blessing represented a sufficient pass for the illegalities. Several months later, in another embarrassing reversal, "Clinton's next major confirmation battle"[15] erupted with the nomination of Lani Guinier to the post of assistant attorney general for civil rights. Guinier's past academic and legal work was subjected to withering, often distorting criticism that labeled her a "quota queen"[16] and her thought a "kind of racism in reverse" that "would push America down the road of racial balkanization."[17] As in the cases of Zoe Baird and Kimba Wood, his second nominee to the attorney general position, Clinton withdrew the Guinier nomination.[18]

These misfires, and Clinton's reactions to them, damaged the new president's credibility and integrity. Jon Sawyer at the *St. Louis Post-Dispatch* wrote an extended piece on what the appointment failures indicated about the new Administration.

President Bill Clinton's abandonment of Lani Guinier capped another politically damaging week for the White House that left even loyal Democrats wondering what else might go wrong. It wasn't so much Guinier or the fate of her specific nomination, as assistant attorney general for civil rights. The issue, critics say, was Clinton himself – both his management of the White House staff and the values for which he is prepared to fight ... The problem with Clinton's abrupt junking of the nomination is that it left so many, across so broad a spectrum, wondering just what it is that Clinton really believes in.

Sawyer continued by quoting Senator Paul Wellstone, a liberal Democrat from Minnesota:

"I just think you've got to be a president who stands for principles," Wellstone told home-state reporters after the collapse of Guinier's nomination. "But now to go this way one day and that way the next, it seems as though there are no valid principles at the White House. That's what the problem is, and it is a real serious problem."[19]

These early steps not only served as "the ultimate wake-up call" to conservative Americans,[20] they also disappointed middle Americans, swing voters, and those disaffected former Reagan and Bush supporters who had taken a gamble and voted like Clinton Republicans. Instead of using his youth, intelligence, and charisma to spark the country out of its economic drowsiness, instead of enacting the New Democratic populism on which he had campaigned, Clinton appeared to be an Old Democrat using the office to push liberal elitist policies through the Democratic Congress.

The expansion of a counter-democratic framework: the budget, health care, and the Hill

The second discursive domain that contributed to building Clinton's presidential identity consisted of the drafting and passing of the White House's first federal budget. The process of drafting the budget indicated how Clinton would handle complex projects and negotiate between competing interests within his Administration. Drafting the budget also communicated the new Administration's priorities; with its campaign promises bumping into one another the new Administration had to begin making compromises. Trying to get the budget passed indicated how Clinton would work with Congress and set the tone for future negotiations with the legislature.

Prone to facilitating free-floating and far-ranging conversations about policy, Clinton was irresistibly drawn to exploring every perspective of a problem or issue. His technique of brainstorming shaped staff relations and influenced policy formation, which appeared meandering if not bordering on mayhem (Woodward 1994: 81), and "an endless stream of 'White House in Chaos' stories" communicated this atmosphere to the public (Klein 2002: 61).[21] The budget plan's creation exposed divisions within the new Administration. For instance, political advisors that had served as campaign strategists throughout 1992 felt ostracized and betrayed by Clinton's increasing dependence on his new team of economic advisors. The strategists had helped Clinton win on a platform of stimulating growth and exercising fiscal responsibility. Based on their strategies, the candidate had given impassioned speeches on creating investment programs, stimulating the economy with a package of "fast-track" spending, lowering the middle class's tax burden, and reducing the deficit.

Clinton's new team of economic advisors joined the Administration with sobering news: the campaign promises would have to be broken. The spending initiatives would cost too much, and the middle class's taxes were essential to the budget and for managing the ballooning deficit (Klein 2002).

Also, reforming health care had been an important plank in the Clinton campaign. Drafting the budget forced the Administration to confront the project's cost and the political realities of passing such sweeping legislation. Health-care reform was further complicated when the new Administration announced that the president's wife, Hillary, would lead the reform initiative from an office in the West Wing, and that the plan would be ready within the first one hundred days of Clinton's tenure (by April 30). Hillary was enthusiastic about the project and Clinton encouraged the drafting of a plan without promising that it would be tied to the budget when the latter was sent to the Hill for Congress's vote.

Yet there was strict disagreement within the Administration over whether or not health-care reform would save money or create an additional drain on the budget. Hillary and Ira Magaziner, who was assisting her with the project, wanted to fold health-care reform into the budget deal, and insisted that universal coverage could save the government money by eliminating unnecessary costs and improving efficiency. All of Clinton's economic advisors, on the other hand, argued that the reform would be an expensive proposition that would aggravate the deficit problem.

Given the current atmosphere on the Hill, Clinton's weak mandate, and the Democrats' slim majority in the Senate, passing the budget by itself represented a difficult political challenge in its own right. While the Democrats controlled the House with 259 members[22] to the Republicans' 176, they only controlled the Senate by 57 to 43 seats. The Clintons knew that it would be politically advantageous to include the package in the budget plan because it would have a better chance of succeeding in the Senate. Due to the Senate's rules, the budget could not be filibustered and only required fifty-one Senate votes or a simple majority approval to pass. As a bill arriving at Congress on its own, health-care reform would require sixty votes in the Senate to override the likely threat of a Republican filibuster. On the other hand, folding health care in with the budget increased the chances that the budget itself would not pass, a political eventuality that Secretary of Treasury Lloyd Bentsen, a congressional veteran with experience in both the House and the Senate, argued would cripple the new Administration. Bentsen was the voice of realpolitik. Passing the budget was essential to projecting power to Congress, he told Clinton, and having it fail or stall in Congress would amount to political suicide (Woodward 1994: 88).

Clinton postponed the health-care reform and ultimately sent to Congress the Omnibus Budget Reconciliation bill, which called for increasing taxes on upper incomes, cuts in spending, and deficit reduction. The budget squeaked by in the House by two votes and passed in the Senate by Vice President Al Gore's single vote, while the stimulus plan Clinton hoped to pass in order to alleviate some of the proposed cuts and to pump fuel into the economy was killed by a Republican filibuster in the Senate (Tatalovich and Frendreis 2000: 48).[23]

The budget's passage represented a limited public victory for Clinton but a victory nonetheless, given that its failure would have been politically devastating for the new president. The general story projected to the public was that it was a difficult, tarring battle, and that a renewed spirit of partisanship was alive in Washington. Instead of a tax cut for the middle class, the Clinton plan had raised taxes on those with higher incomes and added a 4-cent per gallon tax on gasoline (an idea for which Clinton had berated and shellacked Paul Tsongas during the 1992 primaries). The news was not entirely bad, but raising anybody's taxes rarely breeds good cheer, and, indeed, in the 1994 midterm elections, congressional Republicans used the tax increases to run against Clinton with great success.

In the Neustadt model of the bargaining presidency, Clinton's first steps were precipitating adverse conditions. The budget hurt Clinton's reputation on the Hill and inside Washington circles, where the perception set in that he was "a weak president, one who could be rolled" (Klein 2002: 55; see also Schier 2000: 10, 20). Passing the budget had required Clinton to accept enormous compromises and to backtrack on pledges he had made during prior rounds of negotiations. For instance, Clinton had coaxed House Democrats into passing a politically unpopular increase in energy taxes, or Gore's Btu tax, a difficult vote that representatives knew they would dread explaining to their constituents back home. Clinton had promised to stand behind it, but when the tax ran afoul in the Senate, he eliminated it and left the House Democrats with nothing but a record of voting to raise taxes. Such maneuverings helped turn the "notion that Clinton had no 'core values'" into a "Beltway cliché" (Klein 2002: 55). Another critical consequence of the budget episode was what David Broder called the rising "trust deficit," that people were learning to not believe what the new president claimed, a consequence of the fact that people were "discovering that Clinton really played fast and loose with the facts in last year's campaign."[24]

Failing to master the demands of the public presidency as well, a "climate of suspicion"[25] developed and began to take deep root in segments of the culture during Clinton's first year. Scandals mushroomed, fueled in part by the Administration's evasive practices and posture of resistance to the White House press corps. Clinton got around to appointing his White House staff about a month later than presidents-elect usually do. His method of finding people with whom to surround himself, however, was typical. He turned to his campaign staff and emphasized loyalty over long-term Washington experience. In his history of covering the Clinton presidency, Joe Klein (2002) observes that the Clintons settled into Washington with a "cramped, defensive obsession with the forces arrayed against them" (106), and that they preferred to surround themselves with people that were "slavish, unobtrusive, and loyal" while "forceful personalities were not courted" (45). These elements combined to create a garrison-like atmosphere in the White House. Consequently, an oppositional and suspicious culture developed between the White House and the press corps. Evan Thomas, the Washington bureau chief for *Newsweek*, said some reporters covering the White House might have "an element of revenge, because this particular crowd were smug [sic], contemptuous of the press and thought they could go over our heads."[26]

Bad relations with the press began early in 1992 as a result of the incredible amount of scrutiny Clinton's private life received in the early months of his campaign. *Star* magazine had broken the Gennifer Flowers story, but the Clintons most resented the fact that other, more legitimate news producers seemed to be very willing to overlook the questionable sources[27] that were giving rise to the damaging rumors. Many in the press, on the other hand, were left with an uneasy feeling that they had been used, manipulated, and lied to after the Clintons' *60 Minutes* interview with Steve Kroft.

The *Wall Street Journal*, a potent and unrelenting critic of Clinton, had turned the candidate's response to the Vietnam War draft into the campaign-threatening "draft dodging" story, and its editorial page continued to put pressure on Clinton and his appointments well into the Administration's new term. Clinton ran afoul of the *Washington Post* when its columnist Dan Balz asked the candidate in December of 1991 about the rumors swirling that the young Clinton had somehow evaded the Vietnam War draft. Clinton told Balz it was a "fluke," that he had given up his ROTC deferment and asked to be called up out of a matter of conscience and patriotism – the version that Balz published in the *Post* in the middle of January, 1992.[28] A month later the *Wall Street Journal* investigation and a similar piece in the *Los Angeles Times* appeared, each contradicting the story Clinton had told Balz. The *Washington Post* was left with the task of explaining its embarrassingly naïve and under-investigated account to its readership and media critics, and left with a considerable amount of resentment and suspicion of the future president. On the other hand, Clinton was treated like a media darling during a good stretch of his campaign. His performance at the Democratic National Convention was praised, his post-convention bus tour was practically celebrated, and his performances in the presidential debates received vast degrees of positive and enthusiastic press.

After the election, however, the new Administration and the press declined the opportunity to honeymoon together. During its inaugural gala, Clinton's staff made a point of making fun of the press's behavior by showing a video of various journalists making obviously incorrect, doomsday predictions about the Clinton campaign. The *Wall Street Journal* started criticizing the new Administration as soon as it took its first steps. The paper ran two withering critiques of Lani Guinier that helped sink her nomination, and its editorial page ran a four-part series of "Who is ..." pieces[29] that critically investigated three members of the Rose Law Firm in Arkansas with whom the Clintons were closely associated and one piece on the first lady herself, titled "Who is Hillary Clinton?" as if the real person had yet to be presented to the public.[30] In mid-June newspapers and weekly news magazines were running covers that questioned the president's competence and asked if he had any core beliefs. The Clintons hosted a barbeque with the White House press corps to try to mend relations. The day after, Clinton abruptly terminated a press conference after erupting in anger at a reporter's question. Howard Kurtz of the *Washington Post* described the scene:

The reporter said that Clinton's withdrawal of the Lani Guinier nomination and his consideration of federal Appeals Court Judge Stephen G. Breyer for the Supreme Court "may have created an impression, perhaps unfair, of a certain zigzag quality in the decision-making process here. I wonder, sir, if you could kind of walk us through it and perhaps disabuse us of any notion we might have along those lines. Thank you."

Clinton stared angrily at Hume [the reporter] and said in a voice filled with contempt: "I have long since given up the thought that I could disabuse some of you of turning any substantive decision into anything but a political process. How you could ask a question like that after the statement she[31] just made is beyond me."

An Administration official said the president was unable to take further questions because several senators and Hillary Rodham Clinton rose in applause and moved toward the stage.

Kurtz suggested that perhaps the episode played to viewers as if Clinton "were standing up to an arrogant press corps,"[32] and others in the press surmised that the "display of righteous anger" was "calculated to show backbone and toughness." Veteran Washington correspondent Helen Thomas of United Press International summed up the press's suspicions: "We've been framed."[33]

The combination of the Administration's guardedness and secrecy with the press's sense of an entitlement to know, and suspicion that blood was in the water, gave rise to a culture of impending scandal.

In mid-May, as jokes about Clinton shutting down Los Angeles International Airport to receive a $200 haircut filled late night talk show monologues ("Hair Force One"), the new Administration's first scandal, "Travelgate," erupted. Less humorous than the haircut episode, Travelgate was a story about nepotism and allegations of the mismanagement of federal travel funds, and it contributed a concrete example to which critics could pin their growing suspicions about corruption within the Administration.[34] When seven employees of the White House travel office were abruptly fired, White House spokesperson Dee Dee Myers told the press that the Administration had requested that the FBI investigate the office for mismanaging funds. The staff had been dismissed, she claimed, due to "gross mismanagement" and "very shoddy accounting practices."[35] The news grabbed the press's attention, Joe Klein (2002) suggests, because the travel office had developed a friendly relationship with the White House press corps by enabling perks like transporting for free packages that reporters purchased during overseas trips to cover the president (58). Also, the dismissed employees denied the charges, and claimed that they had not been given an opportunity to either face their accusers or defend themselves. Within days, the White House released information that suggested the firings were a typical case of cronyism: the staff had been replaced with friends and family of the Clintons who were interested in providing the travel services for the White House. The *New York Times*'s editorial page summarized the events thusly: one of Clinton's friends, the Hollywood producer Harry Thomason, had communicated to the White House that he knew people who were interested in handling the Administration's travel affairs, and that Catherine Cornelius, a distant cousin of the president, was going to assist by handling the travel demands through an outfit called World Wide Travel in Little Rock. The aide who handled the transition, David Watkins, was a former business associate of World Wide's owner, whose family had political ties to Mr. Clinton.[36]

The cronyism fueled criticism, but the news that the White House had asked the FBI to substantiate its version of the firings – and thus had moved toward undoing "two decades of efforts to insulate the law-enforcement agency from even the appearance of Presidential manipulation"[37] – raised deeper levels of suspicion and apprehension. The FBI's involvement suggested the days of Hoover's unethical tactics waged to shape political outcomes, and conjured images of the Nixon White House.[38] Thus, Travelgate thickened the atmosphere of mistrust, and helped to normalize suspicions that the Administration might be conducting illegal and unethical practices in the secrecy afforded by the White House's power corridors. Suspicion piled up like fall kindling, particularly among some portions of the public like the far Right, some mainstream conservatives, libertarians, and full-time armchair critics. But middle Americans and longtime Democrats were not immune to the atmosphere either. Added to this mix was a sense of titillation and excitement of the suspected but unknown, the kind of feeling one gets just before seeing the first victim in a slasher movie. Writing in the *New York Times*, Anthony Lewis described the atmosphere: "The press is ravenous, ready to see scandal in a speck of dust."[39]

In late July the atmosphere of scandal thickened considerably. Vince Foster, a longtime associate and friend of the Clintons from their days in Arkansas, who was working as the deputy White House counsel, was found dead in a local park, shot in the head in an apparent suicide. Foster's death captured imaginations within the far Right, among whom conspiracy theories spread like wildfire – for instance, theories positing that Foster had been murdered because he knew information that could prove damaging and embarrassing to the Clinton White House. Just as Travelgate gave Administration critics a tangible symbol of a traditional form of Washington corruption, Foster's "death reinforced the fantasy of a lethal immorality about the Clintons" (Klein 2002: 107), and stirred the radical Right into endless webs of exotic conspiracy theories, murder cover-ups, and secret love affairs within the Clinton inner sanctum. The event initiated a galvanization of anti-Clinton sentiment and added an increasingly sinister dimension to Clinton's symbolic framework for far Right segments of the nation, a process catalyzed by right-wing radio talk shows' endless debates on the sources and motives of Foster's death. Yet Foster's death also commanded attention from more than just the far Right. It was the subject of two separate investigations by special prosecutors, which indicates that his death captivated the imagination of more than just the fringe Right. Also, Foster would remain part of the Clinton scandal story through his connection to the Whitewater story, which would crash into public discourse just a few months later.

Throughout the fall of 1993, the scandal atmosphere slowly intensified. News of the Clintons' involvement in a failed real-estate deal and of their friends' and business partners' involvement in a failed savings and loan (S&L) trickled into the *New York Times*, the *Los Angeles Times*, and the *Washington Post*. All of the accounts were laced with language of suspicion accompanied by disclaimers noting that nothing illegal had been uncovered. Hazy links and suppositions continued to form through the fall months. The Clintons, we learned, had friends named Jim and Susan McDougal, who operated the failed Arkansas Madison Guaranty S&L,[40] and with whom the Clintons had invested in the Whitewater Development Corporation, a real-estate investment firm. Madison Guaranty and the Whitewater firm had come under the scrutiny of the Arkansas Justice Department for suspicion of financial fraud. A typical article about Whitewater read like a journalist's efforts to identify characters in a confusing, overly plotted play. The story seemed to refuse to make clear what exactly had transpired, or to identify the relevant parties, investigative agencies, or jurisdictions. At this time, the story's impenetrable details functioned like annoying background chatter to middle Americans.

In the meantime, also during the fall, Clinton's public approval ratings were "stagnating" and his disapproval ratings began to rise after the country witnessed images of dead American Marines being dragged through the streets of Mogadishu, Somalia, and hundreds of American troops fleeing by boat from pro-military, gun-toting Haitians parading around on a dock in Port-au-Prince, Haiti.[41] The president gained a modicum of popular approval, on the other hand, by passing NAFTA (North American Free Trade Agreement), the promotion of which included an impressive ceremony featuring Clinton flanked by former presidents Ford, Carter, and Bush, who were also supporters of the treaty.

Health care robustly re-entered the news when Clinton gave an impressive presentation of Hillary's and Ira Magaziner's plan to joint sessions of Congress. The speech became legendary of Clinton's speaking skills, because for the first nine minutes of his performance, the teleprompter from which he was supposed to read was scrolling the wrong speech. Realizing this, Clinton ad-libbed for the duration until the problem was corrected and the proper text was loaded. Polls indicated that most Americans considered the issue very important and that there was considerable popular support for universal coverage.[42] Several factors contributed to its eventual downfall, however. The project began to turn sour almost immediately after it was announced that a reform proposal would be drafted and that Hillary would be leading the effort. The process by which the plan was designed aroused suspicion and resentment both within the Administration and without. The team drafting the plan was highly secretive and defensive, inquiries into the plan's formation were met with resentment, and suggestions were received with off-putting impatience. The task force was shrouded in a blanket of secrecy and "a know-it-all smugness became the operational style," Klein (2002: 120) reported. Much of the senior White House staff could not understand the content of the plan and felt silenced during briefings. Treasury Secretary Lloyd Bentsen, Woodward (1999: 316) reports, "was disturbed that the healthcare plan had not been subjected to the collegial deliberative process of the economic plan, but was handled back channel," with its architects "trying to keep all the information" to themselves.

The secrecy created a discursive vacuum, and leaks filled the void. Based on a flawed, leaked chart, the *New York Times* reported that "government financial experts have told the White House that President Clinton's health-care plan may require $100 billion to $150 billion a year in new public and private spending by Government, business and consumers."[43] Additionally, the secretive atmosphere was aggravating health-care-related industries which would be directly affected by the plan. Industry leaders who wanted to exercise influence over the plan's formation felt ostracized by the secretive process and distrust fomented in the business community as the plan developed. The insurance industry responded with a highly effective "Harry and Louise" ad campaign, which signaled that the Administration's plan would put "caps" on individuals' coverage and thus limit people's access to doctors. One of the spots ended with Harry asking in exasperation and disbelief, "So what if your health plan runs out of money?" Sensible Louise, his wife, responded, "There's got to be a better way."

Politically the budget victory and NAFTA had consumed most of Clinton's preciously scarce political capital. By the time the health-care plan met expected Republican resistance, Clinton would no longer be in a position to woo many of the congressional Democrats he had already persuaded to support these prior initiatives. Also, the nation was consumed with discourse of an enormous budget deficit. Neither the senior White House staff nor industry experts believed the task force leadership's claims that the plan would actually save the government money and reduce spending. Democratic Senator Daniel Patrick Moynihan went so far as to say the plan's estimates were based on "fantasy numbers," a statement that gained considerable TV news coverage.[44] Finally, if the plan made it to the Senate, it was almost certain to meet staunch Republican resistance because they would not want to hand the Democrats an enormous legislative success heading into 1994's midterm elections.

Lacking sixty Democrats in the Senate, the plan would not have been able to overcome a Republican filibuster.

In the middle of December and through the beginning of 1994, the Clinton Administration's scandal problems merged and metastasized. "Troopergate" erupted when the monthly conservative news magazine The *American Spectator* published the article "His Cheatin' Heart," on December 18. The article set the stage for Paula Jones to enter the public sphere as a symbol of Clinton's sexual appetite and uncontrollable Achilles' heel. The article's principal subject was a colorful account, replete with extensive interview excerpts, of how Clinton used the Arkansas State Troopers that safeguarded the governor to procure for him young women for sexual conquests, hence "Troopergate." The article portrayed the interaction between Jones and Clinton as a mutually agreed-upon sexual encounter. Insulted by the narrative, Jones filed a lawsuit against the president in February of the following year, seeking from the president an apology and financial damages.

The press had been aware of Paula Jones and her accusations for some time prior to the *American Spectator* article. Major papers had declined to robustly investigate or report the story because the people who were promoting Jones and giving her a stage were so clearly ideologically driven and had obvious histories of opposing Clinton's rise to power.[45] Michael Isikoff (1999) of the *Washington Post*, on the other hand, had conducted extensive investigations into Jones's story and thought that it was worth pursuing and reporting. His editors did not agree, explaining that all of the evidence was hearsay, that an apparent "pattern of behavior" was not newsworthy, and that nothing illegal appeared to have taken place. The *Los Angeles Times* too had been courted by Paula Jones's principal advocate, longtime Clinton antagonist Cliff Jackson, to investigate the story. Like the *Washington Post*, the paper had declined. "But [the story] had a ring of truth ... and it gained great, if initially surreptitious, currency in Washington," Klein (2002: 108) admits in his account of the rise of Troopergate. Once the *American Spectator* had published their piece, the *Los Angeles Times* and its mainstream competitors joined in the process of telling the story. The new year looked laden with scandal.

Troopergate proved sensational in the short term. In the long term, while it would accumulate the legal materials ultimately responsible for Clinton's impeachment, it would also become an unpleasant reminder of how long conservative critics had been digging through Clinton's private closet. Whitewater, on the other hand, was explosive from the outset due almost entirely to its potential connection to Vince Foster's death. On December 19, the *New York Times* reported:

Federal investigators are trying to determine whether a file relating to a failed Arkansas savings-and-loan owner and his investment firm was taken from the White House office of Vincent W. Foster Jr. after he committed suicide in July ...

The officials said investigators had been told that Mr. Foster, the deputy White House counsel who died of a single gunshot wound to the head on July 20, kept a file in his office on James McDougal, the savings and loan owner and a former business associate of President Clinton, and on the Whitewater Development Corporation, a real estate investment firm under scrutiny for possible financial fraud in a separate Justice Department inquiry in Arkansas.

But the law-enforcement officials said no such file was listed in the inventory of items in Mr. Foster's office that was conducted by Bernard W. Nussbaum, the White House counsel, in the presence of Federal agents on July 22.

. . .

The law-enforcement officials did not say how investigators learned of the existence of the file, and the circumstances surrounding its disappearance are murky.

The officials also said that the inquiry was being hampered by a lack of cooperation from the White House. They said some Administration officials whom investigators sought to interview had engaged in time-consuming negotiations about being represented by lawyers. They also said that investigators strongly suspected that a few White House officials might not be volunteering all they know.[46]

The missing files thus linked Whitewater to the domain of suspicion surrounding Foster's death, and henceforth Whitewater became an inescapable symbol. The *Washington Post* was adamant that the White House release all of the Clinton's documents related to the Whitewater land development project. Feeling besieged and attacked, and persuaded that a conspiracy was mounting against them,[47] the Clintons categorically refused to cooperate. Aides George Stephanopoulos and David Gergen, the latter a longtime advisor to Republican presidents, and a figure hired by Clinton earlier in the year to curb signs of excessive liberalism, pleaded with the president to cooperate fully and release any and all documents to avoid the appearance of hiding something. Clinton's "response to the scandal-mongering," Klein (2002: 110) reports, "was a furious, self-defeating defiance that overwhelmed the White House and limited his ability to enact the grander goals of his presidency." Hillary exercised considerable influence on the president, and her resistance to cooperating was even stronger than that of the president. The White House refused the *Washington Post*'s request and the atmosphere of suspicion intensified as the new year began.

Symbolic pollution and the weakening of the presidential power

In mid-January Clinton embarked on a trip to central Europe and nations of the former Soviet Union. Travel abroad typically brings a US president positive media attention and bolsters approval ratings. Throughout this trip, however, the media relentlessly probed the Whitewater deal and inquired about the possibility of the attorney general appointing a special prosecutor to investigate it. On January 11, via a telephone conference call from Ukraine, Clinton spoke with his legal and political advisors. White House legal counsel Bernard Nussbaum warned Clinton that a special prosecutor would "broaden the investigation to areas we haven't even contemplated ... [T]his will be a roving searchlight ... They will chase you, your family and friends, through the presidency and beyond" (Toobin 2000: 67). Clinton listened instead to his political team, and the following day George Stephanopoulos announced that the president had asked Attorney General Reno to appoint a special prosecutor, adding that the Administration hoped the step would bring the subject to "a speedy and credible resolution" (quoted in Toobin 2000: 68).

Later in January, upon Clinton's return, Republican opposition to the Clinton health plan was becoming more cohesive and had even picked up support from some powerful Democrats. Sensing the mounting opposition, Clinton confronted the plan's critics in his January 25 State of the Union Address. In a touch of theater that Republican Senator Alan Simpson described favorably as "Reaganesque,"[48] Clinton flourished a black pen and declared, "I want to make this very clear ... If you send me legislation that does not guarantee every American private health insurance that can never be taken away, you will force me to take this pen, veto the legislation and we'll come right back here and start all over again."[49] Though performatively powerful and provocative, it was politically unwise as it only served to further entrench and solidify Republican opposition to the plan.

The following week, highly critical, controversial, and attention-generating critiques of the Administration's health-care plan appeared in the press, warning that the plan would be far more costly than the public had been led to believe, that the government would be making patients' medical decisions, and that the Administration and its spokespeople – that is, Bill and Hillary Clinton – were not telling the American public the truth about the plan.[50] Media interest in Troopergate and Whitewater was at its apex while the Republicans were becoming increasingly organized and disciplined in their opposition to the White House. On February 11, the scandal atmosphere intensified even further when Paula Jones filed a lawsuit against the president, charging that he had sexually harassed her and violated her civil rights.

Through the rest of winter and spring the Republicans waged a highly organized ad campaign through diffuse media outlets to interweave these story lines to portray the Clinton Administration and the Clintons themselves as counter-democratic threats to America's sacred center. For instance, the rising star of conservative radio commentary, Rush Limbaugh, pressed this story line relentlessly as a guest on television shows and on his radio program:

> Because everybody says – or a lot of the critics said, "We've got to get on to other issues." And I think Whitewater is about health care. Whitewater's about Bosnia. Whitewater is about crime and – and welfare reform. And I'll tell you why. Character – the issue of character was put on hold during the 1992 campaign. Nobody cared about it because so many people were upset with the economic situation, they wanted a change. And it's now coming home to roost.[51]

The campaign tied the institutional to the cultural, arguing that the damage the Clintons could do to the White House was only half as harrowing as the threat they represented to American beliefs, values, and morality. Character and policy, the public and private, became deeply intertwined early in the Clinton presidency, and this symbolic boundary would figure prominently in the Clinton–Lewinsky scandal in 1998. While a majority of the public eventually interpreted Clinton's affair as representing a private matter, they also facilitated the conflation of the two much earlier in Clinton's tenure.

The Administration responded by trying to return policy, issues, and the routine work of government to the national discourse. The Republicans' story line, which weaved suggestions of murder and sexual impropriety into representing a threat to the nation, was more compelling, however. Also, the White House's first year of policy initiatives had not been very popular. Middle and centrist Americans had been surprised by the new Administration's perceived liberal excesses. Those that had voted for change and gambled on the rising star from Arkansas reinterpreted Clinton's campaign promises about economic resuscitation and reform as political untruths delivered for personal and political gain. The Democratic Leadership Counsel that had helped bring Clinton to national prominence felt abandoned by Clinton and was left wondering if he had believed in its organization's causes in the first place. Finally, with the 1994 midterms approaching, the Republican juggernaut gaining speed on anti-Clinton rhetoric, and feeling deceived and confused by Clinton's goals and style of leadership, congressional

Democrats were quite willing to disassociate from the Administration and allow it to weather the political storm on its own.

Suspicion and consternation grew among Clinton's base and among Administration-friendly journalists, as well. Joe Klein, for instance, who was generally sympathetic to many of Clinton's policy initiatives and skeptical of charges of corruption, explored the "character issue" thesis in his editorial, "The Politics of Promiscuity," in *Newsweek* in May of 1994. Though Klein emphasized that much of what had been rumored about Clinton's private life remained unsubstantiated, the article suggested that the promiscuity with which Clinton led his private life seemed to exercise considerable influence in his public service as well, and therefore represented a legitimate subject of investigation:

> But a clear pattern has emerged – of delay, of obfuscation, of lawyering the truth. The litany of offenses is as familiar as it is depressing.

> But it seems increasingly, and sadly, apparent that the character flaw Bill Clinton's enemies have fixed upon – promiscuity – is a defining characteristic of his *public* life as well. It may well be that this is one case where private behavior does give an indication of how a politician will perform in the arena. It may be that Clinton's alleged (and it must be emphasized: unproven) behavior toward women is not irrelevant when his behavior toward Haitians, Bosnians – and Americans – is considered, and therefore should be a fit subject for greater scrutiny ...

> With the Clintons, the story *always* is subject to further revision. The misstatements are always incremental. The "misunderstandings" are always innocent – casual, irregular: promiscuous. Trust is squandered in dribs and drabs.

> Does this sort of behavior also infect the president's public life, his formulation of policy? Clearly, it does. Has it made him any less effective? ... It might destroy this Administration insidiously ... by feeding the public cynicism about the nature of politics and politicians.

Clinton's approval rating continued its long downward slide through the summer and early fall. The president tried to reverse the trend at the end of June by dramatically reshuffling his staff and inserting more experienced personnel into key White House positions. Despite the display of house cleaning, with his health-care initiative floundering on the Hill and congressional investigations probing Whitewater, suspicion and frustration continued to mount among the nation's publics.

As Labor Day approached and the congressional midterms loomed in the near distance, the Administration's health-care initiative was pronounced "dead" and subjected to a thorough "postmortem" in the press,[52] much of which heaped blame for its demise on Clinton and his wife for their political fecklessness. Republican opposition had successfully demonized the plan by reframing it as "socialized medicine," a polluted symbol of old Democratic, high cost and big bureaucracy thinking. Also over the course of the year, discourse about the health-care initiative had been sprinkled throughout with references to Clinton's controversial Surgeon General appointee, Dr. Joycelyn Elders, who had publicly advocated the free distribution of hypodermic needles to drug addicts, condom distribution to teenagers, and teaching masturbation as an alternative to sexual intercourse to high school students. For Republican opposition it was a short leap in symbolic practice to frame the Clinton Administration as a radically liberal, if not outright socialist threat to the nation's center, suffused with corruption from the top down.

In this "unsettled political environment," with neither a strong figure in the Executive nor a solid record of recent legislative accomplishments, congressional Democrats grew increasingly glum about their prospects in the approaching midterms.[53] Clinton would play a central role in campaign commercials, but not a role of his own choosing. Taking measure of campaign strategies in September, *New York Times* columnist Richard Berke reported that it was "striking, although hardly surprising, that Democratic candidates' advertising does not feature the president."[54] Instead, Republicans aspiring to unseat Democratic congressional incumbents were featuring Clinton in their commercials and using new digital editing technologies to "morph," or virtually erase the distinction between their opponents and Clinton himself. A testament to Clinton's symbolic problems and low approval ratings, unknown and inexperienced Republican challengers were choosing to run against the president of the United States instead of simply against the congresspersons inhabiting their districts' seats.

More than thirty congressional campaigns used the morphing technique and "almost all exclusively [featured] Clinton as the bad guy."[55] A typical morphing commercial would focus in on an unflattering still image of the Democratic congressional incumbent. A voice-over would begin announcing which Clinton initiatives the congressperson had supported. Slowly and seamlessly, the Democratic incumbent's image would morph into Clinton's and then after a few moments, morph from Clinton's image back into the incumbent's. The technique moved from visual simile to visual metaphor, from "Congressperson X is like Clinton" to "Congressperson X is Clinton." It associated the Democratic congressperson with Clinton to the extent that the two literally became the same person, shared the same identity, and inhabited the same body. The Republicans turned the midterms into a referendum on the Clinton Administration and they succeeded spectacularly.

Not since 1922, in the wake of the Teapot Dome scandal, had a majority party suffered such a devastating loss of political power.

The Republicans took control of both the House and the Senate for the first time since 1954, forty years priorly. Tom Foley, the Speaker of the House, and fifty-one other Democrats lost their House seats, netting a fifty-two seat gain for the Republicans. The Republicans picked up ten seats in the Senate. Bob Dole became the Senate majority leader, and Newt Gingrich became the Speaker of the House. This transferred an enormous amount of institutional power to the Republicans, who treated their sweeping victory as a mandate from the public and as an indictment of the Clinton White House. They immediately began to expand congressional investigations of the Executive Branch.

Earlier that year, Attorney General Janet Reno had appointed Robert Fiske to head the investigation into the Whitewater land and S&L dealings and Vince Foster's suicide (Woodward 1999: 241). November's shift in congressional power enabled the Republican-controlled Senate to remove Fiske and appoint Ken Starr to the role of special prosecutor. Additionally, the House and Senate banking committees both began hearings on Whitewater. And Newt Gingrich, as the new Speaker of the House, became increasingly vocal in his criticisms of Clinton, announcing upwards of twenty new task forces and subcommittees to investigate him – a number he was later forced to reduce.

During his first two years in office, Clinton had achieved an 86.4 percent success score in garnering support in House and Senate roll call votes. In 1995, in what Carroll J. Doherty (1996: 3427) called a "benchmark of futility," Clinton's success score dropped to 36.2 percent, a level that represented "the lowest score of any president" since the *Congressional Quarterly* initiated its survey in 1953 (see also Schier 2000: 10).

In a comment made to Todd Purdum of the *New York Times* in May 1995, an unnamed advisor characterized the US as "a country without a consensus on almost any topic." In this context, Clinton had turned to improvising and speaking about many topics at once in his public statements: "It's called zigging and zagging," the advisor said.[56]

Politically, the midterm loss forced Clinton to pursue the center more strategically, to steal from the opposition's platform, and to aggressively take advantage of Republican missteps. Political scientist Stephen Skowronek (1997: 453) characterized Clinton's tenure as representative of a class of "preemptive presidents," leaders who in their "brazenness ... maneuver around the ideological spectrum, zigzagging in their policy commitments and crafting hybrids that confound the standard labels." Such presidents, Skowronek suggested, are "a constant source of provocation to their opponents" (ibid.), and they "intrude sui generis into our national politics with inconsistent and often explosive effects" (450).

5

The conservative revolution as purification and its subsequent pollution: the rise and fall of Newt Gingrich, and the fall and rise of Bill Clinton

More than simply taking a place on the national stage, Newt Gingrich effectively displaced President Clinton from the symbolic center of America's political sphere:

The face of the federal government becomes transformed this week by a boyish-looking, Southern intellectual from a broken home whose steely determination led him to the pinnacle of political power.

Move over, President Clinton. Welcome to Washington, Speaker Gingrich.

More than anyone else, Newton Leroy Gingrich of Georgia has, at 51, come to symbolize the political revolution that hit Washington Nov. 8.[1]

Signified as both the "Gingrich Revolution" and the "Republican Revolution," the Republicans' midterm victory represented a sea-change in the American political sphere. The election's institutional consequences presaged a profound shift in the government's legislative direction. Symbolically, the election signaled a correction of its political identity and a change in the nation's trajectory. If Clinton had represented an abatement of Reagan- and Bush-era conservatism, the Gingrich revolution signaled a lurching return to the Right.

Unsettling the political center: the rise of Newt Gingrich

Just as Clinton's election was in large part a rebuke to Bush Sr.'s aloofness, Newt Gingrich's rise was structurally enabled by Clinton's varied-to-poor performance during his first two years. The election was a referendum on Clinton, and Gingrich smartly exploited the opportunity.

Just a couple of months prior to the election, Gingrich was virtually unknown to most Americans, and many of his colleagues considered him little more than a "bomb-throwing backbencher"[2] and a "conservative gadfly."[3] Media elites had turned to him occasionally for "inflammatory sound bites" when they needed a "colorful combatant who could be counted on to denounce the ruling Democrats in the harshest terms." These same elites, however, "breezily dismissed his conservative ideas" and "did not take him seriously as an intellectual force."[4] The Republican victory, however, placed his ideas at the center of American political discourse and, to a considerable degree, given how much Gingrich forced Clinton toward the "center," into the annals of turn-of-the-century American law.

Gingrich's meteoric rise led news columnists and editorialists to make political meaning by comparing and contrasting the new Republican leader to President Clinton. Both were baby boomers from the South, and both were raised by adults struggling through broken relationships and various kinds of familial difficulties. Both politicians were constructed as unusually smart and intellectual given their difficult backgrounds, and both were framed as rising to leadership roles through hard work, persistence, and political savvy. During the midterms, the differences between the two broke in Gingrich's favor. The increasing frequency with which news columnists and opinion makers portrayed Clinton's performance as one of fraught indecision, ambiguous political principles, and reversals on major policy issues both foreign[5] and domestic, the more quickly public suspicions solidified into crystal understandings: Clinton was "a chronic waffler."[6] "How many Bill Clintons are there?," the *Columbus Dispatch* editorial page asked, "Count the issues and multiply by two."[7]

The "person on the street" put it this way:

"We elected him without knowing who he really was, only knowing what he said he was," says Katrina Smith, 58, a Mimbres, N.M., drug counselor. "But after watching him in office for a year and a half we know enough now to say he's a disappointment."[8]

And the *New York Times* contrasted the two characters thusly:

One thing that makes this year's election remarkable is its aftermath. Mr. Gingrich and his deputy, Dick Armey of Texas, have continued to say what they believe and do what they said they would without excuses or temporizing. In comparison to the Democrats, their press conferences have been clear, if nothing else. When was the last time Speaker Tom Foley or the majority leader, Richard Gephardt, or the President gave voters a legislative vision undiluted by irreconcilable promises, one for each constituent?[9]

Gingrich, on the other hand, was constructed as resolute, ideologically unwavering, and a bit angry (or "Mad as Hell," as *Newsweek* framed him on the cover of the issue it released the day before November's election [November 7, 1994]).[10] While people wondered about Clinton's political core, Gingrich passionately proclaimed his small and limited government sensibilities. It is important to note early in this chapter, however, that Gingrich's revolutionary identity would be read through a less romantic, but grimmer and cautious lens just half a year after his victory. The Federal Building in Oklahoma City would be destroyed by domestic terrorists in April of 1995. The symbolic fabric in which Gingrich was wrapping himself in the fall and winter of 1994 and early 1995 – as a *revolutionary*, a radical, an anti-government, "return the power to the people" type of leader – was alluring against the background of Clinton's scandal-tinged, Keystone Cop style of governing. In November 1994, Gingrich represented clarity, action, and movement, whereas the Clinton White House represented confusion, "gridlock," and governmental stasis. Oklahoma City would radically shift the interpretive environment in which Gingrich's signifiers produced meaning and would lend the outspoken Speaker a sanguinary hue. In late 1994 and early 1995, however, the revolutionary signs dominated television sets, radio airwaves, and newspapers' broadsheets in a favorable way, one that suggested American publics were again searching for political fresh air:

The "contract with America" offered this week by GOP [Republican party] House members and candidates is a refreshing gamble. Under Gingrich's leadership (either as the ranking Republican or as speaker of the House), they propose to stand for something ... Gingrich has done something else, as well. The contract notion reminds Americans that party labels are supposed to stand for something. The Democratic Party could not produce such a document today, or at least one so detailed. Its disparate wings would collapse into each other, just as they did with [the] health-care reform ... [proposed during] William Rodham Clinton's [first] two years.[11]

Gingrich's authorship of the bold Contract with America helped seal the Republican's November victory, an event which transformed the new Speaker into the symbolic and political leader of the conservative juggernaut. Gingrich and the Contract became icons of the new political order.[12] News columnists and editorialists repeatedly called or likened the new Speaker to a prime minister.[13] By importing this political signifier, news makers suggested that Gingrich was in some intangible way assuming a status and position of power greater than that of a traditional Speaker of the House.[14] For instance, *Newsweek*'s Evan Thomas, on CNN's *Inside Washington*, said of Gingrich:

He is the prime minister of the United States. I mean, the fact is he controls the power. We all made fun of Newt and he's in some ways an easy figure to mock because he's so grandiose about being Churchill and de Gaulle and all that.

The fact is, he's used those models very effectively. He has been a world leader. He has gotten a ton of stuff done. Maybe it's going to get cured in the Senate, maybe some of it's not going to pass, but the fact is he's passed more legislation than anybody since Sam Rayburn, or anybody since the LBJ days.[15]

Time Magazine would name Gingrich their "Man of the Year" for 1995. *USA Today* proclaimed Gingrich the "Man of the Moment" in one of its first headlines of the year (January 3, 1995). In a lengthy two-part series published in the first two months of the new year, the *Washington Post* proclaimed Washington had become a new space, "Mr. Gingrich's Neighborhood" (January 15, 1995), and that America had entered a new time, "The Age of Newt" (February 26, 1995).

Just prior to reconstituting these Cartesian axes of the American symbolic landscape, the *Washington Post* used a headline to report the shift in the nation's attention:

Speaker Tries to Adjust to Life in the Spotlight; Intense Scrutiny Dogs Gingrich as He Assumes Leadership Role.[16]

What is fascinating about this headline is that the *Washington Post* was highlighting as news that the nation's spotlight, its mise-en-scène, had focused on a new subject. It was news about news, which announced that a new main character had taken over the national political drama.

The headline and the article's opening sentences are important for another reason, one that will become more obvious later in this narrative. For now, to foreshadow, the article's second sentence announced,

The nation's newspapers and television cameras have found nothing so fascinating as the Georgian's march through Washington – and the unintended brush fires he has set.[17]

Gingrich's rise thus far had been framed in revolutionary and, at times, in caustic, angry terms; revolutions, after all, are bloody affairs. Analyzing it in its entirety, the sentence invokes the Civil War's revolutionary symbolism: the South's revolt from the North, Union and Confederate citizens killing one another, and, most particularly, General Sherman's bloody and apocalyptic march through Georgia.

The sentence's author demonstrates both a biting cleverness and a guarded awareness that he is playing with inflammatory symbolism. The sentence's cleverness stems from the columnist's reversing of the victors and victims in the symbolic landscape of Sherman's March: this time a Georgian is riding through the federal capital, setting fires along the way. Yet the columnist adds that these are unintended brush fires, which signals that they have been set accidentally, without malice, and that they are containable. These temper the sentence's acidity. On the other hand, Gingrich is portrayed as marching *through* Washington, as opposed to marching *to* it. This connotes that he is penetrating through the capital, that he does not intend to stay, and that he therefore has little stake in its status after he has passed through. And these qualifications only temper slightly the cataclysmic symbolism of Sherman's March, which is known for its scorched earth, total warfare ethos.

The sentence makes for engaging reading. It is this kind of constitutive, performative language, however – language that mixes Gingrich's revolutionary zeal with dimensions of violence and anger – which would bridge the discursive space between Gingrich and the Republicans' symbolic framework, on the one hand, and the symbols and discourse that would come to constitute the domestic terrorists on the other.

Gingrich was far from bashful while leading the "Republican revolution." Rather, he stepped onto center stage and brashly demanded that the spotlight remain on him. He had plenty to say once he had Washington's and the country's attention. Much of his discourse centered on emphasizing the promise that the Contract with America represented for the country, on the one hand, and lambasting the Clintons, on the other.

Character formation and access to the means of symbolic distribution: the Contract with America and the first 100 days of the Gingrich Congress

The Clintons had promised to present a health-care plan to Congress within the first 100 days of the president's first term, a deadline they notoriously failed to meet. Gingrich played on this failure by promising to bring to a vote in Congress the ten bills stipulated in the Contract with America within the same time frame. The tactic highlighted significant differences between his approach to legislating and the Clintons' way of governing. The Contract's promises were clear, succinct, and understandable, and perhaps most importantly, they were visible and accessible to everyone. The point constructed by Gingrich and repeated by the media was clear: the Clintons had failed to deliver on their promise, whereas Gingrich would succeed, and turn his words into deeds within the constraints that he had placed on himself.

The Clinton health-care plan had been coded as created in a secretive environment, written in indecipherable, technocratic language, and as representing an un-American, socialist expansion of the state; that is, Republican opposition successfully made it look like a secretive power-grab by the governing Left elite. Gingrich's plan, to the contrary, could be itemized and discussed in a single newspaper article. Its potential long-term consequences for American society, of course, could not. Critics argued that the list of bills was deceptively simple,[18] but they failed to win many sympathetic ears. Instead, as the process of legislating goes, the Contract's progress through the House drew immense amounts of attention. National and regional newspapers, like *USA Today* and the *Cleveland Plain Dealer*,[19] published easily readable charts and lists detailing which bills had passed and which remained in the legislative process. Gingrich and the Contract were being transformed into the nation's new political icons.

The new Congress succeeded in bringing the Contract's bills to a vote within ninety-three days and within the promised time allotment, passing nine of the ten along the way. To celebrate this legislative triumph, Gingrich made an unprecedented request of CNN that the network grant him free prime-time coverage to mark the completion of the new Congress's first 100 days and the successful passing of the Contract. CNN agreed, thus further cementing the Speaker's control over the national stage.[20]

Other than CSPAN and PBS, CNN represented the only cable news alternative to the dominant three networks in 1995.[21] The Persian Gulf War in 1991 had elevated CNN to national prominence, and gained the news network a significant portion of news consumers' attention. The O. J. Simpson arrest and trial, which would be conducted throughout 1995, furthered CNN's gains in the news production/consumption market. MSNBC and the FOX News channel would not debut on air until 1996. In this context, CNN's agreement to air Gingrich's 100 days speech conferred even greater status on the Speaker.

It is important to note that this cable news media apparatus – CNN, MSNBC, FOX News, and CSPAN (launched in 1979, financed by cable companies and non-profit, the network was not really popular until CNN began its rise, and CSPAN now is considered to have a sizeable "cult" following) – experienced a meteoric rise in popularity in the 1990s. CNN led the way in 1991 with its coverage of the Persian Gulf War, and it is also important to note that MSNBC and FOX were being developed during a period in which the Clinton White House was constantly enmeshed in webs of suspicion and scandal. These latter two networks were launched just two years before the Lewinsky scandal broke, and it seems reasonable to assume that they saw Monicagate as their networks' opportunities to succeed much like CNN had with the Persian Gulf War just five years priorly.

Defining the other by exploiting defusion: Gingrich Republicans attack the Clintons

In addition to promoting the Contract during his ascension, Gingrich used his newfound command over the nation's mise-en-scène to rail against the Clintons and the Clinton White House. Invoking strongly exclusionary and polluting symbolism in the course of his rise, Gingrich described Clinton and his supporters as "enemies of America,"[22] and revived the cultural and political divisiveness of the Nixon era, calling Bill and Hillary "counterculture McGoverniks," who were presiding over a White House of drug-abusing,[23] "left-wing extremists."[24] The name calling carried over into 1995, and became even more bizarrely personal when Gingrich's mother whispered to Connie Chung during a televised interview that her son said of Mrs. Clinton, "She's a bitch."[25]

Gingrich's name calling and symbolic jousting tapped into electoral dismay with the Clintons. It also found a sympathetic and eager audience in the conservative talk radio market, particularly with fans of Rush Limbaugh, whose rise to national celebrity-hood mirrored Gingrich's own. Yet Gingrich's critical discourse was paralleled by still angrier and more inflammatory voices from the Right.

In the weeks following the Republican midterm victory, veteran congressman and, like Gingrich, legendary "bomb thrower"[26] Jesse Helms challenged Clinton's legitimacy by making veiled threats to the president. Representations of Helms threatening the president began when the congressman mailed Clinton a letter requesting that he postpone raising the issue of the GATT treaty for another congressional session. The letter was portrayed in cartoons and editorials as an inappropriate, quirky kind of inversion of authority, and as a threat from the congressman to the president. The second incident occurred while the letter was still being discussed in the press and Helms was interviewed on CNN. Asked if he thought Clinton was "up to the job" of commander in chief given his two years' experience, Helms responded, "I'll give you an honest answer. No, I do not. And neither do the people in the armed forces."[27]

Clinton's relationship with the armed forces was already strained by his personal legacy with the Vietnam draft, his presidential attempts to open the military to participation by homosexuals, and his proposals to reduce military spending. Helms's comment elevated the symbolic stakes, turning a disagreement between the president and the armed forces over policy into a challenge of the democratically sacred institutional order whereby the military branches operate under civilian – namely, presidential – control. Helms challenged the president's authority, and stated that the president was not seen as a legitimate leader in the eyes of many military personnel.

Helms persisted in challenging Clinton's authority, stating that the president was so unpopular in North Carolina that he had "better watch out if he comes down here. He'd better have a bodyguard." The comment introduced the susceptibility of Clinton's body, the idea that physical harm could be visited on the president, into the discursive arena. And the idea came from within the government, conferring upon it perceived legitimacy. Though the comment was roundly criticized, Helms's voiced threat to Clinton's person indicated how much Clinton was defused from the presidential character to part of the conservative Right. Helms's off-the-cuff, commonsensical understanding stated that Clinton was not only accessible or touchable, but woundable or killable (and dispensable, given Helms's senior congressional position), if within the reach of mere foot soldiers and citizen mortals. The statement indicated that, at least to many of Helms's constituents, Clinton was not protected by the sacred veil of the presidential mantle.

Finally, before moving on to Clinton's post-election slump and Gingrich's political decline by overexposure and symbolic association with right-wing extremism, it is worth introducing one additional example of how commentators on the Right were framing President Clinton. In addition to railing against the Clintons, popular radio host G. Gordon Liddy of Watergate fame had repeatedly invoked militaristic and violent language to prescribe how citizens should react to government intervention in their lives. Bureau of Alcohol, Tobacco, Firearms, and Explosives at your door? BATF agents are "bottom-dwelling slugs," Liddy responded, and advised, "Shooting back is reasonable ... I have counseled shooting them in the head."[28] After the midterms, Liddy continued his symbolic assaults, this time focusing on the Clintons: "The way to get rid of Bill and Hillary Clinton is not to bomb and strafe the White House from Cessnas, or use semiautomatic weapons from Pennsylvania Avenue. The way to do it is at the ballot box ... Send 'em back to there the chicken-guts, waste-fouled waters of the rivers of Arkansas."[29]

While these comments from the Right ranged from robust political symbolic warfare to outright inflammatory, they also indicate the degree to which Clinton had become defused from the presidential mantle. Republican Representative Dick Armey's comment to his Democratic colleagues during a House debate about a crime bill earlier in 1994 captured Clinton's fading status: "Your president is just not that important to us."[30] In this case, Clinton's defusion from the role of the presidency represented a crisis of legitimacy.

Darkside of the mise-en-scène: Gingrich's meanness problem walks and talks

While Gingrich had become a virtual prime minister, his capturing of the mise-en-scène proved to be a double-edged sword. Shortly after "leading the House GOP to victory," *USA Today* reported, "Gingrich has become known more for mouth than merit."[31] Columnists reported and opinion makers commented on Gingrich's more bombastic statements. He celebrated himself as a "transformational figure"[32] and a "conservative futurist,"[33] while his spokesman Tony Blankley suggested his boss was like Churchill, de Gaulle, Sadat, and Gandhi, all rolled into one "American revolutionary package."[34] Columnist Joe Klein later commented that Gingrich seemed "even more grandiose and intemperate than before and blinded by the sudden acclaim." Gingrich himself "acted as if he believed" in the prime minister comparisons. "At one point," Klein recalled, Gingrich "told me that he, personally, would lead a 'Wesleyan revolution' in America" (Klein 2002: 140).

Gingrich's omnipresence, unflinching confidence, and gleaming self-pride quickly began to put off the American middle. Poll results published the day before Gingrich officially entered the Speakership role showed that his unfavorability rating was 10 percentage points higher than his favorability rating (36 percent unfavorable, 26 percent favorable), and that 40 percent disapproved of the way he was handling the transition to GOP rule, compared with 31 percent who approved.[35] The new Speaker "is overexposed," the *Christian Science Monitor* reported, and his "manner is too intrusive. He's like getting 50 pounds of fudge as a gift. It's too much at once."[36] Likewise, dissension arose in the new majority's ranks, as some Republicans threatened to vote against some of the articles of the Contract with America, contending that "the reforms were too harsh" or that they "would encourage abortions."[37]

Critics argued that Gingrich was too single-minded, autocratic, and dismissive, and that his leadership style stifled debate and shunned compromise.[38] The *New York Times*'s editorial page commended Gingrich for his honesty and clarity while it attacked his ideas for their "brutality," for being "benighted and mean-spirited," and for expressing an "anti-government theme [that] borders on the fetishistic."[39] In response to those who "love to hate" him due to his "enormous self-confidence and an ambition of even larger proportions," Gingrich concluded that his critics and enemies were in actuality reacting to the scope of his political vision:

I think I am trying to effect a change so large that the people who would be hurt by the change – the liberal, Democratic machine – have a natural reaction, which gets wearying sometimes.[40]

Columnist David Broder, an unwavering centrist, pointed out that Gingrich's snide comments and negativity ratings were combining with Jesse Helms's corrosive statements about Clinton, Senate leader Bob Dole's truculence, and House Majority Leader Dick Armey's fiery partisanship, to create "what you might call the GOP's meanness problem."[41] These four new Republican leaders, Broder noted, were "pit bulls," who were "notably hard-edged and pugnacious, remembered for moments in which they lost their cool and became snarling adversaries."[42]

"Person on the street" interviews in a Republican district showed that even self-described conservatives found the new Speaker overly harsh:

"He's entertaining, he speaks his mind, he makes politics interesting," said Chuck Towne, a 61-year-old sales representative who identified himself as a Republican. "But I don't think he's good for the country."

Another self-professed Republican, Twila Emuryan, a 48-year-old nurse, was less entertained: "I think he's using his situation as Speaker of the House to his own personal advantage," she said. "I don't think he understands life. He wants to stop supporting the food program for schools. Why starve the kids? And welfare. You just can't pull the plug on everyone."[43]

Gingrich's problems with his public persona did not necessarily translate into higher favor for Clinton. Nor did his tarnished image dampen public hopes for the new Congress. Gingrich's reputation, the *New York Times* reported, had not rubbed off on Congress. Rather, surveys showed that "voters think much better of the institution now than they did before he took over in January. And a majority want Congress, not the President, to set the agenda."[44] Indeed, a CBS News poll taken in late January indicated that 78 percent of respondents expected Congress to have more influence in setting the government's agenda than the president.[45]

Defusion as eroding legitimation: Clinton narrated as a one-term president

As described in the prior chapter, Clinton's star was diminishing even before Gingrich's began to shine. When Clinton started to campaign for democratic challengers and incumbents up for re-election, he found many of the candidates vocally and physically distancing themselves from him by choosing to not appear with him at rallies. As much as campaigning for others, some press reported that Clinton seemed to be campaigning for himself. *USA Today* reported that he appeared to be "pleading with voters to let him finish the job," but that his pleas met with "polite, but sometimes silent" receptions, even in places that had been instrumental in bringing him into office two years priorly.[46]

Before the midterms Clinton was being framed by names like "William the Waffler" and "William Rodham Clinton," and described as practicing a "politics of promiscuity" that left him "suffering the death of 1000 cuts" politically, and begging for sympathy from voters.[47] After the midterms, he was increasingly described as gravely in danger of becoming a one-term president. "Tuesday's results put Clinton's presidency in jeopardy," the *Washington Post* reported in its lead story a couple of days after the election. "Given perceptions about Clinton's weakness," the article continued, presidential hopefuls in both parties started to stir into action. Questions about Democratic primary challengers to the incumbent began to percolate, and it was reported that Republican hopefuls were beginning to jockey for position to win the nomination in 1996.[48]

The "weary-looking Clinton"[49] was "dangerously silent"[50] and appeared "utterly forlorn and decisively beaten"[51] in the wake of the midterms, the *Washington Post* and *New York Times* reported. Reasons for Clinton's seemingly precarious hold on office abounded. The *New York Times*'s editorial page said that his first two years had been "helter-skelter" and that they represented "a study in political incoherence," "artless flip-flops," and "confusion." "If the President wishes to salvage any honor from the next two years," the editorial continued, Clinton would have to overcome his "lack of definition" and "shapelessness," and abandon the "wagon-circling style" that had made him "the captive of a small and notably inept set of White House tacticians."[52]

Commentary on how Clinton could regain control of his political future and salvage his presidency flowed into political news. The *Washington Post Magazine* published a sprawling piece by strategist David Osborne titled "Can this President be Saved? A Six-point Plan to Beat the One-Term Odds."[53] In addition to offering its own advice, the *New York Times* reported that Clinton would respond to the electoral defeat by moving rightward:

The advance intelligence indicates that the President will propose middle-class tax cuts and the scaling down, if not the dismantling, of certain units of Government. The intent is twofold: to prove that he heard the message of hostility to big government and heavy spending that the electorate sent, and to seize as his own some of the most eye-catching Republican promises.[54]

The most accessible legislative symbol of Clinton's first two years was the failed universal health-care initiative, a proposal that bespoke Clinton's faith in government's ability to make positive impacts on people's everyday lives. His turn to the Right, however, would look odd against his recent efforts at government expansionism. The perils of an effort to out-republican the Republicans, the *New York Times* deliberated, included further entrenching the "widespread belief" that Clinton was merely a "trimmer and a vacillator":

Deepening rather than erasing his image as a wishy-washy leader is perhaps the greatest peril of the course upon which the President appears to be embarking. If he merely echoes the Republicans, without putting forward at least a few distinctively Clintonian programs or ideas, he risks looking more rudderless and less convincingly Presidential than ever. And he cannot win re-election in 1996 without changing a lot of minds out beyond the Beltway.[55]

The president was in a performative bind. Staying the course by promoting government growth might please his base of core Democratic constituents; however, after the midterm thumping, this hardly looked like a viable script to keep following. Moving to the center Right seemed necessary, yet given that Clinton had already been coded a "waffler" and "flip-flopper," this course risked further entrenching his symbolic framework as lacking core principles as the *New York Times*'s editorial page suggested. Yet move to the center Right is precisely the course Clinton plotted.[56]

Clinton began to move toward the center politically, becoming what has since been called a "preemptive," "wild card," or "zig-zagging" President.[57] Using an approach that strategist Dick Morris infamously called "triangulation," Clinton began to follow Morris's ever-flowing poll data and analysis to gain and exploit public opinion, and to co-opt Republican initiatives, softening them by reducing their excesses, and claiming them as his own. For instance, Clinton began scripting into his public addresses references to cutting taxes on the middle class, limiting government spending, and even a willingness to consider Gingrich's idea of amending the constitution to allow prayer in schools. Meanwhile he had his staff working these and other ideas like increasing military spending into the press as well.

Clinton moved closer to the center, by taking steps that I will discuss below. This political re-scripting, however, failed to lend the president any lasting political or popular heft. Moving closer to Republican stances on policy allowed Clinton to construct himself as being in touch with the nation's political mood. The midterm political defeat was simply too damaging to try to ignore, and it sent too clear a message to not respond to it in kind. While Clinton began talking more like a Republican on policy, he also forcefully and relentlessly described himself as a champion of government's role in people's lives while portraying the Republicans as unreasonably hostile toward, and angry about, government. He began sounding like a Republican on policy, yet he routinely qualified his limited-government stances by referencing symbols and narratives of government's past triumphs.

If the 1994 midterms represented the public rebuking Clinton for his first two years, January 1995's State of the Union Address provided the president with his first opportunity to respond to the message. Invoking religious symbolism, the president used the platform to announce a "New Covenant," which included acknowledging the Republicans' victory, using some of their phrases and ideas, while simultaneously defending the role of an activist government working to improve citizens' lives. Clinton's new political script resembled a kinder version of the Contract with America, a kind of "conservatism with compassion," to paraphrase future president G. W. Bush's 2000 campaign platform.

In his address, Clinton spoke from a script that seemed to accept, if not take for granted, the critical themes that had been leveled against government during the Republican revolution. The nation had entered a new era and a new economic order, which demanded that government change too in order to not place undue burdens on its citizens:

We are moving from an industrial age built on gears and sweat to an information age demanding skills and learning and flexibility. Our government, once a champion of national purposes, is now seen by many as *simply a captive of narrow interests, putting more burdens on our citizens* rather than equipping them to get ahead. (emphasis added)

Instead of arguing against this interpretation of government as burden, the script called for governmental change, while sounding themes of individual liberty, God's will, and both personal and civic responsibility.[58] Changing government in this context – the birth of the Republican revolution – meant reducing it and making it more efficient, which was code for slashing spending on social programs, cutting taxes, and rolling back regulations on the private sector. And Clinton's script intoned the need for governmental change time and time again. Yet it also refused to conform entirely to the Republican vision of "the government is best which governs least," and that politicians and public servants necessarily stand in the way of and obstruct citizens in their pursuits of personal security and happiness.

Clinton cited the symbolically weighty character Franklin Delano Roosevelt as an example of a politician who used government to control changing social and economic conditions in ways that benefited the national community.

More than 60 years ago, at the dawn of another new era, President Roosevelt told our nation new conditions imposed new requirements on government and those who conduct government. And from that simple proposition, he shaped the New Deal, which helped to restore our nation to prosperity and defined the relationship between our people and our government for half a century. That approach worked in its time, but we today, we face a very different time and very different conditions.

The script seemed clear, and yet, in many ways, contradictory: it simultaneously called for less governmental intervention in people's lives, on the one hand, while arguing that government represents the principal tool by which the national community can shape its future for the better, on the other. The script seemed to accept that the need for reduced government was obvious. After all, the government that FDR had built, the architecture of the sprawling liberal state – the embodiment of which Clinton and his health-care plan signified – had worked *in its day*, a day that had occurred long ago in our history.

Within this discursive context, in addition to lines celebrating government's historical triumphs, were performatives inserted to constitute public servants as quasi-religious figures who facilitate the essential interaction between state and people in changing times. Politicians and public servants, Clinton asserted, are

the keepers of a sacred trust and we must be faithful to it [the trust] in this new and very demanding era.

Being faithful to this script meant both heeding the recent popular call for government reformation and reduction, while accepting that government plays an essential and sacred role in preserving the community. In addition to invoking FDR, the script paraphrased John F. Kennedy to lend depth and reverence to Clinton's assertions that people should share his faith in government and be respectful of the institution's centripetal, cohesive force. The script framed public service as representing a form of religious calling, with government playing a critical, though circumscribed, role in delivering a common good:

We must not ask government to do what we should do for ourselves. We should rely on government as a partner to help us to do more for ourselves and for each other.

In this way, Clinton tried to reconcile themes of government's limitations, on the one hand, with government as sacred mediator and keeper of the communal spirit, on the other. People must take responsibility for themselves, he intoned, mimicking the Republicans, yet government must play a role in helping people elevate themselves. And in a much repeated phrase in the press, Clinton said that government should be

smaller, less costly, *leaner not meaner.*

In this phrase lie the roots of the symbolic transformation that would take place when the federal building in Oklahoma City was bombed two and a half months after the address. Clinton's popularity would rise dramatically, while Gingrich's and the Republicans' would plummet. Three dimensions in his post-November approach would enable Clinton to regain the mantle of president in the wake of Oklahoma City. By (1) appropriating softer, kinder versions of the Republicans' platform, (2) combining this shift in policy with critical discourse that portrays the Republicans as intolerant, zealous, and unreasonably angry with the symbol "government," and (3) reiterating the performative that government represents a sacred trust that maintains national community, Clinton situated himself to dramatically reshuffle the nation's symbolic landscape in the wake of the Oklahoma City tragedy.

For the time being, however, Clinton's new script of trying to split the difference between the Republican's agenda and a plea for government's relevance received no critical appreciation or enthusiasm. In fact, reviews echoed the *New York Times*'s prediction that splitting the ideological difference would be read as simply more Clintonian fecklessness and lack of clarity and discipline.

Across the nation, newspaper reviews called the 1-hour 20-minute speech one thing: "long." "As Mr. Clinton spoke," the *New York Times* commented, "his parlous situation was evident to the public." That Clinton's new script was "long on appeals for comity," the *Times*'s editorial continued, demonstrated "just how much [Clinton] has been weakened in the last 12 months."[59] David Broder's review captured the general reaction:

If self-discipline is the requisite of leadership – and it is – then President Clinton's State of the Union Address dramatized his failure. It was a speech about everything, and therefore about nothing. It was a huge missed opportunity – and one he will regret.

Coming into Tuesday night, the president had three tasks: to acknowledge the 1994 election results and offer a credible pledge of bipartisan cooperation with the new Republican Congress; to define, for the doubt-wracked Democrats, the ground he would defend against Republican assault; and to reassert his own command of the office he holds and give a direction to the last half of his term. He did the first passably well; the second, badly; and the third, not at all. It was the third challenge – communicating the sense of focused, disciplined leadership – that was most important of all. And he blew it.

. . .

Instead, Clinton was again – at just the wrong moment – the loquacious, self-centered youth who somehow slipped into the Oval Office, all charm and "aw shucks" humility one moment, full of braggadocio the next, seeking approval rather than setting a course.

. . .

It was disquieting to watch a president behave that way. And it is mind-boggling to see him squander a unique opportunity in such a self-indulgent fashion.[60]

Indeed, Clinton's words found little favor and were not carrying much weight, and his post-midterm stature stood in stark contrast to Gingrich's success. Playing on the familiar political metaphor of a "lame duck president," the *Washington Post Magazine* described Clinton returning from a hunting trip as "blown off the radar, unable to make the front page except by brandishing a pair of dead ducks."[61]

The political stage would remain Gingrich's up to the Oklahoma City bombing. Whereas Gingrich had arranged the unprecedented coverage by CNN of his passing of the Contract with America, Clinton seemed to evaporate from the news altogether. Cast off stage, and, at the time, trying to defend affirmative action, Clinton used his first press conference of the year (March 3, 1995) to rail against the Gingrich production:

The old Washington view, I think it's fair to say, is that the federal government could provide solutions to America's problems. The Republican Contract view reflects in many cases an *outright hostility* to governmental action ... My view, what has loosely been called the new Democratic view of the New Covenant view, is to be skeptical of government but to recognize that it has a role in our lives and a partnership role to play.

. . .

The Republicans now have proposed to cut education, nutritional help for mothers and schoolchildren, anti-drug efforts in our schools, and other things which to me appear to target children in order to pay for tax cuts for upper income Americans. I do not believe that that is consistent with our interest as we build America into the 21st century, and we move into this new global economy.[62]

Reacting to the waning power of the president's dramatic stature, the institutional allure of covering the presidency started to erode among the journalistic elite. The high-profile and highly paid media personnel covering the White House began to complain about their lack of air time. Correspondents began to get nervous about their shrinking time slots on their networks' television news programs. Covering the White House for ABC, correspondent Brit Hume complained that "the administration seems a spent force," while Bill Plante of CBS lamented that even the stature of the presidential office seemed lessened: "Now the president is no longer necessarily seen as central."[63]

Given his tarnished image in the public eye, Clinton's peripheral status helped the president, some mused. "The less the American public sees of Bill Clinton," commented NBC's Jim Miklaszewski, "the better off he seems."[64]

Howard Kurtz, who as a staff writer for the *Washington Post* reported on and critiqued other journalists' reporting, framed the White House beat thusly:

Here at the White House, for half a century the very epicenter of the news universe, things are slow. Real slow. White House correspondents are not getting on the air very much. No one has put their faces on milk cartons yet, but they, and the president they cover, are clearly on the political sidelines.

Since the Republican revolution captured Congress in January, all the political action has been at the other end of Pennsylvania Avenue. Newt Gingrich or Bob Dole is on the news almost every night. President Clinton is in a reactive mode, and that is the stuff of brief sound bites, not lead stories.

Throw in O.J. Simpson, the California floods, O.J., the earthquake in Japan, O.J., the subway gas attack in Japan, and the 22-minute evening newscasts don't have much time for the president of the United States. Even the morning shows aren't terribly interested.[65]

The president as culture structure: character and role

The November midterms unsettled the political stage. The political sphere is always mediated by drama. Politics is always a play, and the president is the central character of the American story. Over the course of the twentieth century the office has become the anchoring node in the nation's mythical structure. Actors move in and out of the role; once they are elevated into it, they either succeed or fail to fuse with the role's mythical and narrative expectations. Actors can be bad presidents, but very limited is their power to turn the presidential office itself into a bad role. While the presidential character is the center of the drama, the two-party system ensures that the actor playing the character is always part hero and part villain or fool.

Clinton's rise in 1992 and his first steps in the White House precipitated fevered indignation among the nation's conservative base. He seemed to threaten the traditional character of the presidential role to this constituency. To this group, his assumption of the role seemed to render the character of the president less important, reduce its symbolic gravity, and make the president into something more akin to a Speaker of the House position.[66]

Clinton represented the first serious challenger for the office from the Baby Boomer generation, and he and his wife presented themselves as products of the 1960s Left. Key parts of his personal character threatened traditional notions of American leadership – such as his relationship with Hillary, which, in Steve Kroft's words, seemed to represent more of an "agreement" than a traditional marriage; rumors of his sexual permissiveness and philandering; his strategy for avoiding the Vietnam War draft; and the rumors of scandal surrounding the Clintons' pre-Washington business and political dealings. For many, these anecdotes, rumors, and suspicions about the Clintons' "private" affairs drew into question the Clintons' character and integrity. Additionally, the Clintons' sleight of hand and evasiveness vis-à-vis the scandal allegations furthered the suspicion that something profoundly corrupting lurked behind the façade. The longer the rumors remained in public discourse, the more they seemed to represent fact for some, and the more traction the rumors gained, the more their polluting potential seeped into and stained the Clintons' political ideology.

Staunch conservatives interpreted Clinton's first steps in office as segueing neatly with the Slick Willie portion of his character. He had sought to roll back restrictions on access to abortion and, while celebrating the diversity of his Cabinet, he had tried to reconcile military culture with movements in the sexual politics field. Further, his health-care plan had effectively been framed as flirting with collectivist and socialist assumptions. Yet these policies, in and of themselves, were not enough to profoundly defuse Clinton from the presidential role to the degree he was experiencing in early 1995. A cultural/emotional-cum-political logic was in play: to varying degrees across constituencies, an emotional logic seemed to encourage the conflation of politics with character. For core conservatives, the climate of suspicion surrounding the Clintons confirmed that these were the politics of a nefarious character. Political ideology, character, morality, and emotion became tightly intertwined for people trying to make sense of the nation's leader.

The Republicans' November victory signified the degree to which Clinton had become defused from the symbolic umbrella, the sacred aura, that the office of presidency affords. It also deepened the defusion. The symbolic robe that protects, elevates, and renders sacred the office holder was slipping from Clinton's shoulders, as Jesse Helms's and G. Gordon Liddy's casual references to the potential for violence being visited on the president indicated.

Yet Clinton's symbolic framework was not a product solely of his policies, marriage, or past dealings. Characters also derive their meanings through their relations to other characters in the plot. As I have shown, the November midterms also unsettled the political stage by elevating the Speaker of the House to inflated symbolic proportions.

Gingrich worked to inflate them further. He was constrained, however, by the symbolic limitations of the role and character. The president is the center of the stage, and the Speaker structurally plays a more peripheral role. To be sure, Speakers have transcended the limits of the role before, such as Sam Rayburn and Thomas Tip O'Neill. However, Rayburn was known for bargaining quietly and diplomatically behind the scenes. Tip O'Neill was modestly more public, yet he was playing his role across from Reagan, a symbolically fused giant of the political stage.

Gingrich's enthusiasm for demanding the public's attention, however, challenged the symbolic logic whereby the president is greater than > the Speaker of the House. The American political drama places the president at the social center much like the role of the father in a traditional American family. Thus Gingrich's meteoric rise unsettled American audiences. The way Gingrich wore his power, and the extent to which the media courted both his love and anger, upset the traditional character roles in the national drama. It was as if the press as mother figure had started flirting with a new man, the interloper Speaker of the House, leaving American publics asking, "What did you do with dad?"

An infelicitous performative

With Congress in spring recess, Clinton decided to stage a formal prime-time news conference, his fourth since taking office.[67] His circumstances were grim, and he wanted to inject himself back into policy debates and regain some of the national spotlight. The president can announce an event, craft his discourse, and perform. He does not, however, control the means of symbolic distribution; that is, he cannot command media coverage. The media's relative autonomy from the state means that the president must be seen as an interesting character with a compelling story in order to gain broad coverage.[68] In addition to CNN and CSPAN, only one network agreed to broadcast the event, giving Clinton "the same access to the airwaves that Speaker Newt Gingrich ... enjoyed 10 days ago, when he made a Presidential-style address carried by those outlets."[69] Commenting on how the office of presidency was steadily losing its dramatic allure, the *Seattle Times* quipped, "What if President Clinton held a news conference and nobody came?"[70] Forced to compete for public attention against the TV sitcoms *Home Improvement*, *Roseanne*, *Frasier*, and *Friends*, Clinton faired poorly, drawing a viewership rating of only "meager numbers."[71]

In addition to not controlling who would broadcast his press conference, Clinton also could not fully control the meaning that would be ascribed to the event. He could control the evening's staging and his own statements; however, he could not control the narrative that would emerge from the night's performance. In addition to press reviews complaining that Clinton covered "no new ground"[72] and said "almost nothing he hadn't said countless times before,"[73] the conference reactivated the unsettled topic of Clinton's relationship to the armed services, and the compromised symbolic framework that had dominated his first steps onto the national stage in early 1992.

A third of the way into the conference, Clinton was asked about Robert McNamara's new book, *In Retrospect: The Tragedy and Lesson of Vietnam*, in which the author detailed the lessons he had learned as an architect of the Vietnam War. Clinton deftly dodged the question,[74] yet the topic's mention alone reactivated the symbolic specter of Clinton's dubious handling of his draft prospects, and drew further into the spotlight the president's rather awkward relationship to his role as commander in chief.

Even more damaging, however, was Clinton's response to a question about his peripheral role in current policy debates in the wake of the Republican revolution. That he occupied the office of presidency, Clinton demanded, ensured his relevance:

Q: President Clinton, Republicans have dominated political debate in this country since they took over Congress in January, and even tonight two of the major television networks declined to broadcast this event live. Do you worry about making sure that your voice is heard in the coming months?

Delivering a quintessential example of an infelicitous performative, Clinton asserted that he was relevant:

President Clinton: ... The Constitution gives me relevance; the power of our ideas gives me relevance; the record we have built up over the last two years and the things we're trying to do to implement it give it relevance. The president is relevant here, especially an activist president, and the fact that I am willing to work with the Republicans ...

In *How to Do Things with Words*, John Austin (1975 [1962]) drew attention to performative utterances in language, differentiating them from "constative," or merely descriptive, statements. A constative statement is something like "He is the President," and is either true or false. A performative, on the other hand, performs an action when it is stated, and has the potential to affect changes in social conditions, statuses, or understandings. Borrowing Austin's example, saying "I promise" creates an assurance on which another person bases his or her expectations. To say "I promise" effectively does the work of making the promise; the statement itself creates a new understanding between people, and nothing more is needed. Performatives, Austin noted, are not true or false, but are evaluated in terms of success or failure. In Austin's terms, if a performative succeeds, and is believed and accepted, it is "felicitous." If something goes wrong, the performative is "not indeed false but in general *unhappy*," or infelicitous (Austin 1975 [1962]: 14).

From defusion to fusion: from a hissing sound to a bomb blast

Clinton sought to re-establish his relevance and authority by stating that he was, indeed, relevant. He wanted to state it, and thus make it so. His critics were not persuaded. Under the headline " 'The President is Relevant'; Clinton Asserts His Role in Political Debate," the *Washington Post* rebuffed Clinton's performative in no uncertain terms:

The President last night declared his relevance to the political debate in Washington ... in remarks at a news conference that offered a stark reminder of how much power has shifted from the White House to Congress.

...

The GOP's ability to propose and pass legislation and Clinton's role as the brake on policy, rather than the engine, have him frequently on the sidelines and awkwardly struggling to get into the debate on grounds other than simply threatening vetoes.[75]

The *Post*'s commentary labeled Clinton's performative an infelicity in the starkest of terms. His statement saying he was relevant, the *Post* flatly asserted, showed exactly how much power he had lost and how much his adversaries now wielded. Making a declarative sentence demanding that one be considered relevant emphasizes that just the opposite of the declaration approximates the actual state of affairs. In other words, declaring one's relevance accomplishes just the opposite of demonstrating relevance; those who are relevant do not feel compelled to declare it. Instead of bolstering his status, through these words Clinton reiterated to critics and publics that the Republicans – the elephant on recess – were leading the government, and that his own position remained extraordinarily precarious.

Clinton's response became a sound bite that dominated the post-conference news coverage. The moment marked what Joe Klein (2002: 140) would later describe as "the lowest point" of Clinton's tenure in the White House. Republicans and conservative commentators seized on the comment in order to symbolically associate Clinton with past struggling presidents. Republican Senator and presidential hopeful Phil Gramm said on CBS's *This Morning* that the moment reminded him of Jimmy Carter delivering his "malaise," or "crisis of confidence," speech. Perhaps engaging in hyperbole, conservative columnists Bob Novak and William Safire separately wrote that Clinton's declaration of relevance reminded them of Nixon proclaiming "I am not a crook" in response to the rising tide of the Watergate scandal.[76] Hyperbole only works in relation to a normative sense of the actual or real, and, in fact, Novak and Safire may have meant their comments to be taken literally. Regardless, Clinton's peripheral status, his defusion from the narrative ideal of what a president should represent, and his office's erosion in symbolic capital, established conditions in which Novak's and Safire's comparisons to the dark days of Watergate could be deployed, and, perhaps, find traction.

Representative of the next day's scathing commentary, the *Washington Post* described Clinton's event as "The Snooze Conference; Networks, Viewers Not Tuned In to Clinton:"

If the whole nation had tuned in to see President Clinton answer questions from the media Tuesday night expecting drama, there would have been a continental chorus of hisses.

Of course, as the overnight ratings make clear, the whole nation was emphatically not tuned in – not even 10 percent.

And so an inescapable conclusion: That hissing noise was coming from the East Room of the White House itself. It was the sound of the air leaking out of the once-mighty Washington institution known as the prime-time news conference.

The sleek, glamorous model rolled out in 1961 by John F. Kennedy – the first president to answer questions on live national television – has become a sputtering old jalopy.[77]

The hissing noise was Clinton's defusion from the presidential role, and the office's diminishing role in the drama of contemporary US politics. Clinton needed a strong force to reverse this steady symbolic erosion. While morning commuters were reading the critical reviews of Clinton's performance the night before, the unthinkable occurred. At 9:02 a.m. on April 19, domestic anti-government radicals detonated a truck bomb at the Alfred P. Murrah Federal Building in downtown Oklahoma City, two years to the day after agents from BATF had stormed and razed the Branch Davidian compound near Waco, Texas.

6

Birth of a symbolic inversion: Clinton (re-)fuses with the presidential character

The bombing of the Federal Building in Oklahoma City on April 19, 1995, initiated the symbolic inversion that would return Clinton to the heights of heroism that only the presidential office can afford. The bombing simply appeared. There was no forewarning.

Meaning pre-exists action, yet meaning must also be enacted; it is brought to the fore and given form when it is narrated and performed. Marshall Sahlins (1976, 1981) described how native inhabitants made sense of Captain Cook's sudden arrival to the Hawaiian Islands by interpreting the newcomers through their existing mythical and cultural structures. In a manner, the natives could not have responded otherwise. Their system of meanings already delineated what this type of arrival would mean, and prescribed how it should be welcomed. In this sense, the Cook arrival activated the natives' ritual response. The Oklahoma City bombing occurred in social and cultural circumstances of a more differentiated kind by an order of magnitude. While the event caused meaning makers to rely on existing, deeply rooted cultural structures, it also occurred in a context of mixed opinions and multiple voices.

Like the native inhabitants' first glimpses of Cook's fleet, the Oklahoma City bombing shook to life cultural codes and national narratives that described what presidential leadership should look like, and prescribed how the president should act. The bombing's meaning did not settle naturally like dust on the rubble. Rather, Clinton and national opinion makers used pre-existing cultural structures to ascribe meaning to the devastation. And at the same time, the reactivation of these cultural structures lifted Clinton back into the presidential role, as national leader, healer, and the voice of vengeance and retribution.

Criticism of Clinton both accelerated to new heights and extinguished itself in Thursday 20th's newspaper coverage. In the same edition of the

New York Times appeared the following two columns. In an editorial titled "Relevance is Not Enough, Mr. Clinton," the paper invoked militaristic language to describe how much Clinton had become defused from the role of national leader. The press conference had resuscitated Clinton's problematic symbolic relationship to the nation's military apparatus by way of the McNamara book, and cast a spotlight on the awkwardness with which he strode in his leadership role. The editorial opened with the lines:

No troops will be marching to battle under a banner that reads "The President is relevant." Yet that is about as inspirational as President Clinton got during his televised news conference.[1]

Vaguely echoing Jesse Helms's heavily criticized belittlement of Clinton's ability to fulfill the role of commander in chief, the *Times*'s opening sentence drew directly into question Clinton's ability to lead metaphorical "troops," and portrayed him as a hollow, inauthentic leader, a leader in title alone. Clinton lacked "passion" or "even a sense of conviction," the editorial continued, and he too often struck a chord that "sounded more like self-pity than self-criticism." The editorial concluded:

Mr. Clinton is still groping for an overarching rallying cry to balance the brilliant if simplistic slogans offered by the Republicans. Proclaiming his relevance is a start, but it is not enough.[2]

Performing events

Clinton's rallying cry was located in page 1's headline, which indicated that the nation's discourse was changing abruptly:

TERROR IN OKLAHOMA CITY: THE INVESTIGATION; AT LEAST 31 ARE DEAD, SCORES ARE MISSING AFTER CAR BOMB ATTACK IN OKLAHOMA CITY WRECKS 9-STORY FEDERAL OFFICE BUILDING.[3]

Klein retrospectively called Clinton's press conference his presidency's "lowest point." A low point is only an absolute low if things turn around and tick upward. Without the Oklahoma City bombing, Clinton's political capital may have continued to dwindle down to a mere change.

The bombing's immediate aftermath created a kind of stillness in the symbolic air; an environment both structured and yet contingent. Symbolic structures like the democratic codes of civil society, narratives of heroism, militancy, and justice, and myths of evil threatening the good structured the interpretive environment of the nation's collective conscience.

Culture structures are like the walls and pillars of a sacred space. Symbols, narratives, and icons are like weapons or paintings of armed heroes in battle scenes hanging on the wall; present but taken for granted, they loom in our midst and constitute our sense of possibility, our perceived strengths and weaknesses, our feeling of security or vulnerability. Events are moments when the weapons are taken off the walls, and stories are told explaining the memorials of past victories and fallen soldiers. Events demonstrate that the interpretive environment is structured by taken-for-granted symbolic boundaries and supports, while they also reveal the contingent dimensions that structures afford: who will tell the story of what is occurring, and which past stories inform the present? Who will grab the weapon off the wall, which weapons are appropriate, how should they be wielded?[4] Who will lead the troops into battle, how, and why?

In many respects, the nation's first response to the bombing was heavily ritualized. Blood sacrifice re-fuses citizens to the nation; it is "a ritual in the most profound sense," Marvin and Ingle (1999: 63) observed, "for it creates the nation from the flesh of its citizens." Early news coverage of the bombing focused on particular symbolic subjects: blood, children, emotions, and the solidarity of citizenship. News reports, accompanied by images of the carnage, emphasized the victims' blood that could be seen in the bombsite's dust and rubble. Reporters focused on the children destroyed in the building's daycare center, and discussed how children witnessing the news coverage should be comforted and their anxieties eased. Commentators made projections about how citizens across the nation were experiencing heightened degrees of fear, anxiety, terror, and anger. As the coverage continued into the day, reports increasingly mentioned that citizens around the country were inquiring into contributing to the relief effort, particularly by donating blood.

Before the bombing, the political sphere was contingent and in flux. Gingrich's startlingly quick rise had unsettled the traditional logic whereby the president is the center of popular attention, and the symbolic epicenter of governmental and national power. The bombing, however, reduced and reversed these recent ambiguities in the landscape, and initiated the reconstitution of a political sphere of a more traditional symbolic structure. The president's central role in the developing drama, as protector and militaristic leader, appeared obvious and commonsensical. The president, not the Speaker of the House, was expected to respond to the event, explain what it meant, and prescribe action. The bombing gave Clinton the opportunity to activate symbolic codes and to adorn himself in symbolic weaponry.

Shortly after 5:00 p.m. on the day of the bombing, Clinton issued his first press conference from the White House briefing room. This time the president "had no trouble getting on all four networks" to broadcast "his angry statement":[5]

The bombing in Oklahoma City was an attack on innocent children and defenseless citizens. It was an act of cowardice and it was evil. The United States will not tolerate it. And I will not allow the people of this country to be intimidated by evil cowards.

I have met with our team which we assembled to deal with this bombing, and I have determined to take the following steps to assure the strongest response to this situation.

First, I have deployed a crisis management team, under the leadership of the FBI, working with the Department of Justice, the Bureau of Alcohol, Tobacco and Firearms, military and local authorities. We are sending the world's finest investigators to solve these murders.

Second, I have declared an emergency in Oklahoma City, and at my direction, James Lee Witt, the director of the Federal Emergency Management Agency, is now on his way there to make sure we do everything we can to help the people of Oklahoma deal with the tragedy.

Third, we are taking every precaution to reassure and to protect people who work in or live near other federal facilities. Let there be no room for doubt, we will find the people who did this. When we do, justice will be swift, certain and severe. These people are killers and they must be treated like killers.

Finally, let me say that I ask all Americans tonight to pray; to pray for the people who have lost their lives, to pray for the families and the friends of the dead and the wounded, to pray for the people of Oklahoma City.

May God's grace be with them. Meanwhile, we will be about our work.

Thank you.[6]

Clinton's address to the nation invoked background collective representations while it identified and brought to the fore a script for interpretation and action. It commingled references to the codes of civil society with intonations of bellicosity, primordialism, and a warrior-like ethos. This initial response contained four subjects: the victims, the perpetrators, the public, and Clinton himself. Invoking one of his favorite images, of a man at work diligently doing his job, Clinton constituted himself as an administrator attuned to the seriousness of the situation before him. At the same time, he also borrowed themes from martial republicanism, and quite effectively portrayed himself as representing a warrior and protector figure.

Sounding the role of administrator, Clinton said he would activate the institutions of government to respond in rational, controlled ways, to investigate the bombing, care for the injured, and protect the remaining members of the nation's citizenry. Yet Clinton's words also connoted that he would be a warrior–protector: a figure of measured anger, a deliverer of vengeance and retribution, a killer of killers, and protector of the innocent. Likewise, by invoking God and prayer, and bestowing grace on the fallen, Clinton framed himself as a source of order and calm in the face of the sublime; as an intermediary between a terrified public and the transcendent realm of comfort and justice. In Durkheim's words, Clinton used the moment to transform himself into a "higher-order mythical personality" (1995 [1915]: 286).

His civil discourse addressed the public as a community of democratic citizens. However, cast against the backdrop of the day's bloody ruins, his speech also contained a hue of primordialism that portrayed his audience as innocent, peaceful tribesmen in need of his protection, as much as rational, autonomous citizens. Clinton clearly delineated between citizens and enemies, us and them; between the innocent and unthreatening, on the one hand, and the evil and cowardly, on the other.[7] The binaries could not have been drawn more clearly:

Us	Them
Citizen	Enemy
Good	Evil
Brave	Cowardly
Innocent	Sinful
Defenseless	Armed
Children	Adults
Justice	Injustice
Certain	Unpredictable
Severe	Weak
Judges	Killers

Coverage reproduced and interpreted Clinton's words, but it also described and assigned meaning to the way he carried his body, focusing in particular on his facial expressions. These interpretive acts involved folding Clinton's body into the activated meaning structures – the developing script and background, collective representations – at work in the moment. Building on Gilbert Ryle's work, Geertz famously argued that the social scientist's task is to produce "thick descriptions" by discerning the code, or "stratified hierarchy of meaningful structures," that, for instance, distinguishes a nervous eye twitch from a conspiratorial wink exchanged between two comrades (Geertz 1973: 6–7). Eyes welling with tears and trembling could be interpreted in any number of ways. News commentators' first order of interpretation of Clinton's facial movements held that they represented emotions: namely, anger and rage. Their second order of interpretation, as it were, posited that anger and rage represented authenticity, strength, control, command, and a kind of admirable form of calmness. Tears could mean a variety of things, and anger could be directed at anything. Hours after the bombing, commentators read them as representative of presidential leadership.

The *Houston Chronicle* described Clinton as "emotional," "straining to hold back his anger," "stern-faced but trembling," and suggestively stated that his "eyes appeared to be welling with tears as he spoke." The *Seattle Post-Intelligencer* reported similar facial cues, saying Clinton delivered his address with "jaw clenched and eyes fixed with anger," while the *State Journal-Register* of Springfield, Illinois, described Clinton with "his jaws clenched and eyes narrow with fury."[8] What did these expressions and modes of comportment communicate? They looked presidential. The *Boston Herald* interpreted them as suggesting "strength, calm and a unifier's healing touch," while the *San Francisco Chronicle* read them as indicating that Clinton "was in command ... as news of the bombing stunned the nation."[9] The nation was shocked and stunned, but Clinton was angry yet controlled, and every bit in command, the coverage suggested. Without a trace of irony, the *Buffalo News* proclaimed that Clinton had "never looked more presidential."[10]

The bombing initiated a symbolic inversion in which Clinton began to re-fuse with the presidential model. The performance made him appear authentic. For instance, consider syndicated columnist Sandy Grady's characterization of Clinton's performance:

For once Bill Clinton spoke and nobody could bicker over his words.

"These people are killers and must be treated like killers," said Clinton, trembling with fury.

Yes, dammit, yes.

Shrinks say a terrorist act like the Oklahoma City blast is supposed to fill us with anxiety, dread of strangers, certainly nervousness about hanging around federal buildings.

Wrong.

First there's blood-boiling anger.[11]

In order to praise Clinton's sincerity, Grady felt he must first signal to his readers that he remained an autonomous, skeptical, and detached critic.

He felt it necessary to first confirm that he remembered that Clinton had a history of using words in deceptive and obfuscating ways to create compelling political theater. To borrow from Geertz once again, Grady was winking to his readers to signal that he remained rational and autonomous, that he had not been duped by a "slick" and cynical symbolic stunt. With that caveat stated, Grady then communicated his identification with Clinton's performance. He too felt the anger that Clinton demonstrated from the podium, Grady stated, and he accepted Clinton's definition of himself as the hunter and punisher of killers. Grady's "Yes, dammit, yes" suggests that the elements of performance – the script, actors, and background representations – were working together in kind of perfect synchronicity. Clinton was fusing with his character. Not only did he seem to be acting like a president, he actually started to seem as if he *was* a good president, embodying the qualities of an admirable and heroic leader. Clinton fused with his role, and his role was an admirable one. The audience was fused with the performance, and accepted the script and characterizations that Clinton had elaborated. It was worthy of emphatic cheering and approval, Grady suggested.

Degraded by scandal allegations, policy blunders and outright failures, and an appearance of political fecklessness, Clinton had looked like a one-term president during the first months of 1995. With Gingrich as the icon of the movement, the Republicans had won control over both houses of Congress by championing themselves as limited-government revolutionaries. They had moved the bills outlined in the Contract with America through Congress in the first 100 days of their new term, and had had President Clinton declaring his relevance to an audience eager to scoff and howl at the irony of his statement.

Yet, as David Broder had identified at the end of 1994, the Republicans had developed a "meanness problem." Soon after the Republican victory, Democrats and the Clinton team had begun to try to exploit this symbolic weakness in small ways. Clinton had called for "leaner, not meaner" government in his State of the Union Address. And he had routinely tried to get Americans to think of the Republicans' Contract as representing a "Contract ON America," but to little effect. In another instance, Democratic congressman Martin Frost, trying to raise campaign funds, had sent a letter to potential donors on March 30, 1995, that opened with:

Newt Gingrich is one of the most dangerous figures to emerge in American politics during our lifetime … He calls himself a "revolutionary" but he promotes the policies of a terrorist by backing legislation that will eliminate anti-drug programs for America's youth.[12]

Frost had continued his rallying cry by accusing Gingrich and "the right-wing political forces he's aligned with"[13] of trying to destroy the Clinton presidency, and of seeking to eradicate social programs that aid the "least powerful and least able to defend themselves."[14] Frost's office sent the letter out again on April 26, a week after the Oklahoma City bombing.

When it was brought to his attention, Gingrich sent Clinton an angry letter deploring the discursive tactics of using the Oklahoma City tragedy for political gain. Consequently, the original letter and Gingrich's reply ended up receiving considerable attention in the press. Though the Administration, and Frost more specifically, apologized for the inflammatory language in that particular letter, the Clinton team pressed forward in a none-too-subtle attempt to further link the Republican revolution and its on-air champions with the domestic terrorists responsible for killing federal employees and the children in the Murrah building. What were the combined effects of the Republican revolution and the Oklahoma City bombing on those inside the Beltway? "Politics is breaking out all over," observed Linda Feldmann, staff writer for the *Christian Science Monitor*.[15]

In a widely broadcast and much-praised commencement speech at Michigan State University delivered two weeks after the bombing, Clinton further solidified the symbolic connection between the philosophers of limited-government and the practitioners of anti-government violence:

I would like to say something to the paramilitary groups and to others who believe the greatest threat to America comes not from terrorists within our country or beyond our borders but from our own government. I want to say this to the militias and to others who believe this, to those nearby and those far away. I am well aware that most of you have never violated the law of the land ... But I also know there have been lawbreakers among those who espouse your philosophy that the government was the biggest problem in America, and that people had a right to take violence into their own hands ...

...

There is no right to resort to violence when you don't get your way. There is no right to kill people. [applause and cheers] There is no right to kill people who are doing their duty or minding their own business or children who are innocent in every way. Those are the people who perished in Oklahoma City. And those who claim such rights are wrong and un-American.

The script eroded the distinction between action and philosophy, violence and ideology. It intermingled overt signs of radicalism like paramilitary groups, militias, and terrorists, with "others" who "philosophize" that "the greatest threat to America comes ... from our own government." It reduced the distinction between those who "have never violated the law of the land" with the "lawbreakers ... who espouse your philosophy." Perhaps most provocatively, Clinton invoked geographic imagery, forcing a symbolic linkage between militias and "those far away" with "those nearby." The imagery operated on two levels. Clinton delivered the speech in Michigan, which was well known (as we all learned) for supporting a large, vibrant, and vocal militia movement. But the imagery also operated at the national level, and played on the understandings of the American collective consciousness. In the early 1990s, media outlets had paid considerable attention to militias and to separatist and anti-government movements in the Rocky Mountain States, the Midwest, and in Texas.[16] In this symbolic context, Clinton's use of the terms "those nearby" and "those far away" furthered the linkage between middle-American radical movements and conservative thinkers inside the DC Beltway; that is, those "nearby" Clinton, and the nation's geographic and political center: namely, the Gingrich Republicans.

Throughout May, Clinton took direct aim at talk radio hosts and right-wing ideologues, calling them "purveyors of hatred and division." "They spread hate," he declared, and "they leave the impression, by their very words, that violence is acceptable." News columns and editorials juxtaposed Clinton's angry words about the "purveyors of paranoia" whose voices push "fragile" people over the edge, to quotations from the likes of conservative radio host G. Gordon Liddy, who proclaimed on air that killing BATF agents required "Head shots, head shots – kill the sons of bitches!"[17] In the *New York Times*, editorialists Bob Herbert and Frank Rich closed the symbolic distance between senior Republicans like Newt Gingrich and Bob Dole, and right-wing radio personalities like Rush Limbaugh, Chuck Baker, Bob Mohan, and G. Gordon Liddy, on the one hand, and militia leaders and radical separatists, on the other. Frank Rich cited Idaho militia and Christian Covenant leader Bo Gritz, calling the Oklahoma City bombing "a Rembrandt – a masterpiece of science and art put together." Rich concluded:

What is clear is how extensively the nation's far-right factions are interconnected, forming a political network that often publicly espouses the same ideology as the terrorists in our midst.[18]

Politicizing the Oklahoma City bombing carried with it potential risks. After all, much of the nation had just helped usher the Republicans into Congress by enthusiastically supporting their limited-government platform. Likewise, conservative talk radio was a pop cultural juggernaut, still very much in the process of accumulating new listeners in large numbers. Republican officials and media personalities fought back,[19] denying the link between criticism of the government and the practice of exercising material violence against federal employees.

For instance, radio talk show host Oliver North, the quasi-heroic soldier from the Iran-Contra hearings, tried to slow this symbolic linkage by portraying the bombers as a fringe element that always existed, regardless of the tenor of political discourse at the center of the political sphere. The bombers represented "a fringe element that is always going to be out there. They're not encouraged by talk-show hosts."[20] Dick Williams, writing for the *Atlanta Journal-Constitution*, also represented the practitioners of violence as fringe elements driven by madness and irrationality. He decried Clinton's politicization of the bombing, saying the president was "making political hay from tragedy and murder." In his criticisms of the Right's advocates in the media, Williams continued, Clinton had "named no names – the very essence of McCarthyism."[21]

In terms of the discursive structure of actors, critics on both the Left and the Right sought to constitute the practitioners of right-wing violence in the counter-democratic codes, as extremists, irrational, hysterical, excitable, passionate, unrealistic, and mad.

The politics "breaking out all over" were discursive battles over how closely the mainstream Right could be symbolically linked to the far Right extremists. Radio personalities like North, Williams, and Limbaugh, as well as Republican politicians like Gingrich and Dole, sought to emphasize their autonomy from the anti-government extremists who would use violence to realize their political ideals. Clinton and liberal commentators, on the other hand, worked to semiotically link the center Right with the far, fringe Right – the militia movement, anti-abortion activists, and, ultimately, the Oklahoma City bombers.

Both sides battled to control the definition of "American" civil and political behavior. Clinton called those who hated their government and claimed a right to violence "un-American." Commentators like Williams, on the other hand, argued that free speech and the right to criticize one's government represented the essence of American citizenship. Invoking a potent symbol of anti-civil political behavior, Williams called Clinton's semi-coded finger-pointing McCarthyist.

The Oklahoma City bombing, however, had elevated Clinton's status as well as rejuvenated the symbolic power of the office. Clinton's promise to bring "swift, certain and severe" punishment to the killers, and his overt references to the death penalty,[22] led commentators to frame Clinton as having "True Grit," a reference to a Western revenge movie (1969) in which John Wayne plays a tough US marshall who helps a young woman find her father's killer. Entering the summer months, political commentator Bill Schneider said that the president was putting "the 'Clint' in Clinton." Watching Clinton respond to the Oklahoma City bombing, and seeing him move on to stand up to the Republicans on issues like the federal budget, welfare reform, and affirmative action, Schneider reflected, made him think of Clint Eastwood's infamous vigilante cop, "Dirty Harry" Callahan. In an approving tone, Schneider said that it was as if Clinton had become Dirty Harry, saying to the GOP, "Go ahead. Make my day."[23]

His status elevated, Clinton was better able to secure national media coverage. Just a couple of months priorly, White House correspondents had been bemoaning the fact that the "president is no longer necessarily seen as central,"[24] and that the "sleek, glamorous model" of the J. F. Kennedy media appeal was turning into "a sputtering old jalopy."[25]

Clinton's performances in response to the Oklahoma City bombing, however, transformed him into a strong and comforting character, a "national paterfamilias,"[26] of sorts. His approval ratings climbed dramatically, rising from 40 percent at the year's outset to 58 percent at the end of April.[27] Far from leaking all of its symbolic strength, the presidency was strong again, and back at the symbolic center: "the Oklahoma City bombing galvanized national attention on the man in the Oval Office in a way that was routine during the Cold War but is rarer now," Todd Purdum wrote in the *New York Times*'s front-page story. Purdum and Schneider were not just responding to Clinton's Oklahoma City performances. Clinton had picked up momentum attacking the Republicans, and continued to deliver "rousing red-meat speeches" on topics ranging from Mideast terrorism, abortion rights, and Medicare, moving adroitly "to rally the traditional Democratic voter groups, whose support he must not lose." Purdum was picking up on a definite turn in Clinton's presidential style, reporting that Clinton had recently been taking "actions that were nothing more or less than Presidential, but that *seemed unusually decisive and rhetorically charged for him*" (emphasis added).[28]

The control presidents can wield over the media is not expressly, or even primarily, legal or financial, but performative and dramatic in nature. Compelling political stories with interesting characters garner coverage. The rules of power and governance in postmodern America are about drama's contours, about how performances are executed and interpreted. Governance and power are about dramatic enactment and symbolic communication.

In his analysis of the events leading up to Nixon's resignation, Jeff Alexander (1988: 198) demonstrates that the political polarization that preceded Nixon's re-election had begun to abate, thus allowing the Left to take a critical universalist stance that did not seem to be clear extensions of specific ideological themes or goals. As ritualization developed and the Watergate scandal progressed, Democratic political elites, "who had been radical or liberal activists," were able to assert a "patriotic universalism" that did not immediately tie them to specific left-wing issues (ibid.: 200). The movement toward "generalization," and the development of a "ritualized atmosphere," allowed political elites on the Left to portray themselves as motivated by universalist and patriotic concerns in ways that would have drawn strong criticism and suspicion in the recent past.[29]

Similarly, the Oklahoma City bombing established a ritualized atmosphere and momentary sense of crisis that allowed Clinton to symbolically and pragmatically recast himself as a more militaristic, warrior-like character. Whereas he had been interpreted as incapable of leading troops into battle, the critical praise he received for his stern-faced condemnation of the bombing allowed him to recast himself as an authentic, patriotic, and more masculine and militaristic presidential character.

The bombing crystallized the Republicans' earlier, intentional, symbolic efforts to frame themselves as the anti-government, "revolutionary" party. Clinton worked hard to elevate those narrative structures to representing more of a crisis than the simple "politics-as-usual" narratives they had represented in 1994. That is, he worked to cultivate a ritualized atmosphere and to move the nation's audiences toward a moment of "generalization."

Through these efforts, Clinton regained the political and national symbolic center. Part of this resumption involved redefining the Republicans out of the center, and portraying them as representative of a partial and particularistic ethos. Clinton used the bombing to portray the Republicans as anti-civil, extreme, exclusionary, and in light of the bombing, as threatening to the nation's sacred center. The Republicans, the Clinton team argued, threatened the solidarity that made Americans "American." The Clinton team voiced in subtle and not-so-subtle ways that the partial and symbolic similarities between the radical, anti-government, militia movement and the Republicans actually represented a deep and dangerous trajectory toward the realization of an anti-civil vision.

The Republicans had been the engine driving the vehicle, while Clinton had been relegated to exercising the brake. After the bombing, the brake appeared desirable and necessary, as somehow more American. The Oklahoma City bombing moved the Republicans out of the center, and Clinton deftly pressured them further outward toward the fringe. Neither Gingrich nor Dole was effective at resisting this movement. The forthcoming battle over the budget and government shutdown in November and December would further this process, and effectively assure Clinton's victory in his forthcoming re-election bid in 1996.

Clinton capitalized on the bombing to fully inhabit the archetypical model of the American president as a strong warrior and protector. He moved to the center politically, and consistently portrayed himself as a principled agent who was willing to compromise with reasonable opposition. In fact, Clinton's discipline in sticking to a new, more broadly "presidential" character was in large part the result of political strategist Dick Morris's return to Clinton's side.[30]

He became more politically focused and assertive. Politically, he moved to the center, and almost as a matter of routine, he adopted Republican initiatives, carved off their excesses, and proclaimed them to be his own principles and goals. He attacked his Republican opposition much more forcefully, largely by proclaiming that the very excesses he would trim to locate his own position represented a threat to the core of the contract that bound American citizens to their state.

Return of the culture of scandal

It is no wonder, in this context of Clinton recovering his symbolic power, that Whitewater would fail to take hold again or represent a powerful threat to Clinton's legitimacy.

As summer unfolded, clouds of scandal returned to shadow the White House. The president continued to be hampered by the Whitewater investigation, and by the "climate of suspicion" that seemed to hover over the "secretive" Administration. In an article titled "Whitewater Tricks: New Hearings Prompt the Clintons to Make New Revelations – Only to be Caught Short Again," *Time Magazine* captured the dynamic whereby the Administration promised to cooperate with investigators only to then appear to "hold back" requested information.[31] The makings of the Whitewater scandal had existed since Clinton had first announced his bid for the presidency. It was in December 1993 and January 1994 that Attorney General Janet Reno had appointed Attorney Robert Fiske Jr. as special counsel to formally investigate the Clinton's involvement in the nebulous business deals.

The term "Whitewater" became a signifier, or the surface and communicative dimension of a symbol. Semiotically, it was loaded with signifying and associative potential. It shared the term "water" with "Watergate," which, of course, had come to represent presidential collapse due to egregious ethical violations, on the one hand, and a crisis of state and nation, on the other. Whereas Watergate connoted notions of the potential energy of dammed-up water, which could be let loose and consequently destroy everything in its downhill path, Whitewater suggested the kinetic energy of water already unleashed into violent and destructive motion.

At issue in the brewing scandal were the contents and makeup of Whitewater's signified; that is, the Clinton Administration and the congressional Republicans battled over what might lie below the surface of the term – what did Whitewater really mean? The battle over White-water's meaning took place on different fronts: on investigative, judicial, and political battlefields. On the investigative and judicial fronts, Whitewater represented questionable exchanges of large sums of money between the McDougals, who operated the Madison Guaranty S&L, and the Clintons, who used the money to cover political campaign costs and for real-estate development.

As described above, Watergate went from signifying mere dirty politics to a crisis of government as a result of shifts in the background cultural environment and as the result of dramatic enactments of investigative hearings. Whitewater, on the other hand, never rose above the level of politics and interests. The Republicans were never able to turn White-water into a symbol of danger that would aggravate the nation's collective consciousness to the extent of "generalization," to the point at which an atmosphere of ritualization could develop.

As I elaborate in the subsequent chapters, the failure of Whitewater to rise to a level of crisis and generalization is due to the fact that the Republicans became too symbolically polluted to tell the tale of what Whitewater could possibly mean. Their explanation of what Whitewater might signify could not be trusted. This was due to the Clinton team's convincing degradation of the Republican effort, and keeping the symbol at the level of scandal and politics, not crisis. The scandal took too long to tell, and the Republicans promised shocking revelations too many times without delivering the dramatic goods.

The Whitewater investigative process continued throughout the summer and fall of 1995 and into 1996, and the Republicans kept the scandal's symbol in the public arena, promising that revelations would be forthcoming, and asserting that the Clintons were "stonewalling" the process. For instance, *Time Magazine* captured the dynamic whereby the Administration promised to cooperate with investigators only to then appear to "hold back" requested information. "Whitewater Tricks," read the *Magazine*'s July 24 national coverage article, "New Hearings Prompt the Clintons to Make New Revelations – Only to be Caught Short Again."[32] The following week's *Time Magazine* ran with a portrait of Bob Dole on the cover, accompanied by the title "Is Dole Too Old for the Job?" presaging the next year's election contest. Clinton's popularity remained steady if not terribly impressive, hovering around the 50 percent mark. The Administration spent $18 million over the course of the year advertising Clinton's re-election bid (Woodward 1994). Polls showed that he would beat Dole narrowly in a two-way race, and the background chatter among GOP leaders expressed that Clinton, being more likeable and the better campaigner, could very well defeat the older, less personable Dole come the next fall.[33]

Showdown and the crystallization of Clinton's performative power

Through late summer and early fall, Clinton and the Republicans exchanged challenges over the drafting of the forthcoming federal budget. The stalemate entered October, when a continuing resolution extending government financing expired. Clinton threatened to veto what he had effectively characterized as a budget that cut too deeply into social spending programs like Medicare, Medicaid, education, and funding for scientific research. Clinton did signal, however, that he would be willing to compromise on the budget, and that he accepted the idea of a balanced budget resolution, just not one that included cuts in spending as harsh and drastic as the Republicans were proposing. Clinton projected the message that he wanted to find "common ground," to avoid "wedge issues" that divided the country, and to build "web issues" in order to form coalitions.[34] Gingrich, knowing that he did not have enough votes to override a veto, adopted a less conciliatory stance, predicting a "train wreck" forthcoming if Clinton did not accept the Republican version.[35] Clinton's willingness to court the Republican plan signaled to congressional Democrats that the president was willing to forsake them in order to secure his own re-election the following year. This continued a pattern established in Clinton's first term, and gives an indication of why fellow Democrats seemed to only halfheartedly support the president when the Lewinsky scandal broke out in January 1998.

By November 9 a government shutdown appeared imminent. After weeks of negotiations, Clinton took the surprising step of vetoing the Republicans' proposed continuing resolution, in which they had smuggled many of their spending cut initiatives. The Clinton team charged the Republicans with engaging in "a form of terrorism" by trying to sneak through conditions Clinton had already signaled were unacceptable. Escalating the symbolic associations, and clearly drawing on the year's earlier tragedy, White House Chief of Staff Leon Panetta complained to the press during a briefing:

Don't put a gun to the head of the president, the head of the country, and say: "You don't accept our priorities, you don't accept what we want to do to Medicare and Medicaid, what we want to do to education, we're going to blow you apart."[36]

Dole responded with slightly more subtle symbolic language, conjuring the image of a corpse and a smoking gun: "It's up to the President of the United States. If the government shuts down, his fingerprints are going to be all over it."[37]

The government shutdown began at 12:00 a.m. on November 14 and lasted for six days. The holidays were coming up, and the media was treating the showdown like a presidential election, offering nightly tracking surveys, and following each day's negotiations and discursive clashes. Polls taken one day into the shutdown showed that almost twice as many people blamed the Republican Congress (46 percent) as Clinton (27 percent) for the stalemate. The showdown appeared to be helping Clinton's re-election efforts as well. The same poll showed that Clinton's advantage over Dole in the following year's election was widening, indicating that Clinton would win 51 percent to 41 percent in competition. If he faced Gingrich, Clinton looked even better, with 62 percent favoring Clinton, and a mere 28 percent favoring Gingrich.[38]

The standoff was framed in two ways: as representing "a childish food fight" and "Kabuki theater," on the one hand, and as a crisis precipitated by "three strong-willed men" – Clinton, Gingrich, and Dole – "each with his vision of what is best for America's future,"[39] on the other. The standoff's policy implications seemed terribly important, loaded with gravity, and its outcome appeared to have the potential to affect the nation's long-term financial trajectory. Its central characters, however, were interpreted as stalwart ideologues who seemed to be behaving in confoundingly adolescent ways. The event took a decisive turn toward the "childish" framework just one day into the standoff.

Israeli Prime Minister Yitzhak Rabin had been assassinated on November 4. Momentarily suspending negotiations over the federal budget to attend Rabin's funeral, Clinton invited congressional elites to join him on Air Force One to attend the event. One week later, back in the States, and one day into the government shutdown, Gingrich announced over breakfast with reporters that the shutdown was in part due to the fact that he had felt snubbed by Clinton during the trip to Israel. In what was described as "an almost stream-of-consciousness" delivery, Gingrich told reporters:

This is petty, [but] you land at Andrews [Air Force Base] and you've been on the plane for 25 hours and nobody has talked to you and they ask you to get off the plane by the back ramp ... You just wonder, where is their sense of manners? Where is their sense of courtesy?

Covering the breakfast for the *New York Times*, John Yang reported that Gingrich "said that the fact that Clinton did not speak to him or Dole during the trip to and from Jerusalem is 'part of why you ended up with us sending down a tougher' interim spending bill." "It's petty," Gingrich admitted, "but I think it's human."[40]

Newt Gingrich reacted to the pressure of the standoff by making a clumsy, politically fatal public confession that his hurt feelings had encouraged him to contribute to shutting down the federal government. Bill Clinton, on the other hand, sublimated his showdown energies in another way. On November 15, Monica Lewinsky entered his life.

Gingrich's admission roiled Congress, blazed through the media, and enraged the nation's publics. The battle over the federal budget had been constructed as serious and imbued with gravity. Gingrich's admission deflated the terms of the battle, and dramatically weakened Gingrich's aura of principled opposition and seriousness (see Figure 6.1).

Due to the fallout from Gingrich's "tantrum," Clinton was well positioned to veto the Republicans' next budget draft, which they submitted in early December. As part of Clinton's "zig-zagging" approach to policy, and in accordance with Dick Morris's polling data, Clinton sent to Congress his own seven-year plan for a balanced budget the day after his veto. The proposal contained far fewer cuts in spending than the Republicans' version, however. The process exemplified Clinton's political strategy: adopt the opposition's political goals while shaving off the characteristics that he found ideologically and pragmatically unpalatable. In effect, Clinton had learned to beat the Republicans at their own game.

Clinton forced another government shutdown in mid-December. He continued to portray himself as the voice of moderation and compromise, and to cast the Republicans as "extremists." Seeing public opinion turn radically against them, the Republicans caved in to Clinton's budgetary demands and a new federal budget was passed in late January 1996.

(Re-)fused and re-elected: a prelude to Monicagate

The prior year's symbolic inversion had restored Clinton's presidential status and rejuvenated public acceptance of his legitimacy. While tough symbolic warfare continued between the two principal parties – the Clintons and the Gingrich Republicans – a majority of Americans were

Figure 6.1   Speaker of the House Newt Gingrich caricatured as a crying baby throwing a tantrum, clothed in a diaper and holding a baby bottle, on the cover of the *New York Daily News*, November 16, 1995.

tiring of the personal attacks and name calling, the partisan bickering, and conservative promises of a scandalous denouement, and were left emotionally deflated by the budget showdown from the prior fall. American publics were coalescing into two camps. A quarter of stolid, conservative Americans remained emotionally invested in the Republican drama, in which Clinton played a polluting, vital threat to the American center. The swayable middle, however, were simply tiring of continued promises from elite Republicans that facts would be produced establishing that Clinton really did embody such a threat. Clinton's approval ratings climbed steadily through 1996, from 46 percent in January[41] to 60 percent in September.[42] The public enthusiasm for the conservative agenda that had lifted the Republicans into control of Congress had waned considerably by the spring of 1996.[43] The election year would be marked by the "mellowing of the American voter," Richard Berke wrote in the *New York Times*; the public wanted a "cease-fire."[44] Nonetheless, the Republicans continued to produce discourse about morality, scandal, and honor, rallying their base and exciting their political class. Their dramatic actions, however, alienated unconvinced, centrist audiences. Commenting on the upcoming election, CNN announced that "scandal fatigue" had spread through the American populace and would leave its imprint on the November contest.[45]

The showdown over the federal budget was displaced by the turn of the new year and the re-entry of Hillary Clinton into the public sphere. She was set to release her new book, *It Takes a Village*, and go on tour to promote it in late January. While Bill Clinton was once again on the rise, Hillary's return to the public stage reignited the flames of scandal.

The White House announced that it had found a misplaced memo detailing the travel office firings that had caused a media stir in December 1993. "Travelgate" returned to the news, and the scandal had Hillary's fingerprints all over it. The "Watkins memo" was a statement written by David Watkins, who was one of the employees fired from the White House travel office. In the memo, Watkins charged that he and six fellow employees had been abruptly fired "under pressure from the first lady," a charge the Clintons had strenuously denied when the event first erupted. The memo's release bolstered the earlier complaints by the fired employees, and once again ignited suspicion that the Clintons had been proffering a series of lies and engaging in suspicious cover-ups. A spokesperson for the chair of the House Government Operations Committee leaked to the press that the memo represented "a smoking gun." Representative Bill Clinger (Republican, Pennsylvania), the chair of the committee, followed up, adding:

I'm not saying [Hillary] is lying, I'm saying that there seems to be a convenient lapse of memory, perhaps a little too convenient ... There's certainly been a very strong effort to obscure or obfuscate a lot of very important facts.[46]

Conservative commentators had been anticipating the revelation of a Clintonian "smoking gun" since the president had first taken office, and now it appeared as though their investigative efforts were beginning to pay off. William Safire leaped at the opportunity to join the fray:

Americans of all political persuasions are coming to the sad realization that our First Lady – a woman of undoubted talents who was a role model for many in her generation – is a congenital liar.

Drip by drip, like Whitewater torture, the case is being made that she is compelled to mislead, and to ensnare her subordinates and friends in a web of deceit.[47]

The symbolic warfare between the Clintons and their critics escalated, analytically, or sank, normatively, to a new level. White House Press

Secretary Mike McCurry said to the press that President Clinton was so angered by Safire's words that he wanted to punch Safire in the nose: "The president, if he were not the president, would have delivered a more forceful response to that on the bridge of Mr. Safire's nose."[48]

In addition to Travelgate and Whitewater once again becoming symbols laden with potential signifying energy, a three-judge panel considering Paula Jones's allegations against Clinton ruled that her lawsuit could proceed against the current president. The legal elements for a case against Clinton continued to fall into place, and Republican desire for another moral and political battle continued to develop. A majority of Americans, however, were growing fatigued of the scandal allegations, and deflated due to expending emotional energy following the budget showdown.

Clinton returned to embodying one of his favorite characters, the typical guy doing the business of the nation. Parrying Republican attacks, and portraying a business-as-usual manner, Clinton continued to co-opt the Republican platform (he would sign welfare reform legislation in late July), proposing a "values agenda," and announcing in his State of the Union Address:

The era of big government is over. (Applause.) But we cannot go back to the time when our citizens were left to fend for themselves. (Applause.) Instead, we must go forward as one America. One nation working together to meet the challenges we face together. Self-reliance and teamwork are not opposing virtues – we must have both. (Applause.) I believe our new, smaller government must work in an old-fashioned American way, together with all of our citizens, through state and local governments.[49]

As the Travelgate and Whitewater scandals brewed, and personal animosities flared between the Clintons and their critics, Republican presidential contenders began fighting among themselves. While Bob Dole was considered the likeliest candidate, he nonetheless faced a formidable group of other conservatives hungry for a shot at the November competition. The Republican primaries proved very competitive, with Steve Forbes and Pat Buchanan both tarnishing Dole's image in their quests for the nomination. Each candidate won a couple of states, and winning the nomination proved damaging and costly for Dole, who entered the final electoral competition with greatly depleted funds.

The party's agenda lacked clarity and focus, and Dole struggled to get an effective campaign organization together. Likewise, the country was going through an extended time of peace and prosperity, while Clinton, despite the lingering atmosphere of scandal, had just finished a year in which he appeared more resolute, more focused, and stronger in the face of his Republican opposition. Gingrich's public image, on the other hand, had suffered considerably due to the federal budget defeat, and from repeated narratives framing him as mean, uncaring, and overzealous in the pursuit of reducing the government.

The ad campaigns leading up to the election crafted two competing narratives: Clinton framed Dole as an extension of Newt Gingrich, as old and backward-looking, and as risky and desperate, while Dole emphasized the importance of truth and trust, stating that Clinton embodied or fostered neither, and he invoked the war-on-drugs themes of the 1980s as a means to portray Clinton as a liar and a playboy. The Republicans had used morphing techniques in the 1994 congressional midterms to symbolically link Democratic candidates with Clinton, and the approach had proved enormously successful. In 1996, the Clinton team repeatedly used video footage of Dole and Gingrich standing behind a lectern at a press conference to encourage a similar kind of visual metaphor, and used the term "Dole–Gingrich" in voice-overs to reiterate the association. For instance, in the ad "Tell," video showed Dole stepping aside to allow Gingrich to take the lectern. The movement suggested deference, and was set against a voice-over stating, if Dole wants to make risky cuts to Medicare, "imagine what Newt Gingrich will go after." In several ads, Dole would appear to be yielding to Gingrich, or Gingrich would appear speaking behind Dole despite the fact that Dole was at the lectern, creating an image suggesting that Gingrich was the real leader of the two, the puppet master working behind the scenes to control Dole's choices. In addition to exploiting the negative associations Gingrich inspired, the Clinton team also worked to craft the president as favoring socially conservative values and legislation. For instance, in an example of how a president's duty has come to encompass almost "every public issue of the moment" (Ryfe 2005: 1), the Clinton team released an ad titled "School," in an effort to craft Clinton as a candidate of values. Against a backdrop of video that shifts from portraying a car accident, to kids at school, to a jail door slamming shut, a voice-over speaks:

Each year in American over 2000 kids die in drunk driving accidents. President Clinton wants to protect our kids by taking away drivers' licenses from teenagers who drive drunk. Drug test teens before getting a driver's license. The president, protecting children. Curfews and school uniforms. Tougher laws to crack down on child pornography. TV ratings. Teen mothers stay in school or lose welfare. All Bob Dole offers are negative attacks. The president is protecting our values.

Under the conditions of the defused presidency, the president shifted his image widely, and in this commercial, the audience witnessed a message that would have seemed bizarre, if not outlandish, just a few years priorly. Bill Clinton had shifted from championing universal health care and correcting social injustices like the prescription against homosexuals serving in the military to being a candidate who favored testing teens for drug use and announcing that the era of big government was over.

Dole's campaign, on the other hand, was steadfastly focused on portraying Clinton as deceitful and dangerous. Bob Dole, his ads stated, was "the better man," who spoke "the truth, first, last, and always the truth." "Does the truth matter?" the voice-over asked plaintively; "Does it matter to you?" it continued, personalizing the appeal. Resurrecting Johnson's controversial ad against Goldwater in 1964, a Dole ad titled "The Threat" opened with video of the "The Daisy Girl" picking at a flower's petals just before a nuclear bomb detonates, and states that the threat against today's youth is drugs, a clear reference to Clinton's marijuana gaffe in 1992. "Bill Clinton said he'd lead the war on drugs and change America," the voice-over states. "All he did was change his mind. America deserves better," it concludes.

Clinton's ads featured children of all ages, who were all lit in bright light, and at times touching the president or being held in his arms. Dole's ad campaign, on the other hand, mired the candidate in images of the past, by referencing his war service, for instance, and by invoking the political warfare represented by the Johnson era's Daisy Girl ad. Whereas Clinton's campaign appealed symbolically to a broad swathe of Americans, Dole's campaign signaled particularism, and was often directed at the candidate's own demographic: namely, older Americans.

The Republican nominating convention performed these themes on the television in August, frequently returning to two subjects – honor in the White House, and old age – neither of which played well with centrist Americans. Intoning the theme of his candidacy, Dole announced during his acceptance speech that "Clinton must be defeated to restore the honor of the White House." Former President George H. W. Bush pressed the theme further:

"It breaks my heart," he said, "when the White House is demeaned, the presidency diminished. Bob Dole will treat the White House with respect; his staff will be beyond even the appearance of impropriety, and, in the process, he will increase respect for the U.S.A. around the world. He will be a president we can look up to. He will do us proud."[50]

Bush personalized and extended his critique of the Clinton White House, introducing his wife by saying that his first lady was "a woman who unquestionably upheld the honor of the White House."[51] The comment was interpreted as an unsavory "personal jab," while Colin Powell's pronouncement that the GOP represented a "big tent party" was greeted with both boos and cheers.[52]

In a warmly received speech, Nancy Reagan spoke to the convention about her husband's struggles with Alzheimer's disease. Despite the favorable reception, the speech raised the semiotic domain of nominee Bob Dole's age, and the generational shift that had occurred four years priorly, when Clinton the Baby Boomer had unseated the World War II veteran, Bush Sr., from the Oval Office. Dole's age continued to hamper his efforts to project an invigorated campaign. While giving an anti-drug speech in mid-September, Dole said that he was going to perform like Los Angeles Dodgers' pitcher, Hideo Nomo, who had pitched a no-hitter the night before. "I'm going to be like Nomo," he said. "I'm going to pitch a no-hitter from now until November 5th. The Brooklyn Dodgers had a no-hitter last night. I'm going to follow what Nomo did and we're going to wipe them out between now and November 5th."[53] The gaffe was repeated continuously on television news, and precipitated an endless number of jokes among sports commentators. The Brooklyn Dodgers, of course, had moved to Los Angeles in 1958, just a few years before Dole had won his first election to Congress. One month later, newspapers across the nation ran on their front pages a photo of a struggling, desperate-looking Dole falling 4 ft to the ground from a podium.

Clinton, re-fused with the presidential aura, won the November election decisively, with an almost 10-percentage point advantage. The Republicans' meanness problem and continual attacks on the Clinton White House had fatigued centrist Americans. "Scandal fatigue" had settled into the American political consciousness deeply. Media outlets spent much of 1997 investigating Democratic fund-raising practices, but to their chagrin, the scandal did not find any traction among the news-consuming publics.[54]

The Republicans continued to pursue their mission to reveal the "real Clinton." In December 1997, Independent Counsel Ken Starr found evidence that Bill Clinton had potentially perjured himself, and suborned perjury from others, in his legal defense of Paula Jones's lawsuit. The stage was set for Monicagate, which dominated all of 1998.

7

The second term: the Republicans' polluting scandal and Clinton's successful performance

As I described in the preceding chapters, November and December of 1995 were dominated by narrative constructions of Clinton versus the congressional Republicans in a battle over the federal budget. Clinton's handling of the stalemate cast the Republicans as the villains responsible for forcing the extraordinarily unpopular shutting down of all government services, twice. The powerful and emotionally charged performances Clinton delivered throughout these battles over the budget solidified a shift in the political arena's symbolic landscape. By the end of the battle over the budget, "scandal fatigue" began to permeate the nation's moderate middle. Whereas during the prior two years Clinton was effectively coded as evasive and worthy of suspicion, the Clinton versus Republicans showdown marked the dramatic recasting of the Republicans in the political sphere's role of the corrupt investigators acting on uncivil motives. The Republicans' various investigative efforts were increasingly interpreted as less motivated by democratic ideals and more driven by counter-democratic forms of partisanship. During this shift in symbolic landscape a critical plot point occurred: Clinton began his intimate relationship with Monica Lewinsky three days into the government shutdown.

Attorney General Reno expanded Independent Counsel Ken Starr's investigative reach to include "Filegate"[1] and allegations of Clinton officials lying to Congress in 1996. This increase in Republican investigative power fueled the symbolic expansion of their villain framework and catalyzed what could be called the "Gingrich-ification" of Independent Counsel Ken Starr. Undaunted by this trend, the Republicans continued to insinuate that the investigative efforts would "reveal" mortally damaging facts about the Clinton White House. Despite the periodic unearthing of White House improprieties and questionable past dealings,[2] none of these instances were symbolically transformed into the damning evidence the Republicans had been promising. As a consequence, (1) the Republicans' continual promises of a mortal blow fueled the "scandal fatigue," (2) Starr's investigative expansion resulted in the symbolic linkage of his political motives with those of Newt Gingrich, and (3) the Republicans were increasingly framed as corrupt investigators or "bad cops" (Mast 2006), driven by counter-democratic motives and by a personal dislike for Clinton.

A critical plot development occurred in 1997. As the investigations continued, an anonymous call was placed to Paula Jones's attorneys alerting them to Clinton's relationship with Lewinsky. An important series of additional plot points followed that led to the public revelation of Clinton's involvement with Lewinsky: Paula Jones's lawyers subpoenaed the former intern; Lewinsky met with Clinton to "practice" for her deposition; she was offered a job at Revlon by Clinton's friend, Vernon Jordan; and Lewinsky shared with her then friend, Linda Tripp, a copy of a document titled "Points to Make in an Affidavit," which contained instructions for responding to questions about the Kathleen Willey case. Shortly after, Tripp contacted Starr and agreed to tape conversations with Lewinsky about her relationship with Clinton. Starr then requested and was allowed to expand his investigation to include possible instances of perjury and obstruction of justice in the Jones case. FBI and US attorneys questioned Lewinsky and offered her immunity in exchange for testimony. And finally, on January 17, 1998, Clinton gave a deposition denying he had been in a sexual relationship with Lewinsky.

In the months to come, the Republican dramatic production worked to frame these events as part of a chain of discovery of facts about Clinton's true nature. They also sought to frame initial public reactions of shock and intense interest as constituting a natural response to what should be considered a clear transgression of both legal and sacred boundaries. The Clinton production team, on the other hand, and Democrats more generally, framed these events dramatically as part of a long-standing, secretive, villainously orchestrated plan to attack Clinton personally for political gain.

Towards ritualization: Monicagate's first phase

The social processes resulting from the news release of Clinton's possible relationship with Lewinsky appeared to take on a life of their own. The breach in social routine occurred on January 21, 1998, at 1:11 a.m. when Matt Drudge posted the headline "Blockbuster Report: 23-Year-Old,

Former White House Intern, Sex Relationship with President" on his website. After learning of Drudge's web-posting, the *Washington Post* ran the story on the 21st as well, with the headline "Clinton Accused of Urging Aide to Lie."[3]

The news's rapid spread sparked massive, widespread shifts in attention among people working in political institutions and news media, and pulled citizens away from their mundane routines to focus on a particular occurrence. One Administration official stated that an "air of unreality" had taken hold in Washington;[4] those in the Washington, DC, area were described as "flabbergasted," "shock[ed] beyond belief,"[5] and "stunned and speechless";[6] and one commentator, reflecting on the qualitatively new tone in the nation's capital at the close of the event's first week, symbolically linked the event with Watergate, stating: "Friday evening brought to close a week [not seen] since the darkest days of Watergate."[7]

Audiences actively engaged the emerging ritual-like process as well. Breaking from their routine affairs, people flooded news websites, crashing many servers due to the heavy traffic, bought newspapers in record numbers, and tuned into cable news networks, which experienced dramatic increases in viewership.[8] Civil spheres mushroomed online, as chatrooms filled with people seeking to discuss and debate the events.

Watergate continued to play a central role in the event's symbolic framing. Conservative critic William Safire invoked a piece of Watergate's naturalistic imagery, characterizing the atmosphere around Clinton as a "*firestorm* that [is] going to break out around him" (emphasis added).[9] The metaphors Watergate and firestorm are images of uncontrollable, natural forces. Safire's use of firestorm symbolically links Clinton with Nixon, and characterizes the press and public reactions as natural, uncontrollable, and furious reactions to the presumed corruption.

Sam Donaldson's spontaneous, oft-repeated response to the breach indicates the event's fused, ritual-like feel of irresistible momentum: "If he's not telling the truth, I think his presidency is probably numbered in days. This isn't going to drag out. We're not going to be here in three months talking about this . . . I sat here during Watergate, we all did. I am amazed at the *speed with which this story is going*" (emphasis added).[10] Actively partaking in the telling of the story, Donaldson nonetheless describes the process as propelled by a momentum all its own.

Clinton was the central character in the initial stages of the incipient drama. In terms of mise-en-scène, the critics rendered him a lone figure at center stage. His physical performance in his initial interview with Jim Lehrer on PBS's *NewsHour* was described as "visibly shaken and unsteady in his responses";[11] he appeared as though a "picture of isolation," and "withdrawn ... secretive and evasive."[12] His verbal performance was framed critically as "legalistic and evasive," "carefully worded ... cryptic, partial, and insufficient," and "dependent ... so heavily on omission and factual elision."[13] In terms of the codes of civil society (Alexander and Smith 1993), Clinton was quickly framed a counter-democratic character. He was cast in the image of a guilty man; a heroic, if flawed, character seemed to have been revealed to be an impulsive fraud.

Clinton's symbolic construction in the discourse of civil society was as follows:

Clinton coded as	*Democratic codes*
Evasive	Straightforward
Dependent on legalistic language	Autonomous
Impulsive risk-taker	Rational
Unreasonable	Reasonable
Furious; emotionally volatile	Calm
Impulsive, passionate, and unrestrained	Controlled

Within the first couple of days after the news's release, polls registered dramatic changes in public opinion, indicating a substantive expansion of a ritual-like process and the fusion of audiences with the Republican drama.[14] The number of Americans who disbelieved both of Clinton's denials – of having an affair with Lewinsky and suborning her to perjure herself – rose substantially, from 28 percent disbelieving Clinton on January 21[15] to 62 percent disbelieving him on January 23.[16] Desires for Clinton's resignation were on the rise as well, with 67 percent wanting his departure from office if allegations that he lied under oath were true,[17] and 48 percent favoring impeachment if he refused to step down voluntarily.[18]

Actors in an incipient social drama respond to a disruption of the social routine and to a mounting sense of crisis by working to control the meaning, and thus the consequences of the news. They invoke symbols with great metaphoric reach, and try to discursively construct and embody favorable symbols, codes, and literary archetypes in their actions. Actors' control over the means of symbolic and emotional production, their access to power, and their approaches to establishing the drama's mise-en-scène contribute to the formation of audiences' interpretations.

The Republicans' dramatic intentions included encouraging ritualization, liminality, and a collective sense of being "out of time." Narratively and dramatically, this involved establishing and maintaining narrative clarity and simplicity, and a sense of narrative boundedness in which the beginning had just occurred with the "revelation" of the Lewinsky affair. The subtext of their early efforts was that "we have discovered an evil in the social center; now we must expel it." Their narrative and dramatic efforts were also aimed at hiding the machinations that went into preparing and bringing the social drama into being. That is, they sought to hide their backstage efforts that went into bringing the Lewinsky plot to stage; or, put theatrically, to hide their multiple "investigative rehearsals" that contributed to the news's outing.

The Republicans sought to encourage spectators' "natural outrage" at the news. Durkheim's (1995 [1915]) and Mary Douglas's (1996) work on the relation between the sacred and the profane suggests the public's shock was in some sense culturally predetermined. Both argue that the profane must be removed from a sacred center via ritual means. The US office of presidency is the most sacred symbol in the United States's national cultural order. Clinton's actions of sexual indiscretion and alleged perjury, if judged by the broad consensus that followed the news, were initially interpreted as representing a profanation of that sacred center.[19] It must be reiterated, however, that in highly differentiated democratic societies the sense of flow that audiences experience when they are fused with a social dramatic production is never self-sustaining. It demands constant effort and performative style to maintain the representation of compelling substance. In this regard, the Republicans found themselves in a dramatic bind.

Despite signs of shock, outrage, titillation, and civic reengagement across American publics, the breach could not sustain itself. Social dramas require that producers claiming interpretive authority and legitimacy engage in a continual process of narration. Yet producers are constrained by their emplotment in the developing social drama. Audiences interpret a producer's claims to nonpartisanship, neutrality, and disinterestedness, for instance, vis-à-vis the claimant's character development in the drama thus far.

In January 1998, the Republicans were confronted with a social dramatic paradox: to successfully pollute Clinton they needed to narrate the breach's meaning and dramatize Monicagate's consequences as representing a dire threat to the nation's political center. Yet, they were prevented from engaging the social dramatic battle for fear of further concretizing the corrupt investigator, or bad cop, image the Clinton team had so successfully attributed to them to date. The genre, elements of which had colored public discourse during the Rodney King incident and the O. J. Simpson trial, posits that bad cops pretend to be heroes but in reality misuse their authority in pursuit of nefarious ends. They use their authority to manufacture crises so that they can benefit from appearing to resolve them. In more concrete terms, bad cops plant evidence only to claim to discover it. Once "discovered," the bad cop removes the social threat – the evidence and the framed criminal – and assumes the role of hero for having protected and restored what is sacred in society.

A memo sent to congressional Republicans during the breach's first week by party strategist Frank Luntz indicates that he sensed that he needed to warn Republican characters against playing into the bad cop genre's logic:

The facts will speak far louder than any of your voices. If you comment, you will take a non-partisan, non-political situation and make it both partisan and political. Do not speculate. Do not hypothesize. Too many Americans justify the President's behavior because they dislike his accusers. Please don't add to that justification.[20]

To have fully engaged the breach and dramatized it as representing a crisis of democracy, the Republicans would have run the risk of portraying themselves as conspirators in a politically motivated investigation, or as having manufactured the evidence against Clinton only to have "discovered" it in order to reap the rewards of a newfound heroic status. Such actions would have solidified the Clinton team's well-developed narrative: that "Monicagate" simply represented the latest installment of Republican machinations to delegitimize the president. Yet, simply acting as if they were neutral onlookers would not prevent the Clinton team from dramatically situating Monicagate's news within a narrative of a long, secretive, meticulously orchestrated Republican plot to frame the president. Dramatically checkmated, the Republicans were unable to engage in dramatic contestation over the news's meaning and consequently they quite quickly lost narrative control over the incipient event. Within two weeks they were effectively coded and dramatically defined as unfit carriers of the ritual project.

The Democratic production faced no such dramatic restrictions. As the main character en-scène in this early phase, Clinton used his vast power and means of symbolic production to contest the veracity, and therefore the meaning, of the allegations. He had at his disposal the media's unwavering attention and the symbolic props of dignity and grandeur afforded by the White House setting, which he employed masterfully. For instance, in what was scheduled to be a press conference on education policy on January 26, Clinton stood dramatically below an image of

Figure 7.1   While performing his denial of an affair with Monica Lewinsky, President Clinton shifted from biting his lower lip to narrowing his eyes and forcefully stabbing forward with his pointed finger. He stated, "But I want to say one thing to the American people, I want you to listen to me, I'm going to say this again. I did not have sexual relations with that woman, Ms. Lewinsky. I never told anybody to lie, not a single time, never. These allegations are false, and I need to go back to work for the American people. Thank you. [Applause]," January 26, 1998.

Teddy Roosevelt, the Rough Rider mounted on horseback, and forcefully denied the charges to the riveted media and nation (see Figure 7.1).

Most critics raved about the performance, suggesting it seemed to flow naturally from Clinton's knowledge of and comfort in the truth. With "his eyes narrowed and his finger stabbing in the air," Clinton performed "his most emphatic denial since the scandal surfaced," and through his use of "the present tense in saying ... that 'there is no improper relationship,'" he appeared "more direct ... in denying the accusations" than he had in the previous days.[21] An editorial in the *New York Daily News* declared:

Clinton looked at the American people in the TV eye. He put on his most determined face and punched the air with his finger to drive his point home. There was none of the parsing of the facts that he used to cover his hindquarters in past scandals. No, these were direct, declarative sentences.[22]

Sympathetic and traditionally moderate critics reasoned the performance was too seamlessly compelling, its authenticity too perfectly embodied and delivered, to be the product of a consciously, intentionally deceptive actor. It would demand an unimaginable will to deceive and unforeseen performative skills for Clinton to achieve felicity through falsity under such extreme conditions, critics assumed. Deception, it was believed, would have left a revealing trace. On the other hand, convinced that Clinton always lied, the Republican base marveled at the performance, reading the president's assertiveness as indicative of a certain degree of pathology.

Clinton received aid from a skilled supporting cast as well. In a powerfully dramatic intervention the following morning, Hillary Clinton appeared on NBC's top-rated morning show, the *Today* show, and synthesized all of the elements of the Administration's dramatic strategy into a succinct, coherent plot. Up to this time Hillary had been a polarizing figure. The core of the Left championed her as a representation of how capable women could serve and improve the public sphere. The core of the Right distrusted her and saw her as inappropriately presumptuous and ambitious in her role as first lady. Neither of these audiences would change their opinions based on her *Today* show appearance. Her performance as a loyal wife who believed and would defend her husband under such embarrassing circumstances, however, won her the respect of the critically important political middle still reeling from the just-released allegations.

During the interview Hillary assumed the authoritative tone and demeanor of a drama's narrator, a role whose interpretive authority stems from its critical distance from, and narrative omniscience of, the action on center stage. Successfully taking on this role would allow Hillary to appear as though she were capable of perspicaciously overseeing the event's overall plot, and would thus cast her as a neutral expositor in the eyes of the drama's followers.

She stated the plot simply and matter-of-factly:

This is the great story here, for anybody willing to find it and write about it and explain it, is this *vast right-wing conspiracy* that *has been conspiring against my husband since the day he announced for president.* A few journalists have kind of caught on to it and explained it, but it has not yet been fully revealed to the

Figure 7.2   Pedestrians stop in Rockefeller Center to watch Hillary Clinton during her appearance on NBC's *Today*, January 27, 1998.

American public. And, actually, you know, in a bizarre sort of way, this may do it. (emphasis added)[23]

People stopped their routines to watch Mrs. Clinton deliver her defense of the president, indicating a "bracketing" experience was developing (see Figure 7.2).

Hillary's unproblematic access to the United States's highest-rated morning news show placed her face in the living rooms and kitchens of millions of people across the nation.[24] The timing was impeccable, though it was emphasized very early in the interview that her appearance had been scheduled weeks in advance and was to address a different subject. In contrast to her husband's performance the night before, Hillary entered people's lives unofficially, during their familiar routines, and she treated her audience as if she were a friend dropping in to discuss a personal problem. Her role and title of first lady brought her added deference from the interviewer, and allowed her to enact her script without interruption, oppositional retorts, or the elaboration of counter-narratives. Of course, it would be either bold or stupid dramatic practice to be interviewed by a hostile critic.

During her performance, Hillary worked to shift the drama's mise-en-scène by emphasizing what her tone and demeanor suggested should be obvious to all witnesses: that "the great story here" was not about her husband but about his accusers. In this manner Hillary helped shift the social dramatic focus from Bill Clinton to his accusers while simultaneously drawing on systems of representation that framed the investigators as counter-democratic villains.

The phrase "right-wing conspiracy" invoked imagery of a secretive, coordinated orchestration to oust her husband from office. Her wording – "against my husband" – conjured imagery of the private sphere, thus emphasizing the sexual dimension of the accusations as opposed to the issues more directly related to Clinton's office. "My husband" instead of "the president" suggested that the accusers were taking aim at an unfair target, the family, which is perhaps the very hub of the private sphere.

Finally, Hillary's use of the phrase "since the day he announced for president" framed the current events in the context of an ongoing, long-lasting historical effort. Hillary's phrase countered the Republican's dramatic intentions by pointing out that the allegations and "the real story" had not begun *that week*. Rather, her dramatic framing of the plot, suggesting that the story had actually started long ago, functioned to erode the audiences' sense of dramatic boundedness; to deflate spectators' senses of being "out of time" and in a "bracketed" moment. It further encouraged the audience to detach from the production to study it for signs of orchestration or manipulation. It suggested that if the audience members looked closely they would be able to see the elaborate history of backstage machinations and rehearsal efforts the accusers had engaged in. Hillary's performance was orchestrated to play as an impassioned though reasoned request of audiences and the media to interpret her husband's initial "evasions" as instances of restrained frustration. She asked onlookers to identify with and understand the hero's careful patience in the face of such personalized, counter-democratic efforts. Her account invoked a romantic narrative of a reluctant hero, a kind of Robin Hood, a generally merry, peace-loving man being forced to fight villainous conspirators seeking to harm him and his family.

Roughly twelve hours after Hillary's performance, Clinton-the-accused entered one of the nation's most sacred physical spaces and delivered his State of the Union Address. Clinton's performance during this highly symbolic event capped Monicagate's first phase, and sealed his dramatic production's dominant, if tenuous, narrative control over the event

Figure 7.3   With hands raised to signal a shift from performing collective effervescence to routine business, President Clinton gestures to
applauding congresspersons at the State of the Union Address that they
return to the routine of the assembly, January 27, 1998.

(see Figure 7.3).[25] As *New York Times* columnist John Broder framed the
evening's performance: "Few other politicians of his generation – or any
other – could have pulled off a performance like that of Mr. Clinton
tonight ... Mr. Clinton sailed forward into the stiff wind of adversity."[26]
In one of the most watched addresses in the late twentieth century,
Clinton made no mention of the scandal or of Lewinsky. His words and
physical demeanor evoked the script "I am going back to doing the work
of the nation."[27] Counter to the Republicans' script, Clinton's emphasized a return to the routine and mundane, and strove to further defuse
the once ritualized atmosphere.

In addition to these performances, many of the Democratic production's lesser characters and sympathetic critics worked vigorously to
discursively frame Clinton's accusers in a counter-democratic light. Independent Counsel Ken Starr, Linda Tripp, and Monica Lewinsky were
all placed en-scène through this supporting cast's efforts.

The loose symbolic framework of bad cop that had dogged Independent Counsel Ken Starr began to crystallize under the pressure of repeated portrayals of him as an abusive investigator relying on strong-arm tactics. For instance, Harvard law professor Alan Dershowitz's direct linkage of Starr's tactics to those of overly aggressive police officers practically casts Starr in the lead role of a "good cop, bad cop" routine, in which the good cop leaves the interrogation room to allow Starr to "work the suspect over":

> Perhaps [Starr's actions] will get [public officials] – and the public – to think about the broad implications of arming prosecutors and the police with untrammeled authority to conduct stings, to record conversations and to coerce cooperation by threatening prosecution. No citizen should be targeted by a sting without a "sting warrant" based on probable cause. Nor should any citizen be subjected to the abusive tactics used against the President by Kenneth Starr.[28]

In another example, Starr's investigation was framed as lacking autonomy, and as representing a case of dirty politics:

> In his *three and a half years as the independent counsel investigating President Clinton*, Kenneth W. Starr has spent more than $25 million, won three convictions in Federal court and obtained 10 guilty pleas ... Mr. Starr's inability to hit a big target after so long meant that his inquiry was causing little public stir except to generate criticism from Clinton supporters that he was on a *political mission*. (emphasis added)[29]

By the end of the Monicagate's first phase Starr was coded as an extension of the Republican party, enacting a conspiratorial plot to destroy the president politically and personally. Seeking to satisfy his personal and political interests, Starr was understood as relentlessly persecuting the president, stretching the law, and exceeding his mandate.

Starr's coding was as follows:

Counter-democratic
Partisan, acting as extension of the Republicans; not autonomous
Personally motivated, invading privacy
Conspiratorial/secretive
Stretching the law
Exceeding mandate
Practicing relentless persecution

To paraphrase Derrida, nothing exists outside the coding, including institutions. The Democratic production worked hard to dramatically frame the Office of the Independent Counsel (OIC) as a counter-democratic

institution that endangered the democratic ideals of the nation by
granting a kind of ambiguous legal protection to the investigator's expansive use of his position's power. Anthony Lewis's op-ed column in the
New York Times stated this sentiment succinctly:

I am sure of one thing. The Constitution was not meant to give us – and we should
not want – a system of government in which a roving inspector general with
unaccountable power oversees the President of the United States ... Altogether,
what we see in these events is the picture of an *exceptionally zealous prosecutor*.
And we see one operating with *no meaningful restraints on his power*. (emphasis
added)[30]

As the first phase of Monicagate drew to an end Democratic opinion
makers had largely succeeded at portraying the OIC as an unconstitutional character in the drama. Polls indicate that Clinton supporters and
sizeable portions of the swayable political middle were beginning to
consider the OIC a counter-democratic institution that granted unlimited
power and resources to an investigator that could assert his authority
arbitrarily.

The OIC's coding was as follows:

Counter-democratic
Arbitrary
Limitless power
Unlimited resources
Used for personal gain
Unconstitutional

Once in place, the symbolic frameworks of Monicagate's breach and
crisis phases remained remarkably steady over the subsequent months.
The majority of skeptical, swayable publics that constituted the political
center had settled into understanding Monicagate through the Clinton
team's dramatic framework. Due to the Democratic production's
dramatic and discursive efforts, the Republicans were not perceived as
legitimate carriers of the ritual project to this sizeable majority. The
machinations of their dramatic production had been rendered highly
visible, their back-stage effectively brought to the fore, and their script
rendered overly artificial and contrived. On the other hand, though now
in the minority, the conservative base remained passionately anti-Clinton,
insisted the president was lying, and interpreted the Clinton team's
response as a farce that threatened the very foundations of American
democracy.

Dramatic erosion: Monicagate's middle phase

Public opinion trends steadied after the State of the Union Address and a polarization between two publics solidified. By the end of July a majority (57 percent)[31] opposed Clinton leaving office under *any* conditions while a smaller but devout 39 percent[32] supported continuing efforts to investigate and expel him. There were two downward shifts in anti-Clinton public opinion after January 1998: pro-resignation sentiments decreased roughly 20 percentage points, and pro-impeachment sentiments decreased approximately 8 percentage points.[33] Yet, alongside these trends, at the end of July, 68 percent of the social drama's audience believed Clinton had had an affair with Lewinsky and lied about it, an increase of 18 percentage points over the same time. These contrasting poll trends indicate that an interesting dramatic dynamic took place between February and early August. A sizeable portion of the general public resisted identifying with the Republican dramatic production *despite* believing Clinton had lied about his relationship with Lewinsky, on the hand, and that he had repeatedly, assertively lied about not lying, on the other. Starr's late July disapproval ratings hovered around 60 percent. These trends indicate the Clinton dramatic production's efforts had succeeded during the previous six months, effectively vilifying Starr and further delegitimating the investigative process. As mentioned above, the Republicans were unable to engage in any vigorous dramatic dueling because the Clinton team had successfully sculpted the dramatic landscape such that vigorous Republican action would be read through the idioms of the bad cop genre. By keeping the prior six years of relentless symbolic attacks on the president by Republicans in Monicagate's script, the Administration's production essentially neutered the Republicans of any performative power and cast in doubt their right to constitute and narrate.

Within this context, two micro-events in the drama's middle phase nonetheless functioned to bring publics back to considering the Republicans' discursive and dramatic offerings, and reinvigorated the event's initial, ritually charged atmosphere. In particular, Starr's investigative pressure eventually led the Clinton production to have its star publicly admit (on August 17) to an "inappropriate relationship" with Lewinsky. This dramatic confession placed Clinton back en-scène and infused the Republican drama with new energy. The confession reinvigorated the Right's base, and caused those at the political center, who had decided to support Clinton because they did not trust his inquisitors, to reconsider their loyalty to a character that had lied to them. Once powerfully deflationary, Clinton's "finger stabbing in the air" performance became his "wagging his finger in shame" performance, and was used forcefully by Republicans to parody Clinton's initial performative enthusiasm and to reiterate his "slickness," the strength of his skills at deception.

Less than a month later the Starr Report's release on the internet and in book form revitalized the event's prior, substantively charged atmosphere as well. The report's internet debut on September 11 triggered another break from the mundane in people's everyday lives.[34] "Americans across the country tried to participate in this unprecedented kind of electronic town hall meeting," a reporter described, but "were shut out because of the overload on the computer network."[35]

The *New York Times*'s editorial page reacted to the report's contents by framing Clinton in terms that could be found in any film textbook's discussion of the gangster genre's anti-hero:

No citizen – indeed, perhaps no member of his own family – could have grasped the completeness of President Clinton's mendacity or the magnitude of his *reck-lessness*. Whatever the outcome of the resignation and impeachment debates, the independent counsel report by Mr. Starr is devastating in one respect, and its historic mark will be permanent. A *President who had hoped to be remembered for the grandeur* of his social legislation will instead be remembered for the *tawdriness of his tastes and conduct* and for the disrespect with which he treated a dwelling that is a revered symbol of Presidential dignity. (emphasis added)[36]

Both of these micro-events reversed previous poll trends. Clinton's *job approval* rating dropped to between 56 and 62 percent,[37] approximately tying with its lowest mark set just after the scandal had broken. Public calls to "just drop the matter" lessened substantially: down 17 percentage points from the prior month's poll, 47 percent of the public favored ending the investigation with the report's publication. On the other hand, 51 percent favored further investigations and congressional hearings on impeachment.[38]

At the culmination of Monicagate's first phase, three audiences had merged into two when the majority of publics in the political center came to understand the event largely through the Clinton team's dramatic narrative. Polls indicated that Clinton's admission to having lied combined with the release of the Starr Report to encourage the audience of Clinton sympathizers to split into two audiences. Once again the public was constituted by three audiences, each with a different interpretation of what was taking place in the political arena. Polls also indicated that some of the skeptical centrists who had come to sympathize with the Clinton team's narrative disassociated from both parties' dramas, indicating there was a likely chance this drama would end without heroes of any sort.

Later, in Monicagate's second, middle phase, on August 21, Clinton's taped testimony before the Grand Jury was aired on national and cable television. The tape's release ultimately backfired on its creators. Seeking a successful degradation ritual, the Republicans intended the tape to shame Clinton in front of the nation. The cinematography framed Clinton like a criminal before a tribunal. He was filmed only from the waist up, similar in style to a classic "mug shot" of gangster film imagery. While reporting on the event varied across the political spectrum, the tape's airing was largely framed as an extreme, unjust attempt to publicly degrade Clinton. Though multiple publics witnessed the event, the broadcast appeared to further delegitimate all parties involved, and fracture any ritual re-substantivization processes that had followed Clinton's confession and the Starr Report's publication.[39] The footage and its ironic consequences for the Republican dramatic effort again illustrate the contingency of such events and the dramatic producers' limited ability to estimate how their production efforts will be received by various publics.

In the November midterm elections the Republicans not only failed to increase their 55–45 margin in the Senate, but the Democrats picked up five seats in the House. This Democratic gain represented the first time since 1934 that the president's party had gained seats in a midterm election.

Failed ritual: Monicagate's third and final phase

The House hearings and impeachment proceedings contained some of the most dramatic settings and formally ritualized proceedings of the entire event, yet the Republicans were still unable to get a broader audience to cathect with their production. From the outset Republican Representative Henry Hyde tried to infuse the proceedings with an atmosphere of grave solemnity, invoking Roman law, the Magna Carta, the Constitutional Convention, and referencing the Civil War's battles of Bunker Hill, Lexington, and Concord.

Democratic representatives Barney Frank (Massachusetts) and Charles Schumer (New York) resisted accepting the Republicans' impeachment script that called for solemnity, reverence, and gravity, by performing comedy. In opposition, Frank and Schumer turned the hearings into a farce by repeatedly cracking jokes and making disruptions that frequently had the House Democrats rolling with laughter:

Frank: Now, by the way, on that subject, my colleague from Arkansas challenged Mr. Craig before and said that the president never admitted to "sexual contact" with Ms. Lewinsky; he used the phrase "inappropriate intimate contact." And I suppose they might have been having an inappropriate intimate conversation about which country they'd like to bomb together. (Laughter.)[40]

Though the hearings provided the Republicans with the opportunity to intervene in Americans' lives more directly and forcefully than before, only a small portion of the American public tuned in their televisions to watch the production. The television-ratings story of the weekend was CBS's decision to break away from coverage of the impeachment vote to televise a football game between the New York Jets and the Buffalo Bills. When CBS cut away to the game, its ratings quadrupled to 12 million viewers, more than doubling CNN's highest-spiked rating of the day at 5.3 million for Clinton's address to the nation.[41]

Clinton's trial in the Senate lasted from January 7 to February 12. The trial was procedural and quiet compared to the House proceedings. A two-thirds vote would have been necessary to unseat the president, and the Republicans only held a 55–45 majority. The House Republicans had moved forward with numerical power in opposition to public opinion. In light of losing seats during the prior November's midterms, and the public's unfavorable reading of the House's performance, Senate Republicans understood that a highly ritualized trial would not play well with their constituents, and that they had little chance of wooing twelve Democratic senators to vote with them to remove Clinton from office. Columnist William Neikirk represented the national mood and the Senate's motives aptly:

The U.S. Senate, proud of its heritage as the world's most deliberative body, takes on the constitutional obligation this week of putting a president on trial for only the second time in the nation's history. But at this moment, one overpowering fact has emerged: President Clinton's popularity appears to be speaking louder than the evidence, louder even than the calls of House prosecutors who want Monica Lewinsky and other witnesses summoned to tell a story that has dominated public discussion for a year.[42]

Senate leaders wanted the trial to move as quietly and quickly as possible, and avoid bringing the drama's main characters before the forum to testify once again, which led to quick proceduralism, particularly cast against the Senate's typically slow and studied process. Clinton's favorability ratings rose above 70 percent and hovered during the proceedings, which sent a clear sign to Senate Republicans that pressing for Clinton's removal would do long-term damage to a party nearly bereft of performative power.

Analysts of the impeachment proceedings have attributed Clinton's successes to pragmatic factors, citing the great economic climate, lasting peace, and Clinton's policy decisions (Zaller 1998; Newman 2002; cf. Brody 1998; Han and Krov 2003; Lawrence and Bennett 2001). The truth was quite different: they were the ineluctable results of a complex symbolic process. Clinton successfully performed himself into the role of a martyr who, threatened and wounded by undemocratic forces, labored through the Republicans' degradation ceremony in order to uphold the law of the land for all of America. He successfully portrayed his foes as uncivil, counter-democratic actors strategically wielding morality in their quest for power. As a social actor, Clinton was able to seize on contingent occurrences and turn them into symbolic events, to reweave, in his favor, the meaning-texture of American political and civic life.

After Clinton was acquitted by the Senate, his approval ratings declined considerably, landing in the 50 percent range in May 1999. With the crisis passed, the public slumped into Clinton-fatigue, and perhaps more so, into politics-fatigue. Political actors, on the other hand, responded to the post-impeachment vacuum by plotting their next career steps. Hillary Clinton launched an exploratory committee to pursue a position representing New York State in the Senate. Presidential contenders started vying for their party nominations earlier than usual. Republican governor of Texas George W. Bush Jr. got off to a quick start in early fall, amassing a large campaign war-chest and positioning himself as the Republican frontrunner. Vice President Al Gore went on to win the Democratic primary, yet the candidate and the campaign struggled to find a stable identity. Gore's campaign offers a textbook example of how difficult it can be to craft a compelling, presidential political character under the conditions of defusion. From the public outing of his campaign hiring Naomi Wolf to coach him into "alpha-male" status, to the awkward blue-collar populism around which he scripted his campaign, to his performative blunders during the debates against Bush Jr., adopting a comfortable, authentic leadership persona eluded Gore. His debate performances suffered not due to a lack of technical knowledge, but for his overly technocratic, standoffish, and prissy demeanor. The Clinton-hangover and politics-fatigue did little to help Gore, who was trying to woo a nation with a budget surplus and a rapidly growing stock market, and a public that was treating itself to light news stories about shark attacks off the coast of Florida throughout the summer of 2000.

8

Conclusion

The symbolic inversions, plot twists, and character transformations on display throughout Clinton's tenure demonstrate how the elements of cultural performance structure the flow of wicked political battles, legislative accomplishments and failures, and the prosperous highs and unseemly lows a democratic nation experiences as it recreates itself under the conditions of defusion. Political actors' authority and legitimacy are battled over more frequently and publicly under these conditions, while audiences are fragmented and yet still so thoroughly enmeshed in the political dramas that their active and intent following of the plot and character developments is not required in order for them to stay informed of the drama's arcs and shifts.

Politics is practiced in the nation's capital, and discussed in the discursive and institutional space of "the news." Yet much like sports, celebrity culture, and the weather, political characters and plots are referenced everywhere and often. They are found in obvious sources like the *New York Times* and the evening news, they are reduced and expressed in readily digestible graphs and charts in *USA Today*, they are the subjects of jokes in late night television comedy monologues, they are lampooned and critiqued on daytime talk radio, and they are the ostensible raison d'être of cable news networks. Political characters and plots represent a pool of shared symbols and narratives that friends, families, coworkers, and strangers are able to reference in order to practice everyday interactions and express their broad and narrow feelings of identity and solidarity.

This is not to say that everywhere people are talking in depth about political issues (Lichterman 1996; Eliasoph 1998). Quite the contrary. It is to suggest that in the United States, political characters and plots are thoroughly mediated, ubiquitous, and omnipresent. These conditions make it possible for people to have opinions of political actors and events without ever really devoting themselves to intently following political news. The reservoir of political symbols and narratives represents the meanings that lie behind poll results suggesting how much public approval a political actor is garnering. Publics do not know politicians personally, of course, and generally they are not able to closely follow issue-politics created by elites. Yet almost everyone has an opinion and can craft an explanation, however rudimentary, for their support or dislike for a contemporary politician or policy. These understandings are composed as much of emotional reactions to the character and plot developments in public discourse as rooted in reasoned and studied engagement with political details, and these public sensibilities shape the nation's political trajectory in consequential ways.

The aim of this book has not only been to provide a sustained social science account of the Clinton presidency, some of the most turbulent and significant years in American history, but also to present an "exemplary" case of a new way of thinking about presidential politics and power more generally. Other analysts of power and politics have tended to approach the Clinton years by focusing mainly on the Lewinsky scandal and Clinton's impeachment. Most agree that public opinion played an important role in shaping 1998's drama; however, they disagree over how the public interpreted the events, and the degrees to which the public even knew about or understood what was occurring. Like experts giving contradictory testimonies at a trial, some analysts argue that the public paid only meager attention to the events, and that people cared very little about the process (Sarfatti-Larson and Wagner-Pacifici 2001; Bennett 2002), while others suggest that the scandal and impeachment process represented a global event (Thompson 2000), and that the American public knew very well what was transpiring (Brody 1998; Brody and Jackman 1999 [cited in Bennett 2002]). Unfortunately a naturalistic explanation has settled over understandings of 1998's events, and, more damagingly, over the ways analysts of politics make sense of power in our time. Political scientist John Zaller (1998), for instance, argues that the politics of 1998 indicate that "however poorly informed, psychologically driven, and 'mass mediated' public opinion may be, it is capable of recognizing and focusing on its own conception of what matters" (186), and that there is "some 'natural' level of support for [politicians] that is determined by political fundamentals" (187). What matters to the public? What are the political fundamentals? "'Bottom line' politics," Zaller argues, citing Brody (1991), which means the "substance" issues of economic prosperity, sustained peacetime, and policy moderation (Zaller 1998: 185). The current study breaks decisively with these approaches and findings by placing Clinton's tenure within a broader historical context of the rise of conditions of defusion. Breaking with overly-realist, bottom-line, *a priori* reasoning, this book explains the politics of the 1990s by bringing the meaning-creating processes of performance and interpretation to the fore, and by identifying the dramatic means through which power is understood and practiced in the late-modern context.

This volume's review of presidential and citizenship studies demonstrates that the nature of social and political power in America has changed dramatically over the course of the twentieth and early twenty-first centuries, as presidents have changed their leadership styles, political news journalism has appropriated greater interpretive authority, and as American publics have become more complex, critical, and individualized. The Nixon versus Kennedy debate demonstrated the power of the televised image, and Kennedy's cultivation of an intimate relationship with the press corps changed the way presidents relate to both media institutions and the American public. Television news journalism strengthened its constitutive power through Kennedy's assassination, and Nixon embraced the medium, turning to it frequently as a means for communicating directly with the American public. Lyndon Johnson's credibility gap vis-à-vis the Vietnam War and Watergate helped solidify the mythological structure of the investigative reporter representing a protector of people against the tyranny of the imperial presidency. Whereas Ford and Carter were victims of television's constitutive power and a more skeptical and investigative press, Reagan used television to great success and suffered fewer counter-constitutive efforts from a more acquiescent press. The power of the televised image and the press's investigative impulses notwithstanding, these presidents succeeded and failed for multiple reasons. What has been inadequately explored is how their leadership styles were enacted within a dramatic context, a relationship of symbolic communications between state actors, media institutions, and the nation's differentiating publics.

Clinton's presidency demonstrates that as the conditions of defusion become more entrenched, late-modern incumbents must work much more diligently to fuse with the office's narrative expectations than presidents of the past. As we have seen, politics in this context of defusion is a constant, relentless exercise in symbolic construction, performance, and interpretation: a process of leaders communicating to publics, media professionals proffering visions of collective life and interpreting and shaping understandings of presidential performances, and publics communicating through polls, the ballot box, and through choosing to follow or ignore both the political and media spheres' efforts to gain their frayed attention.

Early in the twentieth century Woodrow Wilson predicted that future presidents would command great oratorical skill. It should come as no surprise that this context has favored "actorly," performance-oriented personalities such as Reagan, Clinton, and Bush Jr. (the anti-acting actor), and harshly punished personalities that struggle to embody a performative style, such as the aloof Bush Sr., the third-person Bob Dole, and the relentlessly and desperately identity-swapping Al Gore. Once under relentless pressure from his opposition and increasingly scrutinized by investigative bodies, Clinton's character thrived as a gentleman bandit, albeit one of mixed repute: a figure championing community and the protection of the vulnerable from the predations of the powerful while narrowly escaping relentless pursuit by powerful investigative agents himself. Prior to September 11, 2001, George Bush Jr. inhabited characters ranging from a predictable conservative correction to the Clinton years, to a freewheeling but largely inconsequential playboy, to the product of a strong-armed Republican effort to regain the office of presidency through a highly dubious election process. If Clinton accomplished his symbolic inversion in the wake of the Oklahoma City bombing, Bush accomplished perhaps his most significant character development in the ashes of 9/11, by picking up a bullhorn and addressing rescue workers in the attack's aftermath. Proclaiming that he could hear them, and that soon the nation's enemies would hear their reply, Bush Jr. began to transform, in part, into a cowboy figure with a split symbolic framework. Fashioning himself as Marshall Will Kane, Gary Cooper's lonely, heroic character in *High Noon*, Bush invoked symbols from the Western genre like "wanted dead or alive," and effectively chose to stand up to the community's perceived threats alone, without the help of the "debaters" in the United Nations. That was one symbolic structure. The other, more favored by European allies as well as a substantial number of anti-war Americans, saw a cowboy more akin to The Stranger, Clint Eastwood's character in *High Plains Drifter*, a mysterious gunslinger hired to protect a community expecting vengeful retribution. Ultimately, The Stranger proves to be a cure more dangerous, deadly, and disastrous than the disease he was hired to confront. President Obama's term reveals a strikingly similar dramatic structure to Clinton's, with universal health care back on the agenda, a disheartening midterm loss, and a violent domestic tragedy in Arizona that implicated revolutionary political symbolism. During his campaign Obama thrived on stirring oratory, and an image of masterful coolness. Yet he created an archetype difficult to sustain on the messy battlefields of cable-mediated Washington politics, and at the time of writing he faces a right-wing backlash reminiscent of Gingrich's congressional revolution of 1994.

The president represents the nation, and this symbolic dimension weighs heavily upon the incumbent's ability to practice institutional power, or to craft, perform, and enact his agenda. Analysts of political power mistakenly treat the institutional dimensions of the presidency as more real than the symbolic. The symbolic dimensions are treated as less important and consequential, as a mystical if not annoying variable that can inhibit or facilitate "real" political accomplishments. The president's symbolic function, however, is as real and consequential as his agenda, and, in fact, it determines agenda goals as well as the incumbent's ability to achieve them. The nation is a symbolic community, and the state is very much at the center of the imagined community's self-understanding. More than any other character, the president represents the singular, orienting node in the symbolic landscape, defining who the nation is as a collectivity with a particular identity.

Under the conditions of defusion, in which state actors, media critics, and publics negotiate a nation's trajectory, political power refers to the ability to shape understandings. Power is performed within a dramatic context, and the president represents the main character in the drama of democracy. The office conveys upon its incumbent a high degree of institutional and dramatic power. However, the drama of democracy means that the office is not autonomous, but subject to constant critique and evaluation by media critics and publics. Critique means interpretation, and interpretations are formed of symbolic components both tangible and deeply structural. In a democracy, institutional power is contingent upon command of dramatic or performative power. Not only policy choices, but political and legislative actions are developed and pursued within shared contexts of understanding.

Once we accept that culture is like an ocean in which we swim – that our bodies, social relations, and institutions are suspended in complex meaning-flows, that we are pushed and pulled by alternately strong, weak, or even opposing currents of metaphor, metonymy, and synecdoche – we begin to understand that the symbolic dimensions of the presidency must necessarily both enable and constrain the incumbent. If having power means having the ability to shape understandings, then performances are actions taken to constitute meanings. Under fused conditions, the constituted meanings of the powerful differ and meet little resistance from subordinates' interpretations. Efforts to constitute and interpretive receptions are relatively homologous, because the background collective representations shape both the sovereign and the subordinates' understandings in a strong, determining way. Under the conditions of defusion, on the other hand, cultural, social, and institutional conditions are more complex and differentiated. While the materials from which meanings are constituted and interpretations are formed remain relatively stable over time, they are also studied and considered with greater degrees of awareness, intention, and critical distance by actors and audiences alike. Richard Neustadt identified bargaining as the principal means through which political power was accumulated and practiced under conditions in which Washington elites maintained considerable autonomy from press scrutiny and public interest. Replete with memorable performances by the incumbent, his wife, his opposition, and his investigators; a political strategy that aggressively tested and courted public opinion in order to craft and communicate agenda goals; a more differentiated, hungry, and aggressive media landscape; and a complex of publics that were alternately attentive and disinterested, angry and supportive; all of these components indicate that the nation has moved into a new era, one that I have explored in this volume under the rubric of the performative presidency.

Notes

Chapter 1

1 "Web traffic doubled from the previous day when the Starr report was released. CNN was scoring an as-yet-unheard of 300,000 clicks a minute. MSNBC tallied nearly 2 million hits – a one-day record – and about 20 million people read the report within two days" (David Kravets, "Sept. 11, 1998: Starr Report Showcases Net's Speed." At www.wired.com/thisdayintech/2009/09/dayintech_0911starrreport/). In contrast to the public release of the Starr Report, special prosecutor Leon Jaworski's investigative report into the Watergate affair was submitted only to Congress, and the documents remained under seal in the National Archives at the time of Clinton's impeachment (*New York Times*, September 10, 1998. David E. Rosenbaum, "Testing of a President: The Proceedings; As Prologue, the Past Looks Like a Bad Bet").

2 Audiences form their political subjectivities in multiple ways, and do not have to directly witness, live or on television, a political event for them to interpret and form opinions about it. George Bishop (2005: xiii–xvi) cautions against interpreting "knowledgeability" vis-à-vis "how closely are you following event x" poll indicators, and against anchoring broad theoretical generalizations on such poll results. What people know or feel about a subject, Bishop suggests, is not necessarily measured by questions probing viewership practices. For instance, polls taken during the House impeachment hearings indicated modest viewership ratings, high job approval ratings for Clinton, and yet majority support for some form of Congressional punishment (impeachment or censure) of the president. These results indicate that audiences' understandings of the hearings were rooted in past political occurrences as well as current events. See Sarfatti-Larson and Wagner-Pacifici (2001: 736, 767 fn. 3) for an interpretation of the viewership rating, and Richard L. Berke in the *New York Times* (December 15, 1998: A/24/1. "Impeachment: The Public; Polls Find Most Americans Still Oppose Impeachment and Now Frown on the G.O.P.") for press interpretations of the polls.

Despite not "following closely" the hearings on television, most Americans had knowledge about, and understandings of, what was occurring and why (see Brody 1998 and Brody and Jackman 1999, cited in Bennett 2002). Their interpretive frameworks were not based solely on the legal parameters of the House's case against Clinton, or on witnessing any one particular dramatic event, but on broader understandings of the characters involved and the various plotlines available to them, which had been created and recreated multiple times over the prior six years. Finally, critics play an important role in shaping and communicating the meanings of a performance.

3 Altheide and Snow (1979) argue that the institutions that control the means of symbolic distribution impose a "media logic" on politics, whereby political actors have had to adapt to corporate media time schedules and genre specifications, and shape their performances, communication styles, and the length of communicated messages accordingly.

4 In setting the sacred and the profane in binary opposition to one another, I build on Alexander and Smith's (1993) argument that the discourse of civil society is organized around binary codes, or "religiously" charged symbols that "set off the good from the bad, the desirable from the detested, the sainted from the demonic" (157). In his later work, Durkheim (1995 [1915]) failed to specify systematically the exact relationships between the sacred, profane, and the routine. Alexander and Smith (1993) theorize the concepts as standing in binary opposition to one another (202 fn. 36). "Sacred symbols provide images of purity and they charge those who are committed to them with protecting their referents from harm," they note, while "[p]rofane symbols embody this harm; they provide images of pollution, identifying actions, groups, and processes that must be defended against" (ibid.: 157).

The codes of American civil society (ibid.: 162–3) are as follows:

The discursive structure of actors

Democratic code	*Counter-democratic code*
Active	Passive
Autonomous	Dependent
Rational	Irrational
Reasonable	Hysterical
Calm	Excitable
Controlled	Passionate
Realistic	Unrealistic
Sane	Mad

The discursive structure of social relationships

Democratic code	*Counter-democratic code*
Open	Secret
Trusting	Suspicious
Critical	Deferential
Truthful	Deceitful

Straightforward	Calculating
Citizen	Enemy

The discursive structure of social institutions

Democratic code	*Counter-democratic code*
Rule regulated	Arbitrary
Law	Power
Equality	Hierarchy
Inclusive	Exclusive
Impersonal	Personal
Contractual	Ascriptive
Groups	Factions
Office	Personality

Chapter 2

1 Under fused conditions, the person inhabiting the role of leader is relatively unencumbered by audience skepticism about the actor's authority and narration. In fact, the potential for dissension or criticism barely exists, if at all. Scripts in these conditions closely resemble background cultural understandings, and tend to restate what audiences overwhelmingly perceived as obvious narrations of the order of things. Power inhered in the leader: the symbolic frameworks invoked during ritual proceedings were understood and accepted by all participants, and the lead actor's pronouncements were interpreted by sympathetic audiences as gospel. Perhaps the starkest example of the shift from ritual to performance, and a critical step toward defusion, is represented by the emergence of Greek theater from Dionysian religious rituals (Alexander 2004: 540–3). The suspicion of mimesis that Plato expressed in *The Republic* – that it cultivates the potential for duplicity in practitioners, manipulates audiences' emotions, and potentially represents a threat to the polis – and Aristotle's (1987 [384–322 BCE]) analysis of the constituent elements of tragedy represent critical reactions to the rise of a class of new professionals dedicated to creating and staging new texts, and learning and practicing the art of acting in order to be able to convincingly inhabit a variety of roles. In this light, Plato's and Aristotle's works on mimesis and poesis also presage the rise of the critic. If tragedy can work and inspire catharsis, then it can also *not* work; a cultural performance can fail, suggesting that the audience has some critical and interpretive distance from the performance, and is capable of judging the performers' efforts and interpretations as wanting and unconvincing. Nietzsche (1956 [1872]) bemoaned this birth of tragedy and the transformation of formerly marginal ritual participants into distanced, reposed audience members at a step further removed from the proceedings. Arguing that the rise of the genre represented the weakened power of the Dionysian ritual's ability to erode its participants' senses of self and to draw them unquestioningly into participating

in group practice, Nietzsche's elegy for the Dionysian ritual represents a nostalgic yearning for the fused conditions of the ritualized past.

2 Michael Schudson's (1998) examination of how the models of citizenship have changed over the course of America's history, for instance, reveals how the social bases of authority, legitimacy, and trust have become more defused and decentered, and illuminates how the understandings of the very purpose of politics have shifted from shared notions of the public good to an individualized process of defining what politics is for and what the arena should mean. Voting, his work suggests, has transformed from an organic ritual process based on demonstrations of solidarities, to more contingent performances undertaken by individually informed, rights-bearing citizens. The foundations of political *authority* have shifted profoundly, Schudson's characterization suggests: "Eighteenth-century American political authority was rule by gentlemen; the nineteenth century brought rule by numbers, majorities of associated men organized in parties; the twentieth-century American politics is rule by everyone, and no one, all at once" (ibid.: 7). Changes in the bases for *legitimacy claims* constituting who can run for and hold office suggest a similar trajectory, from legitimacy based on social station, "in which no one but a local notable would think of standing for office" (ibid.: 4), to demonstrations of party service and loyalty (6), to the contemporary conditions in which "political candidates [are] set adrift from party" and supported by "well-funded, professionally staffed interest groups" (9). The sources of *trust* on which citizens' have based their understandings of potential leaders have become defused as well, shifting from being based on "locally prominent, wealthy, and well-established families [who] can be trusted to represent" a cohesive polity (ibid.: 5), to solidarity and identification with a party, an understanding in which one's "connection to the party derives not from a strong sense that it offers better public policies but that your party is just your party, just as, in our own day, your high school is your high school," to present conditions in which citizens "trust their own canvass of newspapers, interest groups, parties, and other sources of knowledge, only occasionally supported by the immediacy of human contact" (8). Changes in shared understandings of *what politics means and what it is for* indicate defusion as well, shifting from "an organic view that the polity has a single common good" (ibid.: 5), to being centered on parties "more devoted to distributing offices than to advocating policies" (6), to one in which "multiple claimants compete to set the standards of political life" (8), and one in which "individual citizens empowered by the expansion of 'rights' all bid to define what counts as politics and what the experience of politics might mean" (9).

Schudson's descriptions of how *voting rituals* have changed over the past two centuries reiterate the defusion thesis as well. Certainly, voting day still represents a ritual process, but the character of the ritual has transformed considerably, from an organic proceeding, characterized by voters physically engaging the community, to a more mechanical, cognitive activity, in which the creation of political identities and reengagement with solidarities are more diffuse. Schudson describes voting during colonial and early America as an event in which property owners and then citizens, who "did indeed have a choice of candidates," would cast their selection in a loud clear voice, constituting "an act of restating and reaffirming the social hierarchy of the community" (ibid.: 4), and in the mid- to late nineteenth century as an open process in which the voter would cast a ballot "distinctive enough in shape and size" that it allowed for the voter's "party loyalty to be recognized" by anyone in the audience (6). Finally, by the mid- and late twentieth century, individuals drove to facilities cordoned off by law from the "carnivalesque" atmospheres and electioneering activities that suffused the prior versions, and entered private voting booths to make choices on their secret ballots.

3 Neustadt wrote this in 1979, and the chapter from which it is taken was included in the 1990 edition of *Presidential Power*.

4 "Going public is neither premised on nor does it promote a perception of America as a 'mass' society," Kernell states (2007: 121). "Nor does it reduce politics to a plebiscite in which the president seeks continually to bring the weight of national opinion to bear on policy deliberations in Washington. Governance under individualized pluralism remains largely a process of assembling coalitions both within party teams and across diverse interests and institutions."

5 Certainly defusion can create profound problems for an incumbent's relationship with the public: more often than not contemporary presidents will shudder at the invocation of the "Founding Fathers" in the press because the symbol is frequently used as a powerful source of criticism. Yet defusion can also sustain presidents in symbolic crisis: during the march to impeach Clinton, the president's actions were increasingly interpreted as private transgressions, and Clinton was routinely evaluated favorably vis-à-vis the ghost of Nixon past. His transgressions narrated as being largely confined to the private sphere, "Slick Willie" was deemed less polluting than "Tricky Dick."

6 For comparison's sake, to understand the television's quick rise and expansion: in 1950 there were 108 broadcast stations, in 1960 there were nearly 1,000, and in 1995 there were 1,699 stations (Mickelson 1998: 6).

7 Truman showed that he learned from FDR's public relations acumen as well as from his failures. Generally reluctant to directly court public opinion, as an underdog against Thomas Dewey in the 1948 election following FDR's death, Truman embarked on a "whistle stop" railroad tour through parts of America to build popular support by appealing directly to voters. Truman's was a populist effort, an attempt to speak directly with potential voters, yet he used means of symbolic production that projected presidential power by riding the 1940s version of Air Force One, the presidential railcar designed for FDR named the *Ferdinand Magellan*.

8 Support for Kennedy rose after the debate, from 47 to 49 percent, while support for Nixon dropped from 47 to 46 percent (Bruzzi 2000: 129).

9 *Christian Science Monitor*, March 5, 1981.

10 The *Atlanta Journal-Constitution* responded to Carter's candidacy in 1976 with the headline, "Jimmy Who for What?" Clinton experienced similar treatment from the *Arkansas Democrat Gazette*, whose managing editor, John Starr, introduced the nickname "Slick Willie" to describe Clinton when he was governor of Arkansas (John Tierney, *New York Times*, December 20, 1991).

Chapter 3

1 Clinton was the first two-term president since Woodrow Wilson to fail to win a majority of the popular vote in either election (Schier 2000: 6).

2 *Washington Post*, January 29, 1992: A/16. Thomas B. Edsall, "In New Hampshire; Mixed Feelings in Support Group for the Unemployed."

3 *Washington Post*, February 22, 1992: A/8. David Maraniss, "Tsongas Does Stand-Up for Georgia Democrats; Kerrey Video Memorable for Miscue."

4 *Washington Post*, April 26, 1992: A/18. E. J. Dionne Jr., "Clinton Seeks to Shift Focus toward Bush; Challenger Meets with Jesse Jackson."

5 For a discussion on parody's demands on the audience, see Hutcheon 2000.

6 "One wing of the floor is consultant James Carville's domain. It is where the marketing strategy for candidate Clinton is debated and devised. Carville has a chalkboard in the middle of the room, where he lists the basic rules of how to present the campaign. The key rule never changes. In Carville's blunt language, it is: 'The economy, stupid.' Another rule is to contrast Clinton's message of change with the Bush presidency's 'more of the same'" (*Washington Post*, August 3, 1992: A/8. David Maraniss, "A Paper's Political Afterlife; Ex-Arkansas Gazette Houses Clinton's HQ").

7 The two articles detailed the allegations contained in the lawsuit and Gennifer Flowers's assertion of a twelve-year affair with the governor.

8 See Joe Klein, "The Politics of Promiscuity," *Newsweek*, May 9, 1994: 16; and Klein (2002: 108).

9 Discussions of topics that reside at the boundary of legitimate news, like Clinton's private affairs, led the press to engage in self-critique and self-evaluation. Of course, being media outlets, the press engages in self-critique publicly in print and on talk shows. Its expressions of discomfort and guilt at pursuing boundary topics, on the one hand, are accompanied by rationales and self-justifications, on the other.

10 *Guardian*, January 18, 1992: 23. Martin Walker, "A Sexual History America May Leave on the Shelf; Times Have Changed Since Hart was Hounded." While calling the charges "ridiculous" framed them as the stuff of absurd comedy, suggesting that they were produced by Bush's political team served to inflate Clinton's importance. The framing portrayed Clinton as such a threat to Bush that the president had had to assign "operatives" to focus

solely on controlling the threat. It also portrayed Bush in a counter-democratic light, as working secretively and in the shadows.

11 *Washington Post*, January 25, 1992: A/10. Howard Kurtz, "Clintons Agree to Do '60 Minutes'; Airing Here in Doubt Because of Super Bowl Post-Game Conflict."

12 Reading from a prepared statement, DeeDee Meyers, Clinton's spokesperson, called the allegations "trash and untrue." "This is irresponsible, sleazy tabloid journalism" (*Guardian*, January 18, 1992: 1. Simon Tisdall and Martin Walker, "Democrat Brands Sex Charges 'Trash'"). This approach tends to silence mainstream journalists who want to distance themselves from "sleazy tabloid journalism" and force the press to engage in self-critique and self-justification.

13 *USA Today*, January 28, 1992: D/3. Brian Donlon, "Abbreviated '60 Minutes' Still a Ratings Winner."

14 CBS News Transcripts, January 26, 1992. *60 Minutes*, with Steve Kroft, "Governor and Mrs. Bill Clinton Discuss Adultery Accusations."

15 In an editorial titled "Odd Way to Choose a President," David Broder commented that "[t]he Bill and Hillary show is the latest, but surely not the last, step in the degradation of democracy by televised image-making, of substituting for political thought the audience catharsis of highly contrived dramas. It is the spiritual descendant of Richard Nixon's 1952 Checkers speech, of John Kennedy before the Houston Ministerial Association inquisitors, of Ronald Reagan declaiming, 'I paid for this microphone,' of Oliver North showing his chestful of medals to congressional investigators and Clarence Thomas accusing his critics of a public 'lynching'" (*Washington Post*, January 28, 1992: A/21).

16 CBS News estimated that approximately 40 million viewers watched the *60 Minutes* interview (*Washington Post*, January 28, 1992: E/6. John Carmody, "The TV Column").

17 A search of newspapers, magazines, and television and radio transcripts on Lexis Nexis indicates that the nickname was referenced approximately 4 times in January, 18 times in February, 68 times in March, and 101 times in April.

18 *Washington Post*, February 14, 1992: A/24. Editorial, "The Clinton Candidacy."

19 *Atlanta Journal-Constitution*, February 7, 1992: A/4. A. L. May, "Clinton Denies Ducking Vietnam Draft; Newspaper Says He Got Special Treatment from Arkansas Board."

20 *New York Times*, March 20, 1992: A/16/1. Gwen Ifill, "The 1992 Campaign: Front-Runner; Clinton Campaign Watches as Obstacles to the Democratic Nomination Fall."

21 Clinton's response to his New Hampshire defeat demonstrates the power of performance to constitute an event's meaning, and indicates the need for a robust semiotics of gesture in political analysis.

22 *Washington Post*, February 19, 1992: A/15. David Maraniss, "For Democrats Who Didn't Win, Victory Has Many Definitions."

23 Ibid.

24 *Boston Globe*, January 17, 1992: 1. Scot Lehigh, "Political Messages; Tsongas Seen Hurt by his Low-Key Style."

25 *New York Times*, March 20, 1992: A/16. Gwen Ifill, "The 1992 Campaign: Front-Runner; Clinton Campaign Watches as Obstacles to the Democratic Nomination Fall."

26 Ibid.

27 *Washington Post*, February 19, 1992: A/1. E. J. Dionne Jr., "Protest Vote Cuts Bush's N. H. Margin; Tsongas, Clinton Top Democratic Field; Buchanan Makes a Strong Showing."

28 *New York Times*, February 19, 1992: A/1/3. Robin Toner, "The 1992 Campaign: New Hampshire; Bush Jarred in First Primary; Tsongas Wins Democratic Vote."

29 *Washington Post*, February 19, 1992: C/1. Lloyd Grove, "Campaign Notebook; Buchanan Fodder; The Elephant that Roared: Bush Takes a Pasting."

30 *New York Times*, March 20, 1992: A/16/1. Gwen Ifill, "The 1992 Campaign: Front-Runner; Clinton Campaign Watches as Obstacles to the Democratic Nomination Fall."

31 *New York Times*, March 19, 1992: A/1/1. Kirk Johnson, "The 1992 Campaign: Connecticut; Clinton Taking the Campaign to Tsongas Turf: Connecticut is Looming as Vital Battleground."

32 *Washington Post*, March 20, 1992: A/17. Wílliam Booth, "Brown Unfazed by Ascension to 2nd Place; Reformist Candidate Calls Self a 'Moral Force.' "
   New York Times, March 26, 1992: A/20/1. Richard L. Berke, "The 1992 Campaign: Brown; Dark Horse or Not, Brown Enjoys Being Able to Strut."

33 *New York Times*, April 1, 1992: A/21/1. Elizabeth Kolbert, "The 1992 Campaign: Assessment; Clinton Hopes Debates Return Initiative to Him."

34 Ibid.

35 *Washington Post*, March 30, 1992: A/1. Thomas B. Edsall, "Clinton Admits '60s Marijuana Use; 'A Time or Two' during British Stay Disclosed in TV Debate."

36 Elizabeth Kolbert of the *New York Times* reacted to Clinton's verbal gymnastics thusly: "Watching the New York primary campaign unfold on television recently has been like watching one of those awkward movies in which the leading actor seems to be performing a part from the wrong film. Gov. Bill Clinton arrived in New York last week playing the role of an out-of-towner who comes to the big city, is treated like a hick, but still manages to charm the metropolis. The script that has actually been produced, however, goes more like this: Governor of small state comes to big city, is heckled, loses his cool and finally admits to having smoked marijuana" (*New York Times*, March 31, 1992: A/17/1. Elizabeth Kolbert, "The 1992 Campaign: Media; As Entertainment, this Campaign is Not So Bad").

37 *New York Times*, March 31, 1992: A/17/1. Elizabeth Kolbert, "The 1992 Campaign: Media; As Entertainment, this Campaign is Not So Bad."

38 *Washington Post*, March 31, 1992: Editorial, A/17. Richard Cohen, "Two Bill Clintons."

39 Ibid.

40 Tsongas, who had already officially dropped out, finished second.

41 *Washington Post*, July 18, 1992: A/1. Ruth Marcus and Edward Walsh, "Candidates Court Perot Supporters; Bush and Clinton Portray Selves as Agents of Change."

42 *New York Times*, July 19, 1992: 4/1/1. Robin Toner, "The Bounce; Blunt Reminders that It's Not Over Until Nov. 3."

43 *New York Times*, July 19, 1992: 1/20/1. Gwen Ifill, "The 1992 Campaign: The Democrats; Clinton–Gore Caravan Refuels with Spirit from Adoring Crowds."

44 On June 26, 1990, President Bush signed a bipartisan bill that increased taxes in response to a ballooning budget deficit. A recession set in anyway.

45 In the interview in which he agreed with Reagan's characterization, Bush said he regretted the tax increase because of the "flack it's taking" and because of the "political grief" it caused him, not because of any negative consequences it spurred in the economy (*Atlanta Journal-Constitution*, March 3, 1992: A/1. Dick Williams, "Bush Sorry for Breaking Promise of No New Taxes: 'If I had it to do over, I wouldn't,' he says"). Ann Devroy of the *Washington Post* quoted a Bush senior official as saying that campaign aides believed Bush "would never reestablish his credibility with the American people" if he did not admit he had erred in entering the 1990 pact. Without such a confession, the official said, "all his pledges [would] ring hollow" (March 4, 1992: A/1. "Breaking Tax Pledge a Mistake, Bush says; Repudiating 1990 Budget Deal, President Cites 'Political Grief' ").

46 CBS News Transcripts, July 1, 1992. *This Morning*, Paula Zahn and Harry Smith, "President Bush Answers Questions about His Campaign – Part II."

47 *Washington Post*, July 3, 1992: A/1. Thomas B. Edsall, "For Bush, It's 'Not Good News'; Data Undercut, Campaign Plan."

48 ABC News Transcripts, July 26, 1992. *This Week with David Brinkley*.

49 *Chicago Sun Times*, July 29, 1992: 35. Rowland Evans and Robert Novak, "Obsession with Quayle Stalls Bush Campaign."

50 *Atlanta Journal-Constitution*, July 30, 1992: A/12. George Will, "If George Bush Wants to Help His Party, He'll Withdraw from the Race."

51 CBS News Transcripts, August 17, 1992. Campaign '92: The Republican National Convention. Special Report, with Dan Rather, "Patrick Buchanan Addresses the Convention."

52 *Washington Post*, October 17, 1992: A/23. Jim Hoagland, "Bush's Place in History."

There is ample evidence indicating that Bush failed poorly with many other viewers. John Harris, also a *Washington Post* columnist, reported on a study conducted at Virginia Commonwealth University, which used "debate meters" to gauge uncommitted voters' reactions to what the candidates said. "Bush scored one of his two most negative responses of the evening with his response to Hall," Harris reported. "His other low point was when he attacked Democratic presidential nominee Bill Clinton's character. 'It spoke to the perception that here is someone who is out of touch,' said Robert Holsworth, a Virginia Commonwealth political scientist who helped conduct the debate-meter experiment" (*Washington Post*, October 16, 1992: A/12. John F. Harris, "Putting Them on the Spot Put Her in the Spotlight; At Debate, Va. Woman Sought Human Touch").

53 ABC News Transcripts, October 15, 1992. "Special: The '92 Vote: The 2nd Presidential Debate."

54 Ibid.

55 *MacNeil/Lehrer NewsHour* transcript, October 16, 1992. "Making His Case; '92 – Voice of the People; '92 – Gergen & Shields."

56 *Washington Post*, December 30, 1992: A/19. Robert J. Samuelson, "Bill the Bold, Bill the Pleaser; The Best Thing for the New President to do is Concentrate on a Few Big Problems."

Chapter 4

1 55.1 percent of the voting-age population represents the highest percentage since Nixon's 1972 re-election victory.

2 The high rate of member turnover in the House of Representatives during the election and the loss of ten seats by the majority Democrats, when combined with Democratic challenger Clinton defeating the incumbent Bush for the presidency, amounted to an "unusual year" and an "unusual election" (Jacobson 1993).

3 The editorial's title was "A Monumental, Fragile Mandate" and contained the synopsis "What all that adds up to is an electoral college victory of monumental but tenuous proportion" (*New York Times*, November 4, 1992: A/30/1). In fact, neither of Clinton's electoral victories represented strong mandates. In 1996, Clinton would become the first second-term president since Woodrow Wilson (1913–21) to fail to win a majority of the popular vote.

4 *USA Today*, January 28, 1993: A/7. Richard Benedetto, "Clinton's Poll Numbers Reflect Controversies."

5 Ibid.

6 Clinton had scripted the "economy, stupid" as his foremost concern upon entering office, yet one of his first policy initiatives concerned gays in the military, a cause that found little favor in a citizenry looking for economic relief. Zoe Baird, nominated for attorney general, was revealed to have hired an illegal alien, and Clinton withdrew his nomination of Lani Guinier amid constructions of the nominee as one of "Clinton's Quota Queens" (*Wall Street Journal*, April 30, 1993. Clint Bolick), one who would advocate for instituting racial quotas.

7 *Time Magazine*, June 7, 1993. Michael Duffy, "The Incredible Shrinking President."

8 *US News and World Report*, June 14, 1993: 114/23/40. Matthew Cooper, Kenneth T. Walsh, Donald Baer, and Gloria Borger, "A Question of Competence."

9 The first sentence of Bob Woodward's (1994: 11) introduction to his book on Clinton's first budget is, "At the heart of Bill Clinton's 1992 presidential campaign was his pledge to fix the economy and to use his presidency to do it."

10 ABC News Transcripts, November 4, 1992. *Special with Ted Koppel*, "72 Hours to Victory: Behind the Scenes with Bill Clinton" (referenced in Klein [2002: 44]).

11 Clinton's pursuit of traditionally liberal causes like reducing restrictions to abortions and opening the armed services to homosexuals "evoked disapproval from a sizeable number of Americans and led to the perception that Clinton was paying attention to controversial social issues at the expense of economic issues" (Schier 2000: 128; see also Woodward 1994: 101).

12 The group's leaders estimated their numbers at around 250,000 and claimed it was the largest March to date (*Washington Post*, January 23, 1993: A/1. Amy Goldstein and Richard Morin, "Clinton Cancels Abortion Restrictions of Reagan–Bush Era; Thousands Voice Opposition in 20th March for Life").

13 ABC News Transcripts, November 20, 1992. *Nightline*, Ted Koppel, "Election Promise, Presidential Minefield."

14 Initially Clinton called for the armed services to stop inquiring into service personnel's sexuality and to not treat declared or outed homosexuals any differently from heterosexuals. The latter item was dropped in the compromise, which essentially returned the policy and practice to the status quo ante (see *New York Times*, May 12, 1993: A/1/2. Eric Schmitt, "Compromise on Military Gay Ban Gaining Support among Senators").

15 *New York Times*, May 21, 1993: B/9/3. Neil A. Lewis, "Clinton Faces Battle over a Civil Rights Nominee."

16 *Wall Street Journal*, April 30, 1993. Clint Bolick, "Clinton's Quota Queens."

17 *New York Times*, May 21, 1993: B/9/3. Neil A. Lewis, "Clinton Faces Battle over a Civil Rights Nominee."

18 The nomination and passing of Joycelyn Elders (July 15, 1993) is a good example too. The Left championed her as a refreshing "straight talker" on issues like sex and drugs. The Right saw her as the epitome of permissiveness and moral relativism. Clinton forced her to resign in Dec. '94. Also, in Nov. 1995, the *Boston Globe* published a piece titled "A Growing List of 'Ethically Challenged' Clinton Aides," which listed Clinton appointees that were "either under investigation and/or forced to resign." The article shows how this "discursive domain" remained a resource for a kind of sarcastic criticism of Clinton's leadership.

19 *St. Louis Post-Dispatch*, June 6, 1993: A/1. Jon Sawyer, "Guinier Mess Leaves Some Questioning Clinton's Beliefs."

20 *Washington Post*, January 23, 1993: A/1. Amy Goldstein, "Clinton Cancels Abortion Restrictions of Reagan–Bush Era; Thousands Voice Opposition in 20th March for Life."

21 The internal mayhem at the White House quickly became legendary: "The public image was of callow, arrogant aides wandering about in dungarees, pulling unnecessary all-nighters and littering the West Wing with empty pizza boxes and cans of Diet Coke" (Klein 2002: 59).

22 Congressman Bernie Sanders of Vermont was elected as an Independent but caucused with the Democrats.

23 The stimulus package failed after Senate Republicans led by Bob Dole mounted an "unprecedented party-line filibuster" to its original form (Schier 2000: 11). A stimulus package passed, but it was just a sliver of its original, multi-billion dollar form.

24 *Washington Post*, February 24, 1993: A/19. David S. Broder, "Beware the 'Trust' Deficit."

25 Clinton initially used the phrase "climate of suspicion" to criticize media coverage of his Administration. The *Washington Times* turned the phrase back on the president, using it to characterize the atmosphere surrounding the Clinton White House. In terms of the discourse of civil society, by 1995 the Clinton team recognized the need to change their scandal management techniques. Bob Woodward (1999: 286) quotes Mark Fabiani, the publicity agent for Clinton's "scandal management team" (aka "rapid response team"), stating, " 'Look, we've got to build our reputation for openness' " with the American public to both reduce the climate of suspicion and consequently to become more politically effective in terms of policy.

26 *New York Times*, June 17, 1993: A/22/1. William Glaberson, "The Capital Press and the President: Fair Coverage or Unreined Adversity?"

27 Jeffrey Toobin examines in great detail one person's efforts to bring down the Clintons, that of Bill's old "friend" from Oxford, Cliff Jackson. Jackson helped get Paula Jones's story into the *American Spectator* and the *Los Angeles Times*, helped Michael Isikoff investigate the Jones story, and helped move the topic of Whitewater into the public arena (Toobin 2000: 1–68). Michael Isikoff (1999) is also pretty straightforward about the conservative elements that helped him develop his story, and is aware of the fact that his critics see him as a simple tool or vehicle for the Right. See Joan Didion (2001) for a critical piece about Michael Isikoff's approach to journalism.

28 *Washington Post*, January 18, 1992: A/1. Dan Balz, "Clinton, Kerrey: A New Set of Questions; Old Tensions Resonate in Political Dialogue of Vietnam Generation."

29 Vince Foster had been the subject of one of the *Wall Street Journal*'s "Who is . . ." series (June 17, 1993), in which the paper accused him of "corner-cutting and casual abuses of power." He referenced the editorial in his suicide note, which greatly angered the Clintons and escalated their battles with the press to full-scale war (Klein 2002: 107).

30 The *Wall Street Journal* (January 5, 1996: A/8/1) editorial revisited 1993's Travelgate, the first lady's work at the Rose Law Firm, her commodities trades, and her work on the health-care plan in light of new information that contradicted her original claims that she had played no role in the travel office firings. The editorial indicated that the Clintons were not who they had presented themselves to be, and that they had secret, hidden selves that demanded suspicion and caution.

31 Ruth Bader Ginsburg, who had just given a speech accepting her nomination to the Supreme Court.

32 *Washington Post*, June 15, 1993: A/13. Howard Kurtz, "One Question Too Many for Clinton; Query by ABC's Hume Provokes Outburst."

33 *Plain Dealer* (Cleveland, Ohio), June 15, 1993: A/4. Thomas J. Brazaitis, "Clinton Nips Question in Bud."

34 In early July 1993, the White House released the report from its internal investigation.

35 *New York Times*, May 20, 1993: A/1/5. Richard L. Berke, "White House Ousts Its Travel Staff."

36 *New York Times*, May 22, 1993: 1/18/1. Editorial, "White House Follies; The Gang that Can't Fire Straight."

37 *New York Times*, May 25, 1993: A/18/1. Thomas L. Friedman, "White House Asked Aid of F.B.I. in Dismissals."

38 In June 1996, "Filegate" entered the public sphere.

39 *New York Times*, May 28, 1993: A/29/1. Anthony Lewis, "Abroad at Home; The Clinton Mystery."

40 The *Washington Post* reported the Justice Department's investigative intentions in a front-page story on October 31, 1993, entitled "U.S. is Asked to Probe Failed Arkansas S&L."

41 *Washington Post*, October 13, 1993: A/4. Ann Devroy, "Clinton Weaves Pledge of Security for All Americans; International Events Overshadow Domestic Issues Speech at University of North Carolina."

42 "In a two-week period surrounding his Sept. 22 speech on health care, Mr. Clinton's approval–disapproval rating was 43–43 ... In the days after the speech, the rating shifted to 49–35," while "53 percent favored the Clinton health plan and ... 25 percent opposed it," reported the *Dallas Morning News* (October 7, 1993: A/3. Carl P. Leubsdorf, "Clinton Moves Up in Opinion Polls; Attention to Health Care Cited; Republicans Believe Gains Transitory").

43 *New York Times*, May 3, 1993: A/1/1. Robert Pear, "Health-Care Costs May be Increased $100 Billion a Year." A month later *USA Today* reported that "President Clinton will consider a value-added tax as a way to fund health-care reform," based on an unscripted comment by Secretary of Health and Human Services Donna Shalala (April 15, 1993: A/4. Bill Nichols, "Back and Forth on National Sales Tax; Clinton Says Idea Can't be Ruled Out").

44 PBS News Transcripts, September 23, 1993. *The MacNeil/Lehrer NewsHour*, "About Face; Coming to Terms; Cost of Peace; the People Rest."

45 See Toobin 2000.
46 *New York Times*, December 19, 1993: 1/28/4. David Johnston, "Missing White House File is Sought."
47 Many of the Clintons' friends and advisors contributed to the perception that a conspiracy was behind the Administration's scandal problems. The conspiracy atmosphere "was encouraged by a truly odd, almost Shakespearean retinue of personal advisors – the First Lady always seemed to keep one such about, from her friend Susan Thomases to the former journalist Sidney Blumenthal – who earned their keep by floating vast, obscure, Manichean fantasies about the world outside the gates. (Blumenthal, called 'Grassy Knoll' within the White House because of his conspiracy fetish, was famous for his chart of the Great Right-Wing Conspiracy to unseat the Clintons)," Klein (2002: 106) reported.
48 *Washington Post*, January 27, 1994: A/2. Mary McGrory, "Clinton's Reagan-esque Ritual."
49 Federal News Service Transcripts, January 25, 1994. "State of the Union Address by President Bill Clinton."
50 For instance, an editorial in the *Wall Street Journal* (Wilfried Prewo, February 1, 1994) disassembled Clinton's favorable reference in the State of the Union speech to Germany's universal health-care program, concluding that "if you want to copy pages out of the German social policy book, have your checkbook handy." The typically left-of-center *New Republic* published a fear-mongering editorial that started with the warning, "If you're not worried about the Clinton health bill, keep reading," and warned that decisions about medical practices and treatment "will be made by the government, not by you or your doctor" (*New Republic*, February 7, 1994. Elizabeth McCaughey, "What the Clinton Plan Will Do for You").
51 ABC News Transcripts, April 19, 1994. *Nightline*, with Ted Koppel. Rebroadcast of segment from the Rush Limbaugh radio show.
52 *New York Times*, August 28, 1994: 1/1/3. Adam Clymer, "The Health Care Debate: Washington Postmortem; With Health Overhaul Dead, a Search for Minor Repairs."
53 *New York Times*, September 4, 1994: 1/1/6. Richard L. Berke, "Democrats Glum about Prospects as Elections Near."
54 Ibid.
55 "In the Congressional races there'll be over 30 campaigns using some form of the morph and almost all exclusively using Clinton as the bad guy," said Dan Leonard, director of communications for the National Republican Congressional Committee (*New York Times*, October 29, 1994: 1/9/1. "The 1994 Campaign: Advertising; Now Playing in Politics, Latest Techniques of Hollywood"). See also Richard L. Berke, "The 1994 Elections: Voters the Outcome; Asked to Place Blame, Americans in Survey Chose: All of the Above" (*New York Times*, November 10, 1994: B/1/5.).
56 *New York Times*, May 7, 1995: 1/1/1. Todd S. Purdum, "Desperately in Need of Winning Streak, Clinton Finds One."

Chapter 5

1 *USA Today*, January 3, 1995: A/4. Richard Wolf, "Gingrich: Man of the Moment."

2 *Washington Post*, October 20, 1994: A/1. Dan Balz, "The Whip Who Would be Speaker; Gingrich Sees Role as 'Transformational.' "

3 *USA Today*, January 3, 1995: A/4. Richard Wolf, "Gingrich: Man of the Moment."

4 *Washington Post*, February 26, 1995: W/8. "Spin Cycles: A Guide to Media Behavior in the Age of Newt, Part 1 of 2."

5 Military debacles in Somalia and Haiti fueled these constructions.

6 *USA Today*, July 20, 1994: A/4. Richard Benedetto, "Clinton 'Suffering the Death of 1,000 Cuts'; Public Losing Patience with President's Style."
   USA Today, July 21, 1994: A/4. Jessica Lee, "Democrats in an Uproar."
   Columbus Dispatch (Ohio), December 18, 1994: B/2. Editorial, "U-Turn on Tax Cut; Clinton Changes Course in Bid to Survive."
   Washington Post, September 21, 1994: A/2. Mary McGrory, "Exit William the Waffler."

7 *Columbus Dispatch*, December 18, 1994: B/2. Editorial, "U-Turn on Tax Cut; Clinton Changes Course in Bid to Survive."

8 *USA Today*, July 20, 1994: A/4. Richard Benedetto, "Clinton 'Suffering the Death of 1,000 Cuts'; Public Losing Patience with President's Style."

9 *New York Times*, November 20, 1994: 4/14/1. Editorial, "Clear but Hypocritical."

10 On the timing of symbolic interventions, *Newsweek*'s portrayal of Gingrich as "mad" suggested both anger and instability, the latter of which represents a polluting symbol in the discourse-of-civil-society sense of the term.

11 *Atlanta Journal-Constitution*, October 1, 1994: A/14. Dick Williams, "Gingrich and GOP Take the Initiative."

12 The heights Gingrich reached so quickly registered internationally as well: " 'The mood is evident even abroad,' a senior British minister said, 'no point in trying to deal with the Administration any more. They've had the stuffing knocked out of them,' " the *New York Times* reported (December 15, 1994: B/16/4. R. W. Apple Jr., "Comeback Kid's Tightest Corner Yet"). *Der Spiegel*, Germany's most widely circulated news magazine at the time, asked if Gingrich was now "America's surrogate President," while billboards in metro stations in Paris wondered if Gingrich was now the person who "dictates his law to the U.S.A." (*New York Times*, March 1, 1995: A/2/3. Elaine Sciolino, "As World Sees Gingrich: Hurrah Here, Hoot There").

13 Joe Klein (2001: 140) said of Gingrich: "there was a fair amount of beltway chatter that the Speaker was now a virtual Prime Minister; certainly he seemed the most important politician in America."

14 The symbolic practice of invoking prime minister to describe the new Speaker's status and power represents a cultural sociological opportunity.

As a symbol, the prime minister is like a tool used by journalists to communicate that the new Speaker inhabited a more elevated status and powerful position than a typical Speaker of the House. However, since the tool was drawn from a non-native political-symbolic discursive landscape, or cultural milieu, it probably had the effect of confusing if not disconcerting some in the American audience.

15 *Washington Times*, April 4, 1995: A/9. Alan McConagha, "Nation: Inside Politics." Discussing Gingrich on *Inside Washington, Newsweek*'s Evan Thomas commented that the new Speaker repeatedly compared himself to Winston Churchill and Charles de Gaulle, and then agreed with the comparisons in a qualitative way. The metaphors were reported and repeated, indicating how a political actor's self-understandings morph into a public sign. Yet the process does not advance without critical reflection. A *Washington Post* columnist commented on the use of the metaphors a few days later, writing that "[j]ust this past week a writer for a national newsmagazine compared Gingrich to Churchill and de Gaulle," adding that chants of "Newt! Newt! Newt!" accompanied the new Speaker's swearing-in ceremony, all of which seemed to indicate that "[o]ddest of all is the way we seem to forget our own very recent history, the way the cycle of promise, expectation and disappointment seems endlessly to repeat" (April 9, 1995: C/1. "100 Days of Our Lives; In the Age of OJ, Does the 'Contract' Deliver More Hype than History?").

16 *Washington Post*, January 11, 1995: A/1. Kenneth J. Cooper, "Speaker Tries to Adjust to Life in the Spotlight; Intense Scrutiny Dogs Gingrich as He Assumes Leadership Role."

17 Ibid.

18 *New York Times*, November 20, 1994: 4/14/1. Editorial, "Clear but Hypocritical."

19 *USA Today*, January 20, 1995. The Hotline, "CNN/USA Today: Poll Update."
   Plain Dealer (Cleveland, OH), January 28, 1995: A/8. " 'Contract with America' Makes Some Progress."

20 *Atlanta Journal-Constitution*, March 30, 1995: A/10. Jeffrey Scott, "CNN Grants Gingrich Free TV Coverage." CNN launched on June 1, 1980. The first Persian Gulf War in 1991 elevated CNN to nationwide attention and made it a staple in nationwide news consumption. These events accelerated news coverage, launched the "24-hour news cycle," and increased demand for "live coverage" of "breaking events." Getting CNN to cover his 100 days victory dance was a sizeable coup for Gingrich, as CNN was the only news alternative to the big three networks at the time. All of these networks were aided by the 1995 O. J. Simpson trial, and many emerging television commentators sharpened their broadcast and journalistic teeth during that media parade. Add the increase in home internet usage and MSNBC and FOX News cable channels hitting the airwaves on July 15, 1996, and October 7, 1996, respectively, and 1998's Clinton–Lewinksy scandal, and a perfect storm was created of clashing media outlets.

21 PBS aired *Newshour* and other news-related shows, as well as the BBC's world news coverage.

22 *Washington Post*, October 14, 1994: A/1. Ann Devroy et al., "Gingrich Foresees Corruption Probe by a GOP House; Party Could Wield Subpoenas Against 'Enemy' Administration."

23 *Washington Post*, February 26, 1995: Magazine, W/8, "Spin Cycles: A Guide to Media Behavior in the Age of Newt, Part 1 of 2."

24 *USA Today*, November 11, 1994: A/3. Judi Hasson, "The Bullish Newt: Gingrich Has No Plans to Back Down."

25 CBS News Transcripts, January 5, 1995, *Eye To Eye*, with Connie Chung, "Speaker of the House; Kathleen and Bob Gingrich and Their Daughters Discuss Newt Gingrich's Life and Rise in Politics." The incident polluted news media as much as Speaker Gingrich at the time because interviewer Chung coaxed Mrs. Gingrich into the admission by saying, "Why don't you just whisper it to me, just between you and me?"

26 *Time Magazine*, December 5, 1994. Michael Duffy, "What's on Jesse's Mind?"

27 CNN Transcripts, November 19, 1994. *Evans & Novak*, with Rowland Evans and Robert Novak. Senator Jesse Helms sent Clinton a letter requesting that he postpone action on the General Agreement on Tariffs and Trade (GATT) treaty to a later session of Congress, which he knew Clinton would not be able to do or be interested in doing. The letter was portrayed as Helms sending a "threat" to the president in a political cartoon penned by "Herblock" (*Washington Post* political cartoonist Herbert Block), and was reported as a kind of odd, inappropriate threat by various news producers.

28 *Washington Post*, November 7, 1994: D/1. Kim Masters, "The Politics of Hate."

29 *Washington Post*, November 10, 1994: D/4. Howard Kurtz, "Talk Radio Hosts, Waking Up on the Right Side of the Bed."

30 *Washington Post*, November 30, 1994: A/27. David S. Broder, "Pit Bulls; Jesse Helms is Just a Symptom of What You Might Call the GOP's Meanness Problem."

31 *USA Today*, January 3, 1995; A/4. Richard Wolf, "Gingrich: Man of the Moment."

32 *Washington Post*, October 20, 1994: A/1. Dan Balz, "The Whip Who Would be Speaker; Gingrich Sees Role as 'Transformational.'"

33 *Washington Times*, November 12, 1994: A/13. "Gingrich: 'There Will be No Compromise.'"

34 *New York Times*, March 1, 1995: A/2/3. Elaine Sciolino, "As World Sees Gingrich: Hurrah Here, Hoot There."
    Independent (London), March 26, 1995: 14. John Carlin, "America Turns Against Contract with Newt; US Congress/Gingrich Revolution Hits Trouble."

35 *USA Today*, January 3, 1995, A/4. Richard Wolf, "Gingrich: Man of the Moment."

36 *Christian Science Monitor*, March 24, 1995: 1. Kurt Shillinger, "Splits in the GOP Ranks Mar 100-Day March Through 'Contract.'"
37 Ibid.
38 *San Francisco Chronicle*, March 27, 1995: A/18. Editorial, "Gingrich Must Learn the Art of Compromise."
39 *New York Times*, November 20, 1994: 4/14/1. Editorial, "Clear but Hypocritical."
40 *Washington Post*, October 20,1994: A/1. Dan Balz, "The Whip Who Would be Speaker; Gingrich Sees Role as 'Transformational.'"
41 *Washington Post*, November 30, 1994: A/27. David S. Broder, "Pit Bulls; Jesse Helms is Just a Symptom of What You Might Call the GOP's Meanness Problem."
42 Ibid.
43 *New York Times*, March 19, 1995: 1/24/1. Katharine Q. Seelye, "The Top Man in the House Holds a Lower Place Among the People."
44 Ibid.
45 *New York Times*, January 25, 1995: A/1/4. R. W. Apple Jr., "State of the Union: News Analysis; A Deflated Presidency."
46 *USA Today*, October 12, 1994: A/10. Bill Nichols, "Clinton's Plea to the Voters: Let Me Finish."
47 *Washington Post*, September 20, 1994: A/2. Mary McGrory, "Exit William the Waffler."
   USA Today, October 12, 1994: A/10. Bill Nichols, "Clinton's Plea to the Voters: Let Me Finish."
   Newsweek, May 9, 1994: 16. Joe Klein, "The Politics of Promiscuity."
   USA Today, July 20, 1994: A/4. Richard Benedetto, "Clinton 'Suffering the Death of 1,000 Cuts'; Public Losing Patience with President's Style."
48 *Washington Post*, November 10, 1994: A/1. Dan Balz, "After the Republican Sweep; Clinton, GOP Leaders Offer Cooperation."
49 Ibid.
50 *New York Times*, December 15, 1994: B/16/4. R. W. Apple Jr., "Comeback Kid's Tightest Corner Yet."
51 Ibid.
52 *New York Times*, November 21, 1994: A/14/1. Editorial, "What Now for Mr. Clinton?"
53 *Washington Post*, January 8, 1995: W/12. David Osborne, "Can this President be Saved? A Six-point Plan to Beat the One-term Odds."
54 *New York Times*, December 15, 1994: B/16/4. R. W. Apple Jr., "Comeback Kid's Tightest Corner Yet."
55 Ibid.
56 Breaking his post-midterm silence, Clinton declared "unequivocally that he would run for re-election" and that he "was 'not worried' about the possibility of a Democratic primary challenge" (*New York Times*, December 30, 1994: A/1/3). He reshuffled his staff, a practice which, along with traveling abroad, signals to the public and press that the president is doing *something*. It signaled

activity and resolve. Klein (2002) reported that Clinton's two most important staff decisions were keeping Leon Panetta as his chief of staff and bringing the political strategist Dick Morris back into his sphere of confidence. Clinton had moved Panetta from directing the Office of Budget and Management to chief of staff before the midterms. Panetta used his new role to impose much-needed discipline on the president and his staff, both controlling access to the president, and limiting the president's time in front of the TV cameras. Dick Morris was given the code name "Charlie," in order to keep his influence on Clinton secret, even from Clinton's other advisors and Cabinet members. Morris encouraged Clinton's movements toward the political center, counseled Clinton to co-opt the Republican agenda, and made public polling the principal tool in shaping policy strategies (see Klein 2002: Ch. 6; and *New York Times*, December 30, 1994: A/1/3. Todd S. Purdum, "Two Confident Fighters Ready to Take On a New Year; Clinton's Course: Islands of Constants in Ocean of Political Change").

57 *New York Times*, May 7, 1995: 1/1/1. Todd S. Purdum, "Desperately in Need of Winning Streak, Clinton Finds One." See also Skrowronek (1997: 450, 453), and Klein (2002: 138–9).

58 Clinton introduced his notion of a "New Covenant" thusly:

As we enter a new era, we need a new set of understandings, not just with government but even more important with one another as Americans ...

I call it the New Covenant, but it's grounded in a very, very old idea: that all Americans have not just a right but a solemn responsibility to rise as far as their God-given talents and determination can take them, and to give something back to their communities and their country in return. Opportunity and responsibility, they go hand in hand; we can't have one without the other, and our national community can't hold together without both.

Our New Covenant is a new set of understandings for how we can equip our people to meet the challenges of the new economy, how we can change the way our government works to fit a different time, and above all, how we can repair the damaged bonds in our society and come together behind our common purpose.

We must have dramatic change in our economy, our government and ourselves.

59 *New York Times*, January 25, 1995: A/1/4. R. W. Apple Jr., "State of the Union: News Analysis; A Deflated Presidency."

60 *South Bend Tribune* (Indiana), January 27, 1995: A/7. David Broder, "Address Ranks as an Opportunity Lost."

61 *Washington Post*, February 26, 1995: W/8. "Spin Cycles: A Guide to Media Behavior in the Age of Newt, Part 1 of 2."

62 Federal News Service Transcripts, March 3, 1995. "President Bill Clinton Press Conference: The Old Executive Office Building."

63 *Washington Post*, March 24, 1995: C/1. Howard Kurtz, "The Snooze at 11; White House Correspondents Wait While Nothing Happens."
64 Ibid.
65 The last sentence of the Kurtz article reads: "Mark Knoller, Plante's colleague in the cramped CBS booth, sounds an optimistic note. 'All we need is a good war or a terrorist incident,' he says." The Oklahoma City bombing occurred the following month. (*Washington Post*, March 24, 1995: C/1. Howard Kurtz, "The Snooze at 11; White House Correspondents Wait While Nothing Happens.")
66 The term "gravitas" became an often-used measuring stick during the 2000 electoral competition, a signifier of character and masculinity that mimicked the symbolic inflations and deflations Clinton and Gingrich experienced in the mid-1990s.
67 *New York Times*, April 19, 1995: A/1/4. Todd S. Purdum, "Clinton Seeks New Welfare Bill, Saying G.O.P. Plan is Too Harsh."
68 *Washington Post*, April 20, 1995: D/1. John F. Harris, "The Snooze Conference; Networks, Viewers Not Tuned In to Clinton." Political consultants know this, of course. The article states, "Michael Deaver, who directed communications for Reagan, said Clinton has only himself to blame if his conference had little impact. 'If the president is doing something, is a leader, and is making news, every television station in the world is going to cover it,' he said. Reagan administration officials planned news conferences only when they had big news that they wanted to share, and worked hard beforehand 'to build up the drama.'"
69 *New York Times*, April 19, 1995: A/1/4. Todd S. Purdum, "Clinton Seeks New Welfare Bill, Saying G.O.P. Plan is Too Harsh."
70 *Seattle Times*, April 19, 1995: A/3. Robert A. Rankin and Ranny Green, "Clinton Not Necessarily News, Say Networks."
71 Ibid.
72 *Washington Post*, April 19, 1995: A/1. Ann Devroy and John F. Harris, "'The President is Relevant'; Clinton Asserts His Role in Political Debates."
73 *USA Today*, April 19, 1995: A/10. Bill Nichols, "Clinton Speaking Up to Get His Voice Back; Says Little New in His Attempt to Shoulder Way into the Debate."
74 Q: Mr. President, you've been quoted as saying that you believe that Robert McNamara's new book in which he essentially says that the U.S. had no underlying basis for the war in Vietnam vindicates your own opposition to the war. I wonder if we could hear you talk about that, and also if in this time of reflection you feel vindicated about your handling of your own draft status?

President Clinton: On the second matter I have said all I have to say about it. On the first, I believe our policy was incorrect. I think the book supports that conclusion. But I do not believe that the book should be used as yet another opportunity to divide the United States over that. We should learn from what happened, and resolve not to repeat our mistakes, honor the service of Americans, and go forward together. That's what we should be doing.

75 *Washington Post*, April 19, 1995: A/1. Ann Devroy, John F. Harris, "'The President is Relevant'; Clinton Asserts His Role in Political Debate."

76 Whereas Novak likened Clinton's "relevance" comment to Nixon's infamous November 1973 "I am not a crook" failed performative (*Chicago Sun-Times*, April 24, 1995: 27. "Relevant Concerns about Clinton"), Phil Gramm associated it with President Carter's July 1979 "crisis of confidence" speech (CBS News Transcripts, April 19, 1995. *This Morning*, with Harry Smith, "Phil Gramm, Republican Presidential Candidate, Discusses President Clinton's News Conference and Welfare Reform"). William Safire called Clinton's response "the most defensive declarative sentence spoken by a president since Nixon's 'I am not a crook' " (*New York Times*, May 14, 1995. "On Language; Political Figures of Speech").

77 *Washington Post*, April 20, 1995: D/1. John F. Harris, "The Snooze Conference; Networks, Viewers Not Tuned In to Clinton." See also: *Seattle Times*, April 19, 1995: A/3. Robert A. Rankin and Ranny Green, "Clinton Not Necessarily News, Say Networks."

Chapter 6

1 *New York Times*, April 20, 1995: A/22/1. Editorial, "Relevance is Not Enough, Mr. Clinton."

2 Ibid.

3 *New York Times*, April 20, 1995 (late edition): A/1/1. Headline, "Terror in Oklahoma City: The Investigation; At Least 31 are Dead, scores are Missing after Car Bomb Attack in Oklahoma City Wrecks 9-story Federal Office Building."

4 See Smith's (1991) article on the ritual dynamics of warfare, the moral codes that govern the appropriate use of violence, and the boundaries of attack, in the Falklands conflict.

5 *Washington Post*, April 20, 1995: D/4. John Carmody, "The TV Column."

6 Federal News Service Transcripts, April 19, 1995. "Statement by President Bill Clinton and Briefing by Attorney General Janet Reno. Subject: Bombing of Federal Building in Oklahoma City, Oklahoma."

7 Two points are worth further consideration. First, earlier I mentioned that events like the bombing reveal structures at the same time that they create moments of contingency. Contingencies should be addressed, such as: could the bombing have been interpreted in other ways, celebrated even, or at least met with more vocal support? The symbolic reservoir existed for it: Thomas Jefferson's famous phrase "Every generation needs a new revolution," for instance, or, "I hold it that a little revolution now and then is a good thing, and as necessary in the political world as storms in the physical." And all of the Republican talk about governmental intrusion into Americans' lives and the more socialist tendencies of Clinton's left-of-center administration provided a pool of recent discursive material that had found popular support in the months

preceding the bombing. The counterfactual question of whether interpretations could have been otherwise is in no way meant as normative support
of the bombing, of course, but is posed analytically. The act was terroristic and
political, representative of a sizeable, radical public, and deeply symbolic; that
is, two years to the day of Waco's burning at the hands of Janet Reno's
enforcement debacle. The timing was noticed and reported, but there was very
little attention paid to it. There was very little soul-searching about the way the
Branch Davidian compound had been razed (see Nancy Ammerman [1995,
1998] for sociological interpretations of these events). Second, Clinton's more
bellicose statements demonstrate a startling similarity to G. W. Bush Jr.'s
response to the terror of 9/11, as well as Bush Sr.'s response to Iraq's invasion
of Kuwait.

8 *Houston Chronicle*, April 20, 1995: A/22. Greg McDonald, "Oklahoma City
   Tragedy; Emotional Clinton Vows to Find 'Evil Cowards.'"
   Seattle Post-Intelligencer, April 20, 1995: A/4. "Clinton Calls Bombers Evil
   Cowards; 'Swift, Certain and Severe Justice' Pledged."
   State Journal-Register (Springfield, IL), April 20, 1995: 4. Mark Barabak,
   "Clinton, Reno Vow Tough Action Against Culprits."

9 *Boston Herald*, April 23, 1995: 35. Wayne Woodlief, "Politics Inside Out; Blast
   Shows Clinton at His Best."
   San Francisco Chronicle, April 21, 1995: A/2. Susan Yoachum, "Disaster
   Allows Clinton to Show His Relevance: Oklahoma Bombing Thrusts Him
   Back into Spotlight."

10 *Buffalo News* (New York), April 21, 1995: 10. Alan Pergament, "TV Delivers
   Emotionally Jarring Images of Oklahoma Tragedy."

11 *Times-Picayune* (New Orleans, LA), April 21, 1995: B/7. Sandy Grady,
   "'Evil Cowards' Can't Blast Away Our Shield of Courage."

12 *Boston Globe*, May 6, 1995: 3. Jill Zuckman, "Gingrich Assails Democrats'
   Letter; Calls Criticism 'Irresponsible.'"

13 Associated Press, May 6, 1995. Michelle Mittelstadt, "Democrats Regret
   Saying Gingrich Embraces Terrorist Policies."

14 *Boston Globe*, May 6, 1995: 3. Jill Zuckman, "Gingrich Assails Democrats'
   Letter; Calls Criticism 'Irresponsible.'"

15 *Christian Science Monitor*, April 26, 1995: 1. Linda Feldmann, "How Oklahoma Plays Inside the Beltway."

16 Well-publicized events in 1991/2, like the "Ruby Ridge Incident" between the
   Weaver family and BATF and FBI agents in northern Idaho; the Branch
   Davidian compound in Waco, Texas; and the "Unabomber" drama that
   continued through the early 1990s until Theodore Kaczynski was arrested in
   Montana in April 1996.

17 *New York Times*, April 29, 1995: 1/23/1. Bob Herbert, "In America; Backing
   off Bravery."

18 *New York Times*, April 30, 1995: 4/15/1. Frank Rich, "Journal; Connect the
   Dots."

19 "Conservatives are coming out fighting, rejecting insinuations that a civilized discussion about the need to reduce the role and size of the federal government – a point Clinton himself has made early and often – could have led fanatical anarchists to launch an attack against innocent people" (*Christian Science Monitor*, April 26, 1995: 1. Linda Feldmann, "How Oklahoma Plays Inside the Beltway").

20 *Christian Science Monitor*, April 26, 1995: 1. Linda Feldmann, "How Oklahoma Plays Inside the Beltway."

21 *Atlanta Journal-Constitution*, April 29, 1995: A/14. Dick Williams, "Other Voices; Where Clinton Went Wrong This Week."

22 *Time Magazine*, May 1, 1995. James Carney, "Measure of a President." At www.time.com/time/magazine/article/0,9171,982871-1,00.html

23 *Washington Post*, May 28, 1995: C/1. William Schneider, "Putting the 'Clint' in Clinton; President to GOP: 'Go Ahead. Make My Day.' "

24 *Washington Post*, March 24, 1995: C/1. Howard Kurtz, "The Snooze at 11; White House Correspondents Wait While Nothing Happens."

25 *Seattle Times*, April 19, 1995: A/3. Robert A. Rankin and Ranny Green, "Clinton Not Necessarily News, Say Networks."

26 *New York Times*, April 20, 1995: A/18/1. Todd S. Purdum, "Undertones of Relevance."

27 *Christian Science Monitor*, April 26, 1995: 1. Linda Feldmann, "How Oklahoma Plays Inside the Beltway."

28 *New York Times*, May 7, 1995: 1/1/1. Todd S. Purdum, "Desperately in Need of Winning Streak, Clinton Finds One."

29 In his analysis of the events leading up to Nixon's resignation, Jeff Alexander (1988) shows how "Watergate" was transformed from representing a mere break-in into a critical threat to America's political and symbolic center. Two mechanisms were central for precipitating and allowing this symbolic transformation to develop. First, the social and cultural polarization of the 1960s, which preceded Nixon's landslide re-election in 1972, had begun to abate. Second, because of this reduction in political and cultural tension, members of the Left's political elite were able to perform in 1973's televised Senate hearings and 1974's House impeachment hearings while both projecting patriotism and expressing motives rooted in critical universalist concerns. Put another way, Democratic elites, "who had been radical or liberal activists," were able to assert a "patriotic universalism" that did not compel audiences to react with skepticism and suspicion that the congressmen were motivated primarily by specific left-wing issues (Alexander 1988: 200). The combination of these dramatic mechanisms, enacted in this cultural and social environment, fostered a movement toward "generalization" and the development of a "ritualized atmosphere." To varying degrees, citizens were pulled away from the specificity of their everyday lives by the unfolding drama, and became connected with the social center. "Watergate" transformed from politics-as-usual into representing Nixon's willful obstruction of justice, abuse of power, and contempt of Congress.

30 *New York Times*, May 7, 1995: 4/1/1. Michael Wines, "The Nation; Feeling Down? How about a Pollster?"
   Washington Post, May 20, 1995: A/8. Ann Devoy, "Clinton Turns to Outsiders to Amplify Message; GOP Consultant, Others Recruited to Overcome Perceived Weakness in Communication."
31 *Time Magazine*, July 24, 1995. James Carney, "Whitewater Tricks: New Hearings Prompt the Clintons to Make New Revelations – Only to be Caught Short Again."
32 Ibid.
33 *Christian Science Monitor*, July 25, 1995. Godfrey Sperling, "Clinton's Big Edge: Personal Appeal."
34 *New York Times*, July 23, 19/95: 1/16/1. Alison Mitchell, "Clinton Regains His Voice with Three Speeches."
35 *Washington Post*, June 14, 1995: A/1. David S. Broder, "Choosing Conciliation over Confrontation."
36 *Washington Post*, November 10, 1995: A/10. Helen Dewar and John E. Yang, "Political Stakes are High as Each Side Cries Foul in Budget Showdown."
37 Ibid.
38 *Boston Globe*, November 15, 1995: 1. John Aloysius Farrell, "The Political Drama Plays out with Polls on President's Side." Another poll, a "Times Mirror survey," showed that "public esteem" for congressional leadership was falling while the president's was rising, and that 7 percent of respondents held the president responsible for the shutdown while 35 percent "blamed" Congress (*New York Times*, November 15, 1995: A/1/3. R. W. Apple Jr., "Battle over the Budget: News Analysis; In this Fight, Polls Guide All the Moves").
39 *Chicago Sun Times*, November 15, 1995: 35. Carl Rowan, "War is Hell; Budget Fight Even Uglier."
40 *Washington Post*, November 16, 1995: A/1. John E. Yang, "Underlying Gingrich's Stance is His Pique about President."
41 *USA Today*, January 17, 1996: A/4. Richard Benedetto, "At 3-year Mark, President Hasn't Boosted Support Base."
42 *USA Today*, September 3, 1996: A/4. Richard Benedetto, "Poll Finds Little Going Dole's Way; Approval Rating for President Reaches a Four-year High of 60%."
43 *Washington Post*, March 17, 1996: A/1. John E. Yang, "Democrats Struggle to Develop Agenda; Leaders Seek Unifying Message in Drive to Recapture House."
44 *New York Times*, January 7, 1996: 4/1/3. Richard L. Berke, "Cease-Fire; The Mellowing of the American Voter."
45 CNN Transcripts, June 29, 1996. *Inside Politics*, with William Schneider, "Scandal Fatigue is Story Behind the Story."
46 NPR Transcripts, January 4, 1996. *All Things Considered*, with Robert Siegel, "Republicans Investigate 1993 White House Firings."

47 *New York Times*, January 8, 1996: 1/27/2. William Safire, "Blizzard of Lies."
48 *Washington Post*, January 10, 1996: A/1. John F. Harris, "A Presidential Counterpunch; Responding to Attacks, Clinton Defends First Lady's Character."
49 Federal News Service Transcripts, January 23, 1996. "President Bill Clinton: State of the Union Address."
50 *Boston Herald*, August 16, 1996: 27. Rachelle G. Cohen, "Dole Chances Turn on Generation Gap."
51 *New York Times*, August 14, 1996: A/1/5. James Bennet, "The Republicans: The Broadcasts; Networks vs. the Organizers: Early Rounds Go to G.O.P."
52 *Philadelphia Inquirer*, August 14, 1996: A/1. Dick Polman, "GOP Takes High Road, But Plots a Detour."
53 *USA Today*, September 19, 1996: A/6. Judy Keen, Deborah Mathis, and James Cox, "Dole's 'Nomo' Pitch is out of the Ballpark."
54 *New York Times*, February 12, 1998: A/34/1. Editorial, "The Price of Scandal Fatigue."

Chapter 7

1 "Filegate" is the label given to the White House's improper procurement of hundreds of FBI files on congressional Republicans and past presidential administrations' workers and advisors.
2 The Government Reform Oversight Committee released its "Travelgate" report criticizing the employees' firings and the Clintons' evasiveness in the investigation, for instance.
3 *Washington Post*, January 21, 1998: A/1. Susan Schmidt, Peter Baker, and Toni Locy, "Clinton Accused of Urging Aide to Lie; Starr Probes Whether President Told Woman to Deny Alleged Affair to Jones's Lawyers."
4 *New York Times*, January 22, 1998: A/25/1. James Bennet, "The President Under Fire: The White House Response; In Interviews, President Denies Affair with Intern."
5 *New York Times*, January 22, 1998: A/1/6. Francis X. Clines and Jeff Gerth, "The President Under Fire: The Overview; Subpoenas Sent as Clinton Denies Reports of an Affair with Aide at White House."
6 *New York Times*, January 23, 1998: A/1/6. John M. Broder, "The President Under Fire: The Overview; Clinton and Vernon Jordan Tighten Denials on Affair and on Seeking a Cover-up."
7 *New York Times*, January 24, 1998: A/1/6. John M. Broder, "The President Under Fire: The Overview; Ex-Intern Offered to Tell of Clinton Affair in Exchange for Immunity, Lawyers Report."
8 MSNBC and FOX News posted 100 percent increases, and CNN recorded a 60 percent increase (*Boston Globe*, January 25, 1998: A/10). See also: *Washington Post*, January 27, 1998: D/1. Paul Farhi, "For Some, Scandal Breeds Success; Print Media Sales, TV Ratings Rise with Coverage of Clinton."

9 *New York Times*, January 22, 1998: A/29/5. William Safire, "Presume Innocence."

10 ABC News Transcripts, January 25, 1998. *This Week*, Weekly Roundtable.

11 *New York Times*, January 23, 1998: A/1/6. John M. Broder, "The President Under Fire: The Overview; Clinton and Vernon Jordan Tighten Denials on Affair and on Seeking a Cover-up."

12 *New York Times*, January 23, 1998: A/1/23. Richard L. Berke and James Bennet, "The President Under Fire: The Clinton Camp; Those Closest to Clinton are Left in the Dark."

13 *New York Times*, January 23, 1998: A/20/1. "Tell the Full Story, Mr. President."

14 The number of people believing Clinton had an affair with Lewinsky rose 20 percent in the first three days, and the number believing he had encouraged her to lie about the relationship rose 14 percent. For the first time in his tenure, less than half the public (49 percent) believed Clinton had the "honesty and integrity required to serve effectively" as president (ABC News Poll, January 29, 1998, cited in the *Washington Times*, Joe Curl, "Poll Number on Honesty Falls Below 50 Percent").

15 ABC Poll, January 22, 1998, cited in Associated Press, "Most Believe President Had Affair."

16 ABC News Poll, January 23, 1998, *World News Tonight with Peter Jennings* transcript.

17 ABC News Poll, January 24, 1998, *World News Saturday* transcript, "Immunity, Credibility and Monica Lewinsky," segment.

18 USA Today/CNN Poll, January 26, 1998, cited in Associated Press, "Poll: If Clinton Lied, He Should Go."

19 Clinton's symbolic framework is in part a product of the political and cultural battles of the late 1960s, on the one hand, and more currently a product of the 1980s and 1990s culture wars, on the other. It should be clear that I am not arguing that Clinton's actions in themselves, of necessity, compelled a particular public response.

20 *New York Times*, January 24, 1998: A/8/3. Katharine Q. Seelye, "The President Under Fire: The Defenders; Clinton's Rapid-Response Squad Now Moves in Slow Motion."

21 *New York Times*, January 27, 1998: A/1/6. James Bennet, "The President Under Fire: The Overview; Clinton Emphatically Denies an Affair with Ex-Intern: Lawyers Say He is Distracted by Events."

22 *New York Daily News*, January 27, 1998: 28. Editorial, "America is Listening, Mr. President."

23 NBC News Transcripts, January 27, 1998. *Today*, with Matt Lauer, "Hillary Rodham Clinton Discusses Allegations Against Her Husband, Child Care, and State of the Union Address."

24 NBC's *Today* show registered a 7.2 rating (percentage of the nation's 98 million homes with televisions) and a 29 share (percentage of sets in use)

on January 27, 1998, the day of Hillary Clinton's interview with Lauer. This was the show's second-highest single-day rating since 1987. The previous high was set in 1989, the day after the San Francisco earthquake (*New York Daily News*, January 29, 1998: 4. Richard Huff, "First Family Truly No. 1 with Nielsen."

25 A nuanced distinction began to emerge in a majority of Americans' understandings of Clinton's self in late January, shortly after the address. Clinton's *public self* became understood as autonomous enough from his *private self* to allow him to adequately perform the duties necessary to be president. Additionally, late January polls began to indicate the majority of Americans were willing and able to maintain a subjective distinction between these two selves, and that they were more concerned with Clinton's political than personal actions. After the event's first week approximately 66 percent of Americans favored Clinton's resignation if he committed either perjury or suborning of perjury, a full 25 percentage points greater than the 41 percent that supported his ousting if he had simply engaged in the affair (ABC News Poll, January 28, 1998, cited in *The Bulletin's Frontrunner*, "ABC Poll (1/26)"). It is my argument that this distinction may not have occurred or remained sustainable had Clinton continued to appear "visibly shaken," nervous, and evasive before his intently curious audiences and critics.

26 *New York Times*, January 28, 1998: A/1/6. John M. Broder, "State of the Union: The Overview; Clinton, with Crisis Swirling, Puts Focus on Social Security in Upbeat State of Union Talk."

27 In addition to focusing on his Administration's accomplishments and plans, Clinton tried to cultivate the theme of the American people *getting back to work together* for the good of the nation. For instance: "This is the America we have begun to build. This is the America we can leave to our children – *if we join together to finish the work at hand*"; or "we must work together, learn together, live together, serve together" (*Washington Post*, January 28, 1998: A/24. Transcript of the State of the Union Address, " 'This is Not a Time to Rest. It is a Time to Build' "; emphasis added).

28 *New York Times*, January 28, 1998: A/25/2. Editorial, "Grading the Independent Counsel."

29 *New York Times*, January 23, 1998: A/16/3. David E. Rosenbaum, "The President Under Fire: The Investigation; New Vigor for a Prosecution Once Seen as Flagging."

30 *New York Times*, January 26, 1998: A/19/5. Anthony Lewis, "Lord High Executioner."

31 ABC News, July 31, 1998, cited in *Washington Post*, Peter Baker and Susan Schmidt, "FBI to Test Lewinsky Dress."

32 Post–ABC News Poll, July 29, 1998, archive poll data from www.washingtonpost.com/wp-srv/politics/polls/vault/stories/data093098.htm

33 Pro-resignation sentiments declined from 67 percent in late January to 45 percent in late July, and pro-impeachment sentiments declined from 48 percent in late January to 40 percent in late July (for late January polls on resignation and impeachment sentiments, see ABC News Poll, January 24, 1998, ABC *World News Saturday* transcript, "Immunity, Credibility and Monica Lewinsky," segment, and for late July polls on resignation and impeachment sentiments, see ABC News Poll, July 31, 1998, cited in *The Bulletin's Frontrunner*, "Clinton's Approval at 63% in ABC News Poll").

34 For instance, MSNBC's website more than doubled its previous web traffic record with more than two million people searching for the report before the web-managers could even get it fully posted.

35 *New York Times*, September 12, 1998: A/11/3. Amy Harmon, "Testing of A President: The Internet; Tangled Web Tangles up the World Wide Web."

36 *New York Times*, September 12, 1998: A/18/1. Editorial, "Shame at the White House."

37 ABC News Poll, September 12, 1998, cited in Associated Press, Will Lester, "President's Job Approval Holds Firm," reported a 56 percent approval rate. Reporting for the *New York Post*, Allen Salkin reported that three weekend polls showed Clinton's job approval rating hovering between 56 and 62 percent (*New York Post*, September 13, 1998: 8. Allen Salkin, "A Feeling, President Let Us Down, Polls Show His Support Still High But Weakening").

38 ABC News Poll, September 15, 1998, *The Bulletin's Frontrunner*, "39% Say Clinton Should Resign in ABC News Poll."

39 The tape's airing invigorated the Republican base, with 63 percent of registered Republicans voicing a "strong desire" to see Clinton removed from office (ABC News, September 22, 1998). However, the tape inspired sympathy for Clinton from a majority of viewers with 63 percent of the public agreeing Clinton was justified in his anger toward his interrogators, 61 percent feeling it was wrong for Congress to release the tape, and 62 percent disapproving of the way Republicans were handling the Lewinksy issue (ABC News, September 23, 1998).

40 Federal News Service Transcripts, December 8, 1998. "Hearing of the House Judiciary Committee Re: The Impeachment of the President, Chaired by Rep. Henry Hyde (R-IL)."

41 The many channels from which the ritual's would-be audiences had to choose contributed to reducing the potential for liminality that had characterized Watergate's hearings. The limited channels during Watergate contributed to the sense that everyone was involved in and witnessing history as it was unfolding. See the *New York Times*, December 23, 1998: A/24/2. Felicity Barringer, "Impeachment: The Media; In Poll, Public Says Clinton Scandal Wasn't '98's Most Compelling Event."

42 *Austin American-Statesman*, January 3, 1999: A/1. William Neikirk, "Senate Braces for Burden of Clinton Trial."

References

Alexander, Jeffrey C. 1988. "Culture and Political Crisis: 'Watergate' and Durkheimian Sociology." In *Durkheimian Sociology: Cultural Studies*, ed. J. C. Alexander. New York: Cambridge University Press, pp. 187–224.

2003. "The Sacred and Profane Information Machine." In *The Meanings of Social Life*. New York: Oxford University Press, pp. 179–92.

2004. "Cultural Pragmatics: Social Performance between Ritual and Strategy." *Sociological Theory* 22 (4): 527–73.

2006. *The Civil Sphere*. New York: Oxford University Press.

2010. *The Performance of Politics: Obama's Victory and the Democratic Struggle for Power*. New York: Oxford University Press.

Alexander, Jeffrey C., Bernhard Giesen, and Jason L. Mast. 2006. *Social Performance: Symbolic Action, Cultural Pragmatics, and Ritual*. New York: Cambridge University Press.

Alexander, Jeffrey C., and Jason L. Mast. 2006. "Introduction: Symbolic Action in Theory and Practice: The Cultural Pragmatics of Symbolic Action." In *Social Performance: Symbolic Action, Cultural Pragmatics, and Ritual*, ed. J. C. Alexander, B. Giesen, and J. L. Mast. New York: Cambridge University Press, pp. 1–28.

Alexander, Jeffrey C., and Philip Smith. 1993. "The Discourse of American Civil Society: A New Proposal for Cultural Studies." *Theory and Society* 22: 151–207.

2001. "The Strong Program in Cultural Theory: Elements of a Structural Hermeneutics." In *Handbook of Social Theory*, ed. J. Turner. New York: Kluwer Academic, pp. 135–50.

Altheide, David L., and Robert P. Snow. 1979. *Media Logic*. Beverly Hills, CA: Sage.

Ammerman, Nancy. 1995. "Waco, Federal Law Enforcement and Scholars of Religion." In *Armageddon at Waco: Critical Perspectives on the Branch Davidian Conflict*, ed. S. A. Wright. University of Chicago Press, pp. 282–96.

1998. "Forum: Interpreting Waco." *Religion and American Culture* 8 (1) Winter: 25–30.

Anderson, Benedict. 1983. *Imagined Communities: Reflections on the Origin and Spread of Nationalism*. New York: Verso.

Apter, David. 2006. "Politics as Theatre: An Alternative View of the Rationalities of Power." In *Social Performance: Symbolic Action, Cultural Pragmatics, and Ritual*, ed. J. C. Alexander, B. Giesen, and J. L. Mast. New York: Cambridge University Press, pp. 218–56.

Aristotle. 1987 [384–322 BCE]. *Poetics*. Indianapolis: Hackett.

Aston, Elaine, and George Savona. 1991. *Theatre as Sign System: A Semiotics of Text and Performance*. New York: Routledge.

Austin, John L. 1975 [1962]. *How to Do Things with Words*. Cambridge, MA: Harvard University Press.

Barnouw, Erik. 1990. *Tube of Plenty: The Evolution of American Television*, 2nd rev. edn. New York: Oxford University Press.

Barthes, Roland. 1972 [1957]. *Mythologies*. New York: Hill and Wang.

Bellah, Robert N. 1967. "Civil Religion in America." *Journal of the American Academy of Arts and Sciences* 96 (1): 1–21.

Bellah, Robert N., Richard Madsen, William M. Sullivan, Ann Swidler, and Steven M. Tipton. 1985. *Habits of the Heart*. Berkeley: University of California Press.

Bennett, Stephen Earl. 2002. "Another Lesson about Public Opinion during the Clinton–Lewinsky Scandal." *Presidential Studies Quarterly* 32 (2): 276–92.

Bennett, W. Lance. 2007. *News: The Politics of Illusion*, 7th edn. New York: Pearson Longman.

Best, Steven, and Douglas Kellner. 1997. *The Postmodern Turn*. New York: Guilford Press.

Bishop, George F. 2005. *The Illusion of Public Opinion: Fact and Artifact in American Public Opinion Polls*. New York: Rowman & Littlefield.

Bowler, Shaun, and Jeffrey A. Karp. 2004. "Politicians, Scandals, and Trust in Government." *Political Behavior* 26 (3): 271–87.

Brace, Paul, and Barbara Hinckley. 1992. *Follow the Leader: Opinion Polls and the Modern Presidents*. New York: Basic Books.

1993. "Presidential Activities from Truman through Reagan: Timing and Impact." *The Journal of Politics* 55 (2): 382–98.

Brody, Richard A. 1991. *Assessing the President: The Media, Elite Opinion, and Public Support.* Stanford University Press.

1998. "The Lewinsky Affair and Popular Support for President Clinton." In *The Polling Report*, November 16. Available at www.pollingreport. com/brody.htm (accessed December 5, 2011).

Brody, Richard A., and S. Jackman. 1999. "The Lewinsky Affair and Popular Support for President Clinton." Paper presented at the annual meeting of the Midwest Political Science Association, April 17, in Chicago.

Bruzzi, Stella. 2000. "The President and the Image: Kennedy, Nixon, Clinton." In *Contemporary Documentary: A Critical Introduction.* Florence, KY: Routledge, pp. 127–52.

Campbell, W. Joseph. 2010. *Getting it Wrong: Ten of the Greatest Misreported Stories in American Journalism.* Berkeley: University of California Press.

Carlson, Marvin. 1984. *Theories of the Theatre: A Historical and Critical Survey from the Greeks to the Present.* Ithaca, NY: Cornell University Press.

2001. *Haunted Stage: The Theatre as Memory Machine.* Ann Arbor: University of Michigan Press.

Ceaser, James W., Glen E. Thurow, Jeffrey Tulis, and Joseph M. Bessette. 1981. "The Rise of Rhetorical Presidency." *Presidential Studies Quarterly* 11 (2): 158–71.

Dahl, Robert A. 1961. *Who Governs? Democracy and Power in an American City.* New Haven, CT: Yale University Press.

1989. *Democracy and Its Critics.* New Haven, CT: Yale University Press.

Dewey, John. 1954 [1927]. *The Public and Its Problems.* Chicago: Swallow Press.

Didion, Joan. 2001. *Political Fictions.* New York: Knopf.

Doherty, Carroll J. 1996. "Clinton's Big Comeback Shown in Vote Score." *Congressional Quarterly Weekly Report* 54: 3427–9.

Douglas, Mary. 1966. *Purity and Danger: An Analysis of the Concepts of Pollution and Taboo.* New York: Routledge.

Durkheim, Emile. 1995 [1915]. *The Elementary Forms of Religious Life.* New York: Free Press.

Edles, Laura. 1998. *Symbol and Ritual in the New Spain: The Transition to Democracy After Franco.* New York: Cambridge University Press.

Eliasoph, Nina. 1998. *Avoiding Politics: How Americans Produce Apathy in Everyday Life.* Cambridge University Press.

Friedland, Roger, and Robert R. Alford. 1991. "Bringing Society Back in: Symbols, Practices, and Institutional Contradictions." In *The New Institutionalism in Organizational Analysis*, ed. W. W. Powell and P. J. DiMaggio. University of Chicago Press, pp. 232–63.

Geertz, Clifford. 1973. *The Interpretation of Cultures*. New York: Basic Books.

Gergen, David. 2000. *Eyewitness to Power: The Essence of Leadership: Nixon to Clinton*. New York: Simon & Schuster.

Goffman, Erving. 1951. "Symbols of Class Status." *British Journal of Sociology* 2 (4): 294–304.

    1959. *The Presentation of Self in Everyday Life*. New York: Doubleday.

    1963. *Behavior in Public Places: Notes on the Social Organization of Gatherings*. New York: Free Press of Glencoe.

    1967. *Interaction Ritual: Essays on Face-to-Face Behavior*. Garden City, NY: Anchor Books.

Gorski, Philip S. 2006. "Mann's Theory of Ideological Power: Sources, Applications and Elaborations." In *An Anatomy of Power: The Social Theory of Michael Mann*, ed. J. A. Hall and R. Schroeder. New York: Cambridge University Press, pp. 101–34.

Gray, Caroline. 2009. "Narratives of Disability and the Movement from Deficiency to Difference." *Cultural Sociology* 3: 317–31.

Greenstein, Fred I. 1988. "Nine Presidents: In Search of a Modern Presidency." In *Leadership in the Modern Presidency*, ed. F. I. Greenstein. Cambridge, MA: Harvard University Press, pp. 296–352.

    1993–4. "The Presidential Leadership Style of Bill Clinton: An Early Appraisal." *Political Science Quarterly* 108 (4): 589–601.

    1994. "The Two Leadership Styles of William Jefferson Clinton." *Political Psychology* 15 (2): 351–61.

    1998. "There He Goes Again: The Alternating Political Style of Bill Clinton." *PS: Political Science and Politics* 31 (2): 178–81.

    2000. " 'The Qualities of Effective Presidents': An Overview from FDR to Bill Clinton." *Presidential Studies Quarterly* 30 (1): 178–85.

Gronke, Paul, and Brian Newman. 2003. "FDR to Clinton, Mueller to ?: A Field Essay on Presidential Approval." *Political Research Quarterly* 56 (4): 501–12.

Hall, Stuart. 2005 [1980]. "Encoding/Decoding." In *Culture, Media, Language*, ed. S. Hall, H. Hobson, A. Lowe, and P. Willis. London: Routledge, pp. 107–16.

Han, Lori Cox, and Matthew J. Krov. 2003. " 'Source Material': Out of Office and in the News: Early Projections of the Clinton Legacy." *Presidential Studies Quarterly* 33 (4): 925–33.

Hertsgaard, Mark. 1988. *On Bended Knee: The Press and the Reagan Presidency*. New York: Farrar, Straus and Giroux.

Hetherington, Marc J. 1998. "The Political Relevance of Political Trust." *The American Political Science Review* 92 (4): 791–808.

Hutcheon, Linda. 2000. *A Theory of Parody: The Teachings of Twentieth-Century Art Forms*. Urbana: University of Illinois Press.

Isikoff, Michael. 1999. *Uncovering Clinton: A Reporter's Story*. New York: Crown Publishers.

Jacobson, Gary C. 1993. "Congress: Unusual Year, Unusual Election." In *The Elections of 1992*, ed. M. Nelson. Washington, DC: Congressional Quarterly Press, pp. 153–82.

Jamieson, Kathleen Hall, and Joseph N. Cappella. 2008. *Echo Chamber: Rush Limbaugh and the Conservative Media Establishment*. New York: Oxford University Press.

Kantorowicz, Ernst H. 1957. *The King's Two Bodies: A Study in Mediaeval Political Theology*. Princeton University Press.

Karnow, Stanley. 1997 [1983]. *Vietnam: A History*. New York: Penguin.

Kellner, Douglas. 1992. *The Persian Gulf War*. Boulder, CO: Westview Press.

Kernell, Samuel. 2007. *Going Public: New Strategies of Presidential Leadership*, 4th edn. Washington, DC: Congressional Quarterly Press.

Kertzer, David I. 1988. *Ritual, Politics, and Power*. New Haven, CT: Yale University Press.

Klein, Joe. 2002. *The Natural: The Misunderstood Presidency of Bill Clinton*. New York: Doubleday.

Lawrence, Regina G., and W. Lance Bennett. 2001. "Rethinking Media Politics and Public Opinion: Reactions to the Clinton–Lewinsky Scandal." *Political Science Quarterly* 116 (3): 425–46.

Lichterman, Paul. 1996. *The Search for Political Community: American Activists Reinventing Commitment*. Cambridge University Press.

Lippmann, Walter. 1965 [1922]. *Public Opinion*. New York: Free Press.

Maltese, John Anthony. 1994. *Spin Control: The White House Office of Communications and the Management of Presidential News*, 2nd edn. Chapel Hill: University of North Carolina Press.

Mann, Michael. 1986. *The Sources of Social Power,* vol. 1: *A History of Power from the Beginning to A.D. 1760*. Cambridge University Press.

1993. *The Sources of Social Power,* vol. 2: *The Rise of Classes and Nation States, 1760–1914*. Cambridge University Press.

Marvin, Carolyn, and David W. Ingle. 1999. *Blood Sacrifice and the Nation: Totem Rituals and the American Flag*. Cambridge University Press.

Marx, Karl. 1963 [1851–2]. *The Eighteenth Brumaire of Louis Bonaparte*. New York: International Publishers.

Mast, Jason L. 2006. "The Cultural Pragmatics of Event-ness: The Clinton/Lewinsky Affair." In *Social Performance: Symbolic Action, Cultural Pragmatics, and Ritual*, ed. J. C. Alexander, B. Giesen, and J. L. Mast. New York: Cambridge University Press, pp. 115–45.

Mickelson, Sig. 1998. *The Decade that Shaped Television News: CBS in the 1950s*. Westport, CT: Praeger.

Mills, C. Wright. 1962 [1953]. *White Collar: The American Middle Classes*. New York: Oxford University Press.

Minow, Newton N., and Craig L. LaMay. 2008. *Inside the Presidential Debates: Their Improbable Past and Promising Future*. University of Chicago Press.

Molotch, Harvey, and Marilyn Lester. 1974. "News as Purposive Behavior: On the Strategic Use of Routine Events, Accidents, and Scandals." *American Sociological Review* 39: 101–12.

Neustadt, Richard E. 1990 [1960]. *Presidential Power and the Modern Presidents: The Politics of Leadership from Roosevelt to Reagan*. New York: Free Press.

Newman, Brian. 2002. "Bill Clinton's Approval Ratings: The More Things Change, the More They Stay the Same." *Political Research Quarterly* 55 (4): 781–804.

Nietzsche, Friedrich. 1956 [1872]. *The Birth of Tragedy and The Genealogy of Morals*, trans. Francis Golffing. New York: Anchor Books.

Norton, Anne. 1993. *Republic of Signs: Liberal Theory and American Popular Culture*. University of Chicago Press.

Peters, Julie Stone. 2000. *Theatre of the Book, 1480–1880: Print, Text, and Performance in Europe*. New York: Oxford University Press.

Putnam, Robert D. 2001. *Bowling Alone: The Collapse and Revival of American Community*. New York: Simon & Schuster.

Ranney, Austin. 1983. *Channels of Power: The Impact of Television on American Politics*. New York: Basic Books.

Renshon, Stanley A. 1994. "A Preliminary Assessment of the Clinton Presidency: Character, Leadership and Performance." *Political Psychology* 15 (2): 375–94.

　　2000. "After the Fall: The Clinton Presidency in Psychological Perspective." *Political Science Quarterly* 115 (1): 41–65.

Roach, Joseph. 1996. *Cities of the Dead: Circum-Atlantic Performance*. New York: Columbia University Press.

　　2000. "Cutting Loose: Burying the 'First Man of Jazz.'" In *Joyous Wakes, Dignified Dying: Issues in Death and Dying*, ed. R. Harvey and E. A. Kaplan. Humanities Institute of the State University of New York at Stony Brook, pp. 3–14.

Robinson, Michael J., and Margaret A. Sheehan. 1983. *Over the Wire and on TV: CBS and UPI in Campaign '80*. New York: Russell Sage Foundation.

Roth, Andrew L. 1995. " 'Men Wearing Masks': Issues of Description in the Analysis of Ritual." *Sociological Theory* 13 (3): 301–27.

Ryfe, David M. 2005. *Presidents in Culture: The Meaning of Presidential Communication*. New York: Peter Lang.

Sahlins, Marshall. 1976. *Culture and Practical Reason*. Chicago University Press.

　1981. *Historical Metaphors and Mythical Realities: Structure in the Early History of the Sandwich Islands Kingdom*. Ann Arbor: University of Michigan Press.

Sarfatti-Larson, Magali, and Robin Wagner-Pacifici. 2001. "The Dubious Place of Virtue: Reflections on the Impeachment of William Jefferson Clinton and the Death of the Political Event in America." *Theory and Society* 30 (6): 735–74.

Schechner, Richard. 1985. *Between Theater and Anthropology*. Philadelphia: University of Pennsylvania Press.

　1990. *By Means of Performance: Intercultural Studies of Theatre and Ritual*. New York: Routledge.

　1993. *Future of Ritual:Writings on Culture and Performance*. New York: Routledge.

　2003 [1988]. *Performance Theory*. New York: Routledge.

Schier, Steven E. 2000. "A Unique Presidency." In *The Postmodern Presidency: Bill Clinton's Legacy in U.S. Politics*, ed. S. Schier. University of Pittsburgh Press, pp. 1–16.

Schlesinger, Arthur Meier. 1973. *The Imperial Presidency*. Boston: Houghton Mifflin.

Schudson, Michael. 1992. *Watergate in American Memory: How We Remember, Forget, and Reconstruct the Past*. New York: Basic Books.

　1995a. "The Politics of Narrative Form." In *The Power of News*, ed. M. Schudson. Cambridge, MA: Harvard University Press, pp. 53–71.

　1995b. "Trout or Hamburger: Politics and Telemythology." In *The Power of News*, ed. M. Schudson. Cambridge, MA: Harvard University Press, pp. 113–23.

　1995c. "National News Culture and the Informational Citizen." In *The Power of News*, ed. M. Schudson. Cambridge, MA: Harvard University Press, pp. 169–88.

1998. *The Good Citizen: A History of American Civic Life*. New York: Martin Kessler Books.

Sewell, William H. Jr. 1985. "Ideologies and Social Revolutions: Reflections on the French Case." *The Journal of Modern History* 57 (1): 57–85.

1996. "Historical Events as Transformations of Structures: Inventing Revolution at the Bastille." *Theory and Society* 25 (6): 841–81.

Shils, Edward, and Michael Young. 1953. "The Meaning of the Coronation." *Sociological Review* 1: 63–81.

Skocpol, Theda. 1985. "Bringing the State Back In: Strategies in Current Research." In *Bringing the State Back In*, ed. P. B. Evans, D. Reuschemeyer, and T. Skocpol. Cambridge University Press, pp. 3–37.

2003. *Diminished Democracy: From Membership to Management in American Civic Life*. Norman: University of Oklahoma Press.

Skowronek, Stephen. 1997. *The Politics Presidents Make: Leadership from John Adams to Bill Clinton*. Cambridge, MA: Belknap Press of Harvard University Press.

Smelser, Neil J. 1963. *Theory of Collective Behavior*. New York: Free Press.

Smith, Philip. 1991. "Codes and Conflict: Toward a Theory of War as Ritual." *Theory and Society* 20 (1): 103–38.

Spillman, Lyn. 1997. *Nation and Commemoration: Creating National Identities in the United States and Australia*. Cambridge University Press.

Stephens, Mitchell. 2007. *A History of News*. New York: Oxford University Press.

Tatalovich, Raymond, and John Frendreis. 2000. "Clinton, Class, and Economic Policy." In *The Postmodern Presidency: Bill Clinton's Legacy in U.S. Politics*, ed. S. E. Schier. University of Pittsburgh Press, pp. 41–59.

Taylor, Diana. 1995. "Performing Gender: Las Madres de la Plaza de Mayo." In *Negotiating Performance: Gender, Sexuality, and Theatricality in Latin/o America*, ed. D. Taylor and J. Villegas. Durham, NC: Duke University Press, pp. 275–305.

Thompson, John B. 2000. *Political Scandal: Power and Visibility in the Media Age*. Cambridge: Polity.

Tocqueville, Alexis de. 1969 [1835–40]. *Democracy in America*, vols. 1 and 2. New York: Doubleday.

Toobin, Jeffrey. 2000. *A Vast Conspiracy: The Real Story of the Sex Scandal that Nearly Brought Down a President*. New York: Simon & Schuster.

Tulis, Jeffrey K. 1987. *The Rhetorical Presidency*. Princeton University Press.

Turner, Victor W. 1974. *Dramas, Fields, and Metaphors: Symbolic Action in Human Society*. Ithaca, NY: Cornell University Press.

1977 [1969]. *Ritual Process: Structure and Anti-Structure*. Ithaca, NY: Cornell University Press.

1982. *From Ritual to Theatre: The Human Seriousness of Play*. New York: Performing Arts Journal Publications.

1986. "Dewey, Dilthey, and Drama: An Essay in the Anthropology of Experience." In *Anthropology of Experience*, ed. V. W. Turner and E. M. Bruner. Urbana: University of Illinois Press, pp. 33–44.

Van Gennep, Arnold. 1960 [1908]. *The Rites of Passage*. University of Chicago Press.

VanDeMark, Brian. 1991. *Into the Quagmire: Lyndon Johnson and the Escalation of the Vietnam War*. New York: Oxford University Press.

Wagner-Pacifici, Robin E. 1986. *The Moro Morality Play: Terrorism as Social Drama*. University of Chicago Press.

Warner, W. Lloyd. 1959. *The Living and the Dead: A Study of the Symbolic Life of Americans*. New Haven, CT: Yale University Press.

Weber, Max. 1946 [1922–3]. "The Social Psychology of the World Religions." In *From Max Weber*, ed. H. H. Gerth and C. W. Mills. New York: Oxford University Press, pp. 267–301.

1958 [1904–5]. *The Protestant Ethic and the Spirit of Capitalism*. New York: Charles Scribner and Sons.

1968. *Economy and Society*, vols. 1 and 2. Berkeley: University of California Press.

Woodward, Bob. 1994. *The Agenda: Inside the Clinton White House*. New York: Simon & Schuster.

1999. *Shadow: Five Presidents and the Legacy of Watergate*. New York: Simon & Schuster.

Zaller, John R. 1998. "Monica Lewinsky's Contribution to Political Science." *PS: Political Science and Politics* 31 (2): 182–9.

Zelizer, Barbie. 1992. *Covering the Body: The Kennedy Assassination, the Media, and the Shaping of Collective Memory*. University of Chicago Press.

Index